Lessons on Profiting from Diversity

Lessons on Profiting from Diversity

Edited by

Gloria Moss

First published 2012 by
PALGRAVE MACMILLAN

Palgrave Macmillan in the UK is an imprint of Macmillan Publishers Limited,
registered in England, company number 785998, of Houndmills, Basingstoke,
Hampshire RG21 6XS.

Palgrave Macmillan in the US is a division of St Martin's Press LLC,
175 Fifth Avenue, New York, NY 10010.

Palgrave Macmillan is the global academic imprint of the above companies
and has companies and representatives throughout the world.

Palgrave® and Macmillan® are registered trademarks in the United States,
the United Kingdom, Europe and other countries.

ISBN 978–0–230–25020–8

This book is printed on paper suitable for recycling and made from fully
managed and sustained forest sources. Logging, pulping and manufacturing
processes are expected to conform to the environmental regulations of the
country of origin.

A catalogue record for this book is available from the British Library.

A catalog record for this book is available from the Library of Congress.

10   9   8   7   6   5   4   3   2   1
21 20 19 18 17 16 15 14 13 12

Printed and bound in Great Britain by
CPI Antony Rowe, Chippenham and Eastbourne.

Contents

v

Figures

Figures

Tables

Notes on Contributors

Audrey Becuwe, PhD (managment sciences), is Assistant Professor at the University of Limoges and researcher at CREOP-EA 4332, Limoges, France.

In addition to her publications on management competencies, diversity management and homophobia in the workplace, she has carried out several studies related to gender and entrepreneurship. Before taking up her appointment at the University of Limoges, she co-headed the Observatory and the Entrepreneurship Research Center at the Ecole des Dirigeants et Créateurs d'Entreprise, France. She is the winner of several prizes (e.g. winner of the thesis prize of the University of Lyons-France, and Paris Chamber of Commerce best prizewinner of HRM study case 2008 and 2007, with C. Falcoz).

E-mail: audrey.becuwe@unilim.fr

Holly Buchanan is the owner of Buchanan Marketing LLC, a consultancy specialising in marketing to and selling to women. She is the co-author (along with Michele Miller) of *The Soccer Mom Myth – Today's Female Consumer: Who She Really Is, Why She Really Buys*. She also has her own blog – *Marketing to Women Online* – and is a guest columnist at *Be Branded*.

Holly has worked with hundreds of clients, including brands like Waterford, GE Healthcare, HP, 1-800-Flowers, American General Life and Genworth Financial. She does sales training, and creates marketing campaigns for many industries, including healthcare and financial services.

E-mail: buchanan.holly@gmail.com

Alan David, MBA (Liverpool University), Alan worked in the Strategic Planning team at Courtaulds before joining the University of Westminster, where he is currently module leader of the Strategy Dynamics MBA elective. He attended the Advanced Management Programme International at Harvard Business School. His research focuses on how systems thinking interventions impact on organisational learning and how a range of intervention techniques, ranging from 'soft systems' approaches and scenario thinking, to strategy dynamics, can enrich managers' 'mental models'. These techniques offer insights into improving performance in organisations, policy design and making strategic choices.

E-mail: alan.david@blueyonder.co.uk

Ian Dodds, MA (Oxon), PhD (University of Reading), is Head of Ian Dodds Consulting, leading a global team of more than 50 consultants who have strong experience of delivering inclusion and diversity solutions for bottom line gains and to increase customer or client satisfaction. He works with major clients globally, including Adecco, Allianz, AstraZeneca, Barclays Bank, Cisco Systems, Coca Cola Enterprises, Deutsche Bank, DSG International, The Economist Group, Goldman Sachs, Herbert Smith, JPMorgan Chase, IBM, Linklaters, McDonald's, Philips, Pitney Bowes, Sainsbury's, Sodexho, Wates Group and UK Government departments. He was Global Head of Organisation and People Development for ICI, then the largest chemicals company in the world, and responsible to its main board for the business and leadership development of its top 1500 executives. He subsequently headed up the European Diversity Practice of Towers Perrin.

E-mail: iandodds@iandodsconsulting.com

Alice Garnier is a PhD student in strategy at the University of Lyon/ Coactis Research Center – University of Lyon 2, EA 4161, France. Her master's thesis project was entitled 'Gender: differences in factor business growth'. Her doctoral research concerns the evolution of portfolio decision-making concerns of SME managers and dynamic growth of their business. Her research interests focus mainly on the critical role of the leader in business growth. Alice is a member of a research project investigating the trajectories of hypergrowing firms, funded by the French National Agency for Research.

E-mail: Alice.Garnier@univ-lyon2.fr

Marion Hersh, PhD, is a senior lecturer in biomedical engineering at the University of Glasgow. Her main areas of research are assistive technology and disability studies, including the employment of disabled people.

She recently completed a Leverhulme Research Fellowship on Mobility for Blind People: New Strategies and Solutions, which resulted in the receipt of a Lady D award from the Polish Government. Follow-up work resulting from the fellowship includes the development of an intelligent and/or robotic travel aid and modelling of the spatial representations of congenitally blind people. She has co-authored two books entitled *Assistive Technology for Visually Impaired and Blind People* (2008) and

Assistive Technology for the Hearing-impaired, Deaf and Deafblind (2003). She is also the organiser and chair of the CVHI Conference Series on Assistive Technology for People with Hearing and Vision, which receives funding from the European Commission.

E-mail: m.hersh@elec.gla.ac.uk

Thomas J. Jordan is the Chairman and Chief Creative Officer of HY Connect, an independent, fully integrated communications firm in the US with offices in Chicago and Milwaukee. The author of two books, *What's a Saatchi and How Come We Have Two of Them?* (2002) and *Re-Render* the Gender (2009), he is a frequent guest speaker at conferences and universities, sharing research and insight on marketing to women. In addition, he has won numerous international creative awards, including prestigious 'Lions' from the Cannes Advertising Festival held each year in France.

E-mail: tjordan@hyc.com

Valeriya Karuk is Business Development Manager at Westminster Business School, the University of Westminster, and she has recently been involved in a number of diversity-related projects. She has won two LDA-funded projects: 'Diversity Case Studies project' and 'Strategic impact of diversity to business performance'. She has also coordinated the 'Implementing Diversity Employment Policies: Examples from large London companies' project for London First as well as research projects for the World Bank, USAID, Coca Cola and Philip Morris. She has run a small student-owned consultancy representing about 18 nationalities specialising in different subject areas.

E-mail: VKaruk1@westminster.ac.uk

Isabelle Maque, PhD (finance), is Assistant Professor at the University of Poitiers, IAE, and researcher at CEREGE-EA 1722, Poitiers, France.

Isabelle's research and publications concentrate primarily on bank–firm relationships focusing on SMEs (multiple-banking, relational vs transactional exchanges, optimisation of banking relationships, French bank–firm relationships and international comparisons). She recently won a grant to pursue her research at international level (Canada, Spain and Scotland). Her latest work involves participation in *Management de la banque: Risques, relation client, organisation* 3rd edition (2011).

E-mail: imaque@univ-poitiers.fr

Gloria Moss FCIPD, PhD, is Reader in Human Resources at Buckinghamshire New University and Visiting Professor at the Ecole Superieure de Gestion, Paris. She combines a background in human resources as Training Manager for Courtaulds and Eurotunnel, where she was responsible for management training with research on leadership, teamwork and design. She has published more than 30 peer-reviewed journal articles investigating the impact of gender, nationality and personality on behaviour, with a book, *Gender, Design and Marketing* (2009), focusing on the impact of gender on behaviours in the area of design and marketing. Another book, *Profiting from Diversity* (2010), is a companion volume to this one and focuses on the business case for diversity as well as the obstacles to achieving progress.

E-mail: Gloria.moss@bucks.ac.uk

Hilary Mullen, MBA, DipM, MMII, has research interests focused on aspects of e-business strategy development, e-marketing and ethical issues in electronic environments, including e-government. She is currently a senior lecturer in the Department for New Media and Technologies at Buckinghamshire New University. In addition to her research activities, Hilary teaches e-business management, strategy development and management. Before academic life, she was actively involved in market-based research consultancy, running her own company in London. She has worked for organisations such as Taylor Nelson Sofres, British Airways, Allied Irish Bank and the Irish Export Board. In her advancing years, she has developed an interest in electronic and mobile marketing to baby boomers.

E-mail: Hilary.mullen@bucks.ac.uk

Isabelle Prim-Allaz, PhD (marketing), is Assistant Professor at the University of Lyon/Coactis Research Center – University of Lyon 2, EA 4161, France. Her research and publications focus primarily on bank–firm relationships, particularly SMEs (relational vs transactional exchanges French bank–firm relationship dissolution). She is also working on relational orientation in the health sector and is a member of a research project on the trajectories of hypergrowing firms, a study funded by the French National Agency for Research.

E-mail: Isabelle.Prim-Allaz@univ-lyon2.fr

Peter Urwin PhD, is Director of the Centre for Employment Research and Professor of Applied Economics at the University of Westminster. He has written papers for *Work Employment and Society* (2001) and produced *Age Matters* for the (then) Department of Trade and Industry (2004). Over the past decade, Peter has carried out work for the Ministry of Justice (2010) on the resolution of conflicts across discrimination jurisdictions; for the Institute for Fiscal Studies on *Ethnic Parity in Jobcentre Plus* (2008); and with Diversity Works for London on the business case for diversity. He is currently investigating issues of generational diversity.

E-mail: urwinp@westminster.co.uk

Lorraine Watkins-Mathys, PhD, PGCE, has research interests focused on aspects of international management and entrepreneurship in emerging and transition economies, including Russia, Central and Eastern Europe, India, Sri Lanka, Vietnam and China. She is currently Head of the School of Applied Management & Law at Buckinghamshire New University. In addition to her research activities, Lorraine teaches international business, aspects of strategy and entrepreneurship. She has been actively involved in consultancy and training with organisations such as Atkins and Veolia, and she is committed with other stakeholders to supporting community and economic development in her local region.

E-mail: Lorraine.Watkins-Mathys@bucks.ac.uk

Catharina Wulf, PhD, has taught in the field of business and managerial communication in France since 1996. She has taught international students at both undergraduate and postgraduate levels in Canada, the US and France. Her primary research interests revolve around e-learning and e-behaviour, virtual teams and leadership, intercultural communication, and organisational behaviour (people skills in management positions). She has presented academic papers at international conferences (IFSAM, Paris; AMS, Lille; EDINEB, Malaga, Spain; University of Maastricht, the Netherlands) in these areas. She has studied in the US, Germany, Canada and France and speaks German, English, French and Italian fluently. Other than teaching, Catharina has worked in the theatre as well as in the field of television screenwriting and production in Canada, Germany and France.

E-mail: catwulf@gmail.com

1
Lessons on Profiting from Diversity

Gloria Moss

This is the second title examining the benefits to be derived from organisational diversity, with the first one, *Profiting from Diversity*, having been published in 2010. The first book focused on the advantages diversity can offer organisations as well as the considerable obstacles to progress, while this volume continues the discussion, focusing on how organisations can best capture these benefits. The latter continues with a discussion of the advantages that diversity can provide organisations. Understanding difference is very much at the heart of this.

In many ways, this positive focus bucks the trend of a lot of writing on diversity. For example, a recent book on the subject, *The Value of Difference* (Kandola, 2009), states that 'We've spent a lot of time, energy and money chasing the ideal of diversity and we have precious little to show for it...we're not getting anywhere with diversity because nothing is compelling us to' (ibid., 1). Elsewhere, Kandola writes that 'Diversity in observable attributes has constantly been found to have negative effects on affective outcomes' and that 'deep seated prejudices some people hold against people who are different from themselves on race and gender may be adding to the difficulty of interaction' (ibid., 53).

The chapters presented in this book, *Lessons on Profiting from Diversity*, all carry a positive message about how diversity can be achieved. They also highlight the diverse elements in people that can be factored into organisational actions in order to boost success. We are not saying that diversity is unproblematic but several chapters show how an understanding of diversity can help reduce barriers to its positive use in organisations, thereby improving competitive advantage.

1

The book is organised into three parts, with the first section discussing diversity in context, and with a focus on the diversity issues relating to web design. The second section then moves into a discussion of diversity in relation to the segmentation variables of age, personality, gender and disability. The final section focuses on diversity's contribution to the bottom line, showing how a new tool can assist in the identification of financial benefits.

1   Definitions

What do we mean by diversity? Researchers have classified differences between people in a number of ways. Wilson and Iles (1999), for example, have categorised them as 'primary' (e.g., age and gender) and 'secondary' (e.g., class and personality). Conversely, Kandola and Fullerton (1994) refer to visible (e.g., race and gender) and non-visible differences (e.g., some aspects of disability). Both the visible and the non-visible are the focus of this book, with chapters examining the implications of **gender** for specific activities such as web design, advertising and enterprise activity, and a chapter also exploring the progress of women in professional service firms and the way masculine organisation cultures can be overturned. **Age** is another visible factor, with chapters on grey entrepreneurs and seniors, and internet/mobile technology. Turning to non-visible differences, there is a chapter on **personality** and how website text can be adapted to different personalities, and a chapter on the benefits a hard-of-hearing population can bring to an organisation. To bring these themes together, the final chapter examines the range of visible and non-visible factors and the benefits that these can bring organisations. The reader will see, spanning the full range of diversities presented in this book, how organisations really can profit from diversity.

2   Benefits

Advocates of the diversity approach argue that customer and employee differences, however defined, should be viewed as an asset (Wilson and Iles, 1999). This implies, then, that individuals should be treated differently according to their characteristics so as to achieve business advantages. By valuing and harnessing the individual differences of staff, such as their age or race, organisational creativity and innovation is reported to improve through the formation of new ideas (Copeland, 1988). The image of the organisation is also reported to improve through a broadening of its appeal to different types of customers and potential job applicants (Thomas and Ely, 1996; Whitehead, 1999). Moreover, customers also may be drawn to an organisation where they can interact with sales staff who share their visible diversity, like age and ethnicity (Johnson-Hillery et al., 1997; Shanmuganthan et al., 2003). Extending the argument, customers will be drawn to products and product sales environments (e.g., websites) that match the preferences of the end-user.

Why is embedding diversity such a priority? There is a growing recognition of the significance of multiple stakeholders in corporate decisions. Increasingly, there is a realisation that managers need to strike a balance among the varied interests of several audiences and the marketing function in order to connect with external players (Chakravorti, 2010). Of course, there are obstacles in the way of achieving greater diversity in organisations, and in the last book, *Profiting from Diversity* (Moss, 2010), several chapters were devoted to the difficulties standing in the way of greater success. It is true to say that 'diversity is being held back by unconscious bias' (Kandola, 2009), but in this book you will see cases where unconscious bias can either be harnessed to advantage (the case, for example, of website text honed to the preferences of the end-user as described by Holly Buchanan), or can be overcome through careful strategic plans (as described in Chapter 6 by Ian Dodds on ways of modifying masculine organisation cultures. Another tactic is transmitting the message that continuation of the *status quo* can damage business, as Tom Jordan does in highlighting the masculine nature of the advertising aimed at women, and Gloria Moss does in highlighting the masculine nature of much web design.

3   Wide range of diversities

The importance of understanding how best to use the Internet to connect with customers is something that has become an increasing priority since the dot.com burst in late 2000. Before that, few organisations had pondered whether there was a need to boost corporate profits by customising marketing communications (Kim et al., 2001), but with the increasing importance of online sales and the growing number of shoppers purchasing from online stores it has become more important for marketers to develop a better understanding of Internet surfers and shoppers (Donthu and Garcia, 1999).

This book presents information on a wide range of diversities, from the visible to the non-visible, and with contributions from people from a range of backgrounds, from academics to practitioners. The reason for having this range is to present a broad perspective on the complex issues presented by diversity. Next we will summarise the contributions that make up this book, examining them in the order in which they appear in this book.

4   An overview

There are two chapters examining the way websites need to reflect the growing diversity of their audiences. Chapter 2, by **Gloria Moss** explores the impact of a range of diversity variables on the design of websites (what is referred to here as *performances*) and on people's *preferences* for these websites, with the main variables explored being personality, nationality and gender. The all-important variable of age is explored in Chapter 3 by **Hilary Mullen, Gloria Moss** and **Catharina Wulf**, while a case study showing how website appeal can be adjusted to suit personality is provided by **Holly Buchanan** in Chapter 5.

In Section A, Chapter 2, **Gloria Moss** explores the impact of a range of diversity variables on a particular context, that of the design of websites. She examines the impact of personality, gender and nationality on *performances* (what people produce) and *preferences* for websites, showing how complex is the process of factoring diversity into strategic thinking. The model presented in this chapter is one which could be used in any sector but the focus on the Internet is justified by the size of this sector. By June 2010, the world Internet user population reached 1.9 billion (http://www.allaboutmarketresearch.com/internet.htm) and annual growth of the World Wide Web is in the order of 20 per cent (Van Iwaarden et al., 2004). This speedy growth brings immense advantages for business since the Internet is thought to offer many advantages compared to conventional channels. For example, it is estimated to produce ten times as many units [sold] with one-tenth of the advertising budget' (Potter, 1994) to facilitate a flexible response, an advantage with shrinking product life cycles (IITA, 1994) and to ease customer retention (Van Iwaarden et al., 2004). Together, these factors are said to have 'transform[ed] the way business is conducted' (Grover and Saeed, 2004). An article written in 2007 on Internet design, for example, makes the following point:

> As the Internet continues to grow and more markets are developed, e-commerce businesses must learn how to use this technology to appeal to their customers' values in the highly competitive e-retailing environment. The potential for enhancing the appeal and usability of business to consumer websites is enormous ... website designers creating websites targeted at mass audiences need to incorporate all of

the different preferences in their design. However designers who are creating sites for a specific audience such as engineering technicians, should understand the specific needs and preferences of this distinct audience and design accordingly. (Cunningham et al., 2007, pp. 2–5)

The international nature of the Internet is a given, and the global audience for the Internet taken with the fact that 'a worldwide, standardised treatment of customers is not the "golden path" of internet marketing' (Barnes et al., 2004) makes it imperative to understand the preferences of an international market. In fact, cultural aspects have been 'recognised as major issues in the internationalisation of e-commerce' (Ksheri, 2001) and cultural factors involve ensuring compatibility between the Internet and the value of society so that design can be matched to the preferences of the end-user (Kurosu, 2003). For there is rich evidence highlighting the persuasiveness of design elements on the Internet (Winn and Beck, 2002), with this as an important element in the 'stickiness' of the Web environment, in other words the sum of website qualities that induce visitors to remain at the website (Cyr and Trevor-Smith, 2004).

Chapter 2 by **Gloria Moss** shows how great an impact these variables can have on the look of a website. Where personality is concerned, it shows how all graphic expression bears the imprint of the maker of that expression and that this is true of drawings and paintings as it is also of electronic media. In an experiment quoted in the chapter, ten 9–10-year-old children produced 153 drawings using computer software as well as 235 freehand drawings, and teachers viewing these productions were asked to infer from this information about the children's learning styles, school subject preferences, behaviour patterns and any other information that occurred. These assumptions were then compared with statements about the children by the children themselves, their parents and their teachers, and the statements were a response to a request to describe the children's most and least favourite school subjects, problem-solving methods, social interaction patterns, personal life philosophies and activity preferences. The inferences made by viewing teachers were found to be correct in 69 per cent and 68 per cent of cases of inferences made about the online and freehand drawings respectively, showing a high ability to infer personality from online expression (Harris, 2007). This result strongly suggests that information about personality is transmitted through online graphic expression.

Where the impact of nationality on web design is concerned, the author conducted a comparison with Dr Rod Gunn of 60 personal websites produced by students at higher education institutions in the

UK and France. It transpired that there were 12 significant differences between the UK and French websites, with the French websites having fewer subjects, more pages, less expert language, more rounded lines, greater number of typeface colours, more informal typeface, greater use of certain colours, greater use of a welcome message, 2D images, colours in the background, use of a crest and reference to one's own achievements. Of the elements that typified the French websites, three-quarters were features that typified female-produced websites in the UK (Gunn and Moss, 2006a), suggesting that French websites are more feminine in character than UK websites. This is not a surprising finding, incidentally, since a well known study of international cultures (Hofstede, 2001) found that France was a more feminine society than the UK.

As far as gender is concerned, a comparison of student-produced websites in the UK revealed statistically significant differences on 13 (56 per cent) of the 23 elements tested in the nationality experiment (Moss et al., 2006b). These elements registering significant differences were spread across the three areas of navigation, language and visual content. The elements on which there were significant differences related to the number of separate subject areas covered (with men favouring more subjects than women), the character of the language (men favoured formal and expert language, self-promotion and infrequent abbreviations), the thematic features of the images used (men favoured use of own logo, images of men and formal images, and women images of women and informal images), non-thematic visual elements (men favouring the use of straight lines, and a conventional layout) and the character of the typography (men favoured formal typography and a smaller or greater number of typeface colours). In terms of navigation, men were more likely to include a site map.

These results across the three variables of personality, nationality and age show the extent to which website design is influenced by personal variables. The next question addressed in this chapter concerns the extent to which preferences vary according to personal variables. Issues related to age are discussed in Chapter 4 by Lorraine Watkins-Mathys but the focus on preferences in this chapter is on gender since this is the only area on which work has been done on preferences. The chapter reports that preference tests show a statistically significant tendency for each gender to assign higher ratings to websites produced by people of their own gender and this finding illustrates the importance of taking diversity into account in the selection of web designer with a view to satisfying the preferences of the end-user.

5 Age and web design

Continuing the theme of digital communications, the link between age and digital communications is explored in Chapter 3 by **Hilary Mullen, Gloria Moss and Catharina Wulf**. They set the scene for a discussion on the use of communications technology by older people by describing the growth in the numbers of this sector of the population in the UK and France, showing how in 2007 the number of Britons aged over 65 exceeded the number of those aged under 16 for the first time; by 2015, half of the adult UK population will be aged over 50 (Young, 2002/3). In France the situation is similar with, in 2009, the 50+ population representing one-third of the population, with youngsters below 20 accounting for just a quarter of the population. It is projected that by 2030, one in two French people will be older than 50 (Guérin, 2009, p. 32), by 2040 the number of people over 75 will double, and by 2050 the number of those who are over 85 will increase from 1.1 million (the figure in 2009) to almost 5 million (Guérin, 2009, p. 19).

Most of the public debates about older people and ageing societies have set a rather pessimistic tone, stressing the problem of providing future pension plans and the potentially negative impact on welfare and care services. Instead of contributing to this pessimistic debate, the authors of this chapter focus on the potential business opportunities generated by the 50+ generations because of their utilisation of the Internet. For example, in the UK it has been found that people aged 50+ were responsible for the majority of the increase in UK Internet usage over the period 2009–10. The size of the UK Internet audience grew by five per cent – from 36.9 million people in May 2009 to 38.8 million people in May 2010 – and according to UKOM, of these 1.9 million new Internet users, 1 million (53 per cent) were at least 50 years old. Of this increase in Internet usage by the 50+, men over 50 were primarily responsible for this growth, accounting for 722,000 (38 per cent) new British Internet users, followed by women over 50 who accounted for 284,000 (15 per cent) new users. This increase in usage by the 50+ population in the UK has produced a situation in which one in four Britons using the Internet today are 50 to 64 years of age.

The chapter compares classification of this older age group in France and the UK and concludes that the Internet is not best being used for this older age group. The evidence for this comes from a 2002 survey of 2,000 people carried out by Millennium, a consultancy specialising in the mature market, showing that 86 per cent of 50+ consumers do not relate to the marketing they see. Similar figures were released in a study by Age Concern entitled 'How Ageist is Britain?' (2004). This shows that more attention could be given to ways of profiting from the diversity that is found in the 50+ generations.

6   Personality and web design

If more could be done to target older people in an appropriate way on the Internet, Chapter 5 by **Holly Buchanan** shows how the wording on the Internet can be adjusted so that it chimes with the preferences of the personality types using the site. We see here how the author analysed the language used by those contributing to onsite reviews of a website specialising in women's clothing in order – following the homogeneity or congruity principle – to identify the style of language that should be used on the website. The author read hundreds of customer reviews and, following analysis, judged that the preferred communication style was SFP, the Sensing Feeling Perceiving type. All these traits are in fact opposite in type to that of the owner/copywriter and so, in order to satisfy the preferences of the end-users, the author changed the voice of the website and emails from NTJ to SFP (NTJ is the Myers-Briggs Intuitive Thinking Judging type).

In an A/B email test, one version was written in the old style (NTJ) and another was written in the new style (SFP); the new style (SFP) achieved a 27 per cent higher click-through rate. The client was convinced that the new copy was effective, clearly recognised the benefits of diversity and made changes throughout the site.

7   Grey entrepreneurs

The subject of age recurs in Chapter 4 by **Lorraine Watkins-Mathys** looking at the phenomenon of grey entrepreneurs. This is one of two chapters in the book examining entrepreneurship characteristics, with the second one by Isabelle Maque, Audrey Becuwe, Isabelle Prim-Allaz and Alice Garnier looking at how to profit from diversity in the banking sector. Where age is concerned, **Lorraine Watkins-Mathys** explains that Europe is ageing fast, that people are living much longer than previously, and more men over 50 will be out of work. She discusses estimates that by 2050 the 'age dependency ratio' – those dependent on being supported by those in employment within the EU countries – will rise to 55 per cent.

Against this background, the chapter aims to provide an overview of grey entrepreneurship obtained from a literature review and attempts to find out the following: what entrepreneurial activities grey entrepreneurs are engaged in; who they are; what their characteristics are; what drives them to become entrepreneurs later on in life; and how the future might render grey entrepreneurship important. On the basis of the findings, the author seeks to make recommendations to policy-makers, researchers and entrepreneurship educators.

The chapter findings affirm that there is an economic and demographic need to promote grey enterprise even though the greatest contribution in entrepreneurial activity is still currently being made by younger entrepreneurs. Grey entrepreneurs tend to start up a business in order to supplement their pension, resulting mainly in low-growth ventures, although a few high-growth businesses set up by grey entrepreneurs are focused on making a business idea happen and making money. In terms of their characteristics, grey entrepreneurs, like their younger counterparts, are mainly white, male, and educated to degree level or equivalent. They are not very likely to have had a parent who ran their own business and are very unlikely to be female or from a different ethnic origin.

Researchers confirm that the topic of grey enterprise remains under-researched, especially in areas relating to the behaviour and experience of grey entrepreneurs, and the growth and turnover of grey start-up businesses. Equally, cross-country comparisons of grey entrepreneurship are relatively sparse. Other obvious gaps include research into older female and older ethnic entrepreneurs, and how to stimulate opportunity-driven grey entrepreneurship that leads to high-growth enterprise. Furthermore, much of the literature on grey entrepreneurial activity is quantitative, providing opportunities for qualitative researchers to collect data that can give rich and contextualised insights into the experiences of grey entrepreneurs.

Finally, the chapter recommends that policy-makers, researchers and entrepreneurship educators pay more attention to promoting grey enterprise because tomorrow's demographic and economic data demand it.

8 Gender and diversity

8.1 Masculine organisational cultures

Four chapters examine how a greater understanding of gender can help organisations profit from diversity. Two offer a UK perspective and one a perspective from the US. Chapter 6 from the UK, by **Ian Dodds**, introduces us to the masculine nature of organisations. He explains how, in the West, government, industry and commerce, education and health have historically evolved under the direction of white males, with the effect that the cultures within them have developed masculine cultures in line with the values and characteristic practices of this group. These result in individuals who are not white and male experiencing unconscious bias which can limit both their contribution and their career progression. It not only manifests itself in the workplace, but also at customer, client and service-user interfaces, resulting in lost revenue and business development opportunities.

Ian Dodds discusses interventions based on his extensive experience which can reverse a masculine organisational culture. These interventions often begin with initial research to determine how unconscious bias plays out in the workplace and in the interface with the market, and then, in order to engage at an intellectual and emotional level, having actors act out scenarios to illustrate the findings from the research. These help make an emotional impact, generating in executives the will to act to change the situation. In one specific case, the executives at this point challenged everyone to behave inclusively both in internal and external interactions, with a key message being that promotion was dependent on demonstrating inclusive behaviour. In this case this initiative was followed up by training, and the success of the intervention was measured by a comparison of a diversity and inclusion assessment before and after it had taken place. Moreover, the annual employee engagement survey was structured so as to enable an inclusion index score to be generated for each of the diversity strands, with progress measured in terms of both the 'softer' change in inclusion (for example through measuring engagement indices for different diversity strands) as well as in terms of 'harder' business-related outcomes (for example, retention of high-potential under-represented employees, new business gains, and customer satisfaction indices by diversity identity group).

8.2 Profiting from positive marketing cultures

Moving to the specific environment of advertising, in Chapter 7 **Tom Jordan** begins from the starting point that the management of most Fortune 500 companies consists mostly of older, white men. He points out how this male domination typifies the advertising industry as well 'with a complete lack of diversity where it matters quite a bit; in the creative departments of the advertising agencies'. He cites the fact that over 70 per cent of all advertising is created by men (Farris, 2005) and if the filters of approval are added in, the creative directors (over 90 per cent men), you arrive at a situation where advertising is created by men, approved by men and appeals mostly to men.

He asks why this is a problem, and part of his answer resides in the fact that the statistics show that women are responsible for over 80 per cent of all purchases (Barletta, 2006). Moreover, research by his agency shows that the percentage of women influenced can be higher in the case of dual decisions, over 90 per cent of which are influenced by the woman. The other part of the answer resides in the fact that an online survey (Greenfield, 2002) found that 91 per cent of female respondents took the view that 'advertisers don't understand them'.

So there is much about the advertising industry to confound the reader, and **Tom Jordan** probes the reasons why it is configured the way it is. One of the reasons suggested is the lure of the rewards for creative people in advertising agencies via the international creative competitions. Jordan points out that if you win a 'Lion', the prestigious award at the Cannes International Advertising Festival, 'your reputation in the creative community increases, your chance for job advancement increases, and there is a good chance that your salary could increase as well'. He goes on to explain that the standards set by Cannes govern the Awards Annuals and these in turn set the tone for the Portfolio Centres which teach writers and art directors how to do award-winning work.

What is the way forward? **Tom Jordan** outlines six principles which he has found bring success in reaching women, and he suggests initiating a discussion around these with the creative directors, art directors and Internet creatives, making it clear that new thinking is called for. Like **Ian Dodds**, he has shown through his own work in organisations that this change is possible.

8.3 Masculine professional services firms

In Chapter 8 **Gloria Moss** examines the world of the professional services firm and the moves and motives there to increase gender diversity. The sectors examined include the legal sector, accountancy, management consultancy, design and software, and she shows how Maister's (1997) view that competitive advantage in professional service firms can be achieved through success with clients and staff can be assisted through the attainment of diversity. For example, a match between the gender of the client and the client-facing member of staff can help in building a successful relationship, while the retention of capable people of both genders can ensure that the firm builds competitive advantage from its human resources, the principal differentiating factor in professional service firms.

Interviews in each of the sectors reveals that these two are major factors in the firms' drive for greater gender diversity, making it clear that there is a very strong business case for greater gender diversity. Having said that, some sectors appear to have a long way to go before they reach anywhere close to equity in terms of male/female partner split. Diversity initiatives can be categorised as having limited or far-reaching effects and many of the diversity initiatives in this sector appear to be of a conservative nature, matching the first two levels only of Wheeler's progressive model of diversity initiatives. This leaves space for initiatives focused on what Wheeler terms 'valuing' and 'leveraging', which would entail far-reaching changes in organisational culture and the management of unconscious bias. Given that the barriers to achieving a fully diverse workforce can only be overcome with structural, cultural and behavioural changes (Holvino et al., 2004), one can imagine that achieving real change can only be achieved through a focus on organisational culture and, as part of that, informal mental models and norms (Senge et al., 1994; Trefry, 2006). One can conceive that initiatives in these areas would provide a major boost to the achievement of diversity in these sectors.

9   Profiting from diversity in the banking sector

Chapter 9 by **Isabelle Maque, Audrey Becuwe, Isabelle Prim-Allaz and Alice Garnier** explores the characteristics of entrepreneurs in France in Rhône-Alpes, a French economically dynamic region. The sample was limited to firms older than four years and with a turnover of at least 500,000 euros per annum. Altogether, responses were received from 382 French small and medium-sized enterprises.

The study highlighted a total of 19 significant differences in the responses of the men and women. These differences related to entrepreneurs' characteristics, with women being slightly younger, having less experience in terms of creating other companies, being more likely to have accounting and finance as a prime skill, and being less likely to be a serial entrepreneur. Differences also emerged in terms of business characteristics and objectives, with women's turnover being lower than men's, and stability in growth having a higher priority for women than men. Consistent with this last point is a lesser intention on the part of the women to sell the business than was expressed by the men. Other differences relate to the fact that women place less reliance on external investors, and higher levels of satisfaction with the support received from a bank. In terms of the management of the business, the women were shown to be more concerned about improving the well-being of employees compared to the men in the sample. These results indicate the need to take gender into account in future research and also in the way that financiers and banks deal with women. Awareness of these differences can lead financiers and banks to profit from diversity by honing their products to the preferences of male and female entrepreneurs.

In contrast to these differences, the results do not highlight any significant differences between men and women in their level of formal education and choice of sector.

10 Deafness in the workplace

Finally, Chapter 10 by Marion Hersh is devoted to disability and issues relating to deafness in the workplace. It concerns the employment of people for whom deafness is a problem. Three and a half million people of working age (16 to 65) out of a total working population of some 37 million (i.e. c. 10 per cent) have some degree of hearing impairment, with 160,000 of them severely or profoundly deaf.

The chapter makes the point that studies relating the positive impact of equality and diversity policies to organisations (EEOT, 2008) have related primarily to gender and race rather than disability. For instance, studies show that high achievers prefer to work in organisations with diversity policies, practices and values (Ng and Burke, 2005), and that such policies, practices and values generally result in improvements in productivity, sales, morale, staff retention, human capital, market access, reputation and employment relations (Kirton and Greene, 2005; Monks, 2007). More than half of the 200 companies surveyed by the European Commission identified the benefits as improved long-term competitiveness, as well as sometimes improved short-term performance. Thus, increasing the diversity of the workforce will generally have significant benefits for an organisation, unless it is badly managed and/or the organisation is marked by systemic discrimination.

Marion Hersh highlights a number of benefits from employing deaf people, with these categorised as follows:

- extending the talent pool;
- retaining skilled employees who become deaf;

- benefiting from the skills, aptitudes and approaches which deaf people may bring to the organisation;
- seeing positive impacts on the organisation of a more diverse workforce;
- improving public relations and wider markets.

Since deaf people have the same spectrum of skills as hearing people, employing them increases the pool of potential employees (HREOC, 2005), thereby increasing an employer's choices and chances of finding a suitable employee with the desired skills and qualities. While of value in general, this is particularly important when there are either general or specific skills shortages. It also increases the talent pool and consequently the likelihood of finding unusually talented and creative employees, or employees with specialised skills who are likely to make a significant contribution to the organisation.

In addition to their job-related skills, training and experience, many deaf employees may additionally have particular skills, aptitudes and approaches as a result of their experiences of deafness. Deaf (and other disabled) people are likely to bring this adaptability and creativity into the workplace with them and may therefore be better at finding innovative and useful solutions to a range of workplace problems.

Moreover, **Marion Hersh** makes the point that several (small-scale) studies show that deaf and hearing people have different 'preferred' hemispheres for processing complex stimuli, such as pictures and letters, as well as detecting target shapes in the peripheral visual field (Phippard, 1977; Reynolds, 1993). There are therefore likely to be advantages for organisations which employ both deaf and hearing people so that both preferences are fully represented. Many deaf people use largely visual communication strategies and are therefore likely to use visual thinking processes and approaches to problem solving. Thus, deaf people with relevant aptitudes and qualifications may be particularly suited to professions such as architecture, design, fine arts, surgery and astronomy, where visual perceptions, visual judgements and/or hand–eye coordination are important.

Since the incidence of deafness increases with age (RNID, undated a), it is important that organisations are 'deaf friendly' so that they can retain skilled employees who have become hard of hearing or deaf with age, and also make the best use of the skills and experiences of these employees. Employers who do not provide appropriate adjustments, practices and policies or where the attitudes of managers and co-workers are hostile, may lose the skills and accumulated experience of valuable employees due to age-related hearing impairment. Alternatively, these employees may stay with the organisation but take great pains to hide their hearing impairments. This will prevent them accessing appropriate accommodations and may subject them to stress, lead to misunderstandings and possibly even conflict with co-workers, and to a deterioration in performance as communication becomes more difficult.

11   Evaluating the business returns from diversity

The final section of the book, evaluating the returns from diversity, is ground breaking. Authors **Ian Dodds, Alan David, Gloria Moss, Valeriya Karuk and Peter Urwin,** having been commissioned by the Mayor of London's Diversity Works for London programme, examine the strategic benefits of implementing diversity in organisations. Chapter 11 thus provides an edited version of the final report, which is available at www.diversityworksforlondon.com. The aim of the project was to demonstrate how diversity initiatives can have a positive impact on business performance, and in doing this identify measurement tools and a methodology for calculating the financial contribution of the effective management of diversity. The aim was also to track the overall business benefits of diversity on the bottom line.

In order to do this, the project team conducted in-depth research in six companies representing different industries and varying in size and turnover, from micro-businesses to global corporations. After examining the selected companies with a view to determining the impact of diversity on the bottom line, the team developed and piloted the Diversity Return on Investment (ROI) tools. These consisted of the Diversity Scorecard (adapted from Hubbard's model) and the Value Analysis Tool within the companies, details of which are provided in the chapter. Overall the pilot demonstrated that it is possible to obtain estimates with acceptable levels of confidence for targeted improvements arising from equality and diversity initiatives. The pilot also showed that the tools work well regardless of company size, the only difference reflecting in the scale of the analysis and the level of detail. The main challenge was a need to estimate the extent to which the targeted improvement can be attributed to equality and diversity factors as opposed to other initiatives. Although Diversity ROI is already being measured in other countries such as the US, we believe that this project is the first attempt to measure Diversity ROI in the UK, and we hope that the results will encourage other organisations to use the tools presented here to measure bottom-line benefits of diversity.

12 Conclusion

This range of chapters provides plentiful evidence of the practical benefits to organisations of ensuring that diversity is fully reflected in the workplace. A failure to do this can only dent an organisation's ability to compete in an increasingly harsh and competitive world, and it is hoped that the range of experience reflected in this volume will lead practitioners and academics alike to further explore the enormous benefits to be gained by greater organisational diversity.

References

Age Concern (2004), *How Ageist is Britain?* (Age Concern: London).
Barletta, M. (2006), *Marketing to Women: How to Increase Your Share of the World's Largest Market* (Kaplan Publishing: United States).
Barnes, B., Fox, M., and Morris, D. (2004), 'Exploring the linkage between internal marketing, relationship marketing and service quality: a case study of a consulting organisation', *Total Quality Management and Business Excellence*, 15 (5/6), 593–601.
Chakravorti, B. (2010), 'Stakeholder marketing 2.0', *Journal of Public Policy and Marketing*, 29 (1), 97–102.
Copeland, L. (1988), 'Valuing diversity, part 1: making the most of cultural differences at the workplace', *Personnel*, 65 (6), 52–60.
Cunningham, D., Thach, L. and Thompson, L. (2007), 'Innovative e-commerce site design: a conceptual model to match consumer MBTI dimensions to website design', *Journal of Internet Commerce*, 6 (3), 1–27.
Cyr, D. and Trevor-Smith, H. (2004), 'Localisation of web design: an empirical comparison of German, Japanese and United States web site characteristics', *Journal of the American Society for Information Science and Technology*, 55 (13), 1199–1208.
Donthu, N. and Garcia, A. (1999), 'The internet shopper', *Journal of Advertising Research*, 39 (3), 52–8.
Equal Employment Opportunities Trust (EEOT) (2008), *Diversity and Equality – A review of the literature, June 2008* (Auckland).
Farris, K. (2005) *Motivated Reasoning and Social Basis* (University of Texas: Austin).
Greenfield Online for Arnold's Women's Insight Team (2002).
Grover, V. and Saeed, K. (2004), 'Strategic orientation and performance of Internet-based businesses', *Information Systems Journal*, 4, 23–42.
Guérin, S. (2009), *Société des seniors* (Paris: Michalon).
Gunn, R. and Moss, G. (2006a), 'An interactive aesthetic for French and UK E-commerce', *International Journal of Technology, Knowledge and Society*.
Harris, J. (2007), 'Personal projections in artists' work: implications for branding', *Journal of Brand Management*, 14 (4), 296–313.
Hofstede, G. (2001), *Culture's Consequences: Comparing Values, Behaviors, Institutions, and Organizations Across Nations* (New York: Sage).
Holvino, E., Ferdman, B. M. and Merrill-Sands, D. (2004), 'Creating and sustaining diversity and inclusion in organizations: strategies and approaches'.

In Stockdale, M. S. and Crosby, F. J. (eds), *The Psychology and Management of Workplace Diversity*, pp. 245–76 (Malden, MA: Blackwell).

HREOC (2005), 'WORKability I: Barriers', Human Rights and Equal Opportunity Commission. http://www.accc.gov.au/content/index.phtml/itemId/287 231/fromItemId/815972/quickLinkId/816517/whichType/

IITA (1994), 'Electronic commerce and the NII', Information Infrastructure Technology and Applications.

Johnson-Hillery, J., Kang, J. and Tuan, W. (1997), 'The difference between elderly consumers' satisfaction levels and retail sales personnel's perceptions', *International Journal of Retail & Distribution Management*, 25 (4), 126–37.

Kandola, B. (2009), *The Value of Difference* (Cornwall: Pearn Kandola Publishing).

Kandola, R. and Fullerton, J. (1994), 'Diversity: more than just an empty slogan', *Personnel Management*, 26 (11), 46–50.

Kandola, R. and Fullerton, J. (1998), *Diversity in Action: Managing the Mosaic*, 2nd edition (London: CIPD).

Kim, J. W., Lee, B. H., Shaw, M. J., Chang, H. L. and Nelson, M. (2001), 'Application of decision-free induction techniques to personalised advertisements on internet storefronts', *International Journal of Electronic Commerce*, 5 (3), 45–62.

Kirton, G. and Greene, A. (2005), *The Dynamics of Managing Diversity. A Critical Approach*. 2nd edition (Oxford: Elsevier).

Ksheri, N. (2001), 'Determinants of the locus of global commerce', *Electronic Markets*, 11, 251–57.

Kurosu, M. (2003), 'A cultural comparison of website design from a usability engineering perspective'. In Ratner, J. (ed.), *Human Factors and Web Development*, 2nd edition, pp. 47–165 (Mahwah: Lawrence Erlbaum Associates).

Maister, D. H. (1997), *Managing the Professional Service Firm*, new edition (New York: Free Press Paperbacks).

Monks, K. (2007), *The Business Impact of Equality and Diversity* (Dublin: The International Evidence, Equality Authority).

Moss, G. and Gunn, R. (2006b), 'Some men like it black, some women like it pink: consumer implications of differences in male and female website design', *Journal of Consumer Behaviour*, 5 (4), 328–41.

Ng, E. S. W. and Burke, R. J. (2005), 'Person-organisation fit and the war for talent: does diversity management make a difference?', *International Journal of Human Resource Management*, 16 (7), 1195–210.

Picard, R. (1998), *Affective Computing* (Cambridge, MA: MIT Press).

Potter, E. (1994), 'Commercialisation of the World Wide Web', WELL topic in the Internet conference on the WELL. 16 November.

RNID (undated a), 'Facts and figures on deafness and tinnitus' (factsheet), http://www.rnid.org.uk/information_resources/factsheets/deaf_awareness/fact sheets_leaflets/facts_and_figures_on_deafness_and_tinnitus.htm, accessed 26 November 2008.

Senge, P., Kleiner, A., Roberts, C., Ross, R., Roth, G. and Smith, B. (1999), *The Dance of Change: The Challenges to Sustaining Momentum in Learning Organizations* (New York: Doubleday).

Shanmuganthan, P., Dhaliwal, S., Stone, M. and Foss, B. (2003), 'Does ethnic focus change how banks should implement customer relationship management?', *Journal of Financial Services Marketing*, 8 (1), 49–62.

Thomas, D. and Ely, R. (1996), 'Making differences matter: a new paradigm for managing diversity', *Harvard Business Review*, 74 (5), 79–90.

Trefry, M. (2006), 'A double-edged sword: organizational culture in multicultural organizations', *International Journal of Management*, 1 September, http://www.allbusiness.com/company-activities-management/management-corporate-cult ure/13477475-1.html

Van Iwaarden, J., van der Wiele, T., Ball, L. and Millen, R. (2004), 'Perceptions about the quality of web sites: a survey amongst students at Northeaster University and Erasmus University', *Information and Management*, 41 (8), 947–59.

Wheeler, M. (1998), 'Measuring diversity: a strategy for organisational effectiveness', *Employment Relations Today*, Springer, 61–68.

Whitehead, M. (1999), 'A time for buy-in', *People Management*, 2 (11), 54–6.

Wilson, E. and Iles, P. (1999), 'Managing diversity – an employment and service delivery challenge', *International Journal of Public Sector Management*, 12 (1), 27–48.

Winn, W. and Beck, K. (2002), 'The persuasive power of design elements on an e-commerce web site', *Technical Communication*, 49 (1), 17–35.

Young, G. (2002/3), *The Implications of an Ageing Population for the UK Economy*, www.publications.parliment.uk/ld200203/ldselect/ldeconaf/179/1, accessed 1 March 2011.

Section A
Diversity in Context

2
Diversity and Web Design

Gloria Moss

1 E-commerce: a growth area

By June 2010, the world Internet user population reached 1.9 billion (All about market research), and commentators are agreed on the speedy growth of the World Wide Web, with annual growth estimated in 2004 at 20 per cent (Van Iwaarden et al., 2004) and recently, by Dr Odlyzko of the University of Minnesota, as 50 to 60 per cent per year (Economist, Technology Quarterly). This speedy growth brings immense advantages for business since the Internet is thought to offer many advantages compared to conventional channels. For example, 'it is estimated to produce ten times as many units [sold] with one tenth of the advertising budget' (Potter, 1994), to facilitate a flexible response, is an advantage with shrinking product life cycles (IITA, 1994), and to ease customer retention (Van Iwaarden et al., 2004). Together, these factors are said to have 'transform[ed] the way business is conducted' (Grover and Saeed, 2004).

In terms of web usage, critical independent variables are those of location, gender and age. Where the first of these is concerned, the percentage of the population using the Internet varies enormously from continent to continent, as can be seen in Table 1.

The table shows that web visitors increasingly represent a multicultural community. In 2008, the consultancy 'Global internet Advisors' wrote that 'In the last 10 years the Internet has radically de-Americanized with profound strategic consequences for Internet CEOs, boards, VCs, investment bankers, government policy makers, and the entire U.S. economy. Over the *next* 10 years the most money, the largest audiences, and the biggest opportunities for Internet growth will happen *outside* the United States' (Global Internet Advisors, 2008).

Table 2.1   Internet usage statistics, June 2010, Miniwatts Marketing Group

Continent	Penetration (% population)	Growth in penetration 2000–2010 (%)	Users (% of table)
Africa	10.9	2,357	5.6
Asia	21.5	621	42.0
Europe	58.4	352	24.2
Middle East	29.8	1825	3.2
North America	77.4	146	13.5
Latin America	34.5	1,032	10.4
Australia	61.3	179	1.1

Source: http://www.internetworldstats.com/stats.htm.

Slicing the Internet population by the further variable of gender reveals similar proportions of men and women using the Web in the US and the UK (Ono and Zavodny, 2003; Jupiter Communications, 2004) but with women as less frequent and less intense users than men, and less frequent online purchasers (Bimber, 2000; Allen, 2001; Van Slyke et al., 2002; Ono and Zavodny, 2003; Rodgers and Harris, 2003; Garbarino and Strahilevitz, 2004; Simon and Peppas, 2005). As far as age is concerned, the following data were collected for Internet users in the US, showing great variations in usage by age.

Table 2.2   US Internet users by age

Generations explained			
Generation name	Birth years, age in 2009	% of total adult population	% of Internet-using population
Gen Y Millenials	Born 1977–90, age 9–32	26	30
Gen X	Born 1965–76, age 33–44	20	23
Younger boomers	Born 1955–64, age 45–54	20	22
Older boomers	Born 1946–54, age 55–63	13	13
Silent generation	Born 1937–45, age 64–72	9	7
G I generation	Born 1936, age 73+	9	4

Source: Pew Internet and American Life Project, December 2008. N = 2,253 total adults.

If location and age are brought together, great variation in usage across Europe emerges. In Scandinavian countries, for example Denmark, Norway and Sweden half of 55–75 year olds regularly surf the Web, while in the UK 43 per cent of those in this age group frequently use the Internet, higher than the frequency of top European heavyweights Germany and France, where only 33 per cent and 40 per cent respectively of this age group regularly use the (Eurostat, 2010).

Moreover, if gender is brought into the equation, research by the (Nielsen Wire, 2010) powered by Nielsen reveals that people aged 50+ were responsible for the majority of the increase in UK Internet usage over the period 2009–10. The size of the UK Internet audience grew by 5 per cent from 36.9 million people in May 2009 to 38.8 million people in May 2010 and, according to UKOM, of these 1.9 million new Internet users, 1 million (53 per cent) were at least 50 years old. Of this increase in Internet usage by the 50+ age group, men over 50 were primarily responsible for this growth, accounting for 722,000 (38 per cent) new British Internet users, followed by women over 50 who accounted for 284,000 or 15 per cent of new users. This increase in usage by the 50+ population in the UK has produced a situation in which one in four Britons using the Internet today is 50 to 64 years of age.

In the overview that follows, we will investigate the role that web design can play in web-user interfaces.

2 Design and web design

Why the focus on design? Quite simply, design is acknowledged to be the 'central feature of culture and everyday life in many parts of the world...replacing nature as the dominant presence in human experience' (Buchanan and Margolin, 1995, p. xii). It is also described as one of the elements of the marketing mix that shapes a person's overall reactions to a product (Roy and Wield, 1989). Moreover, it has been shown that the physical form of a product is an important element in its design (Bloch, 1995), creating certain effects in buyers (Kotler, 1973–74) and evoking emotions that can play a critical role in communicating with customers (Chen and Dhillon, 2002).

In terms of defining these effects, research has shown that products perceived as pleasurable are preferred (Yahomoto and Lambert, 1994) and used more frequently than those not perceived as pleasurable (Jordan, 1998), a factor leading to enhanced purchasing (Groppel, 1993; Donovan et al., 1994). Moreover, recent research has shown that products with visual appeal not only attract greater attention (Maughan et al., 2007) but also enhance perception of the product's usefulness, enjoyment, ease of use and satisfaction (Van der Heijden, 2003; Van Iwaarden et al., 2004) as well as usability (Hassenzahl, 2007). What is more, a product with visual appeal can induce a preparedness to pay a premium (Bloch et al., 2003) of up to 66 per cent as compared to products without visual appeal (Hassenzahl, 2007).

Where research specifically on web design is concerned, previous information systems research has largely followed a functional approach, focusing more on what one set of researchers (Eroglu et al., 2003) have described as high 'task relevant' cues (functional and utilitarian issues) rather than low 'task relevant' cues (emotional/hedonic factors) (Wang et al., 2010). Despite this greater emphasis on task relevant cues (ibid.), research has found factors such as text, imagery and navigation to play a significant role in the Internet user's experience (Zhang and von Dran, 2000), with effectiveness related to technical aspects (e.g., speed of loading), content (Joergensen and Blythe, 2003) as well as design and form (Schenkman and Jonsson, 2000; Chen and Dhillon, 2002; Lavie and Tractinsky, 2004). In fact, the quality of graphics is highlighted as an important design element (Chau et al., 2000), and the specific importance of graphics emerges in a later study in which graphics are listed as one of ten factors contributing to user dissatisfaction in the US and Netherlands (Van Iwaarden et al., 2004).

In terms of specifics, the emotions evoked by design can add to perceptions of a site's credibility, a term used as referring to the believability, perceived quality, trustworthiness and level of expertise of the site (Fogg et al., 2002). Design and form can also influence user preferences (Chen and Dhillon, 2002; Cyr and Bonnani, 2005) with, in the words of Chen and Dhillon (2002), the appearance and structure of the website:

> encourag[ing] or discourag[ing] a consumer's purchasing intentions. In the marketing literature, website features such as layout, appeal, graphics, readability, and ease-of-use have been considered to affect consumers' clicking frequency. (Ibid., pp. 310–11)

Given that 'clicking frequency' registers individual and group interest in a site, Chen and Dillion are signalling the impact of visual factors on time spent online. A separate study, moreover, found that satisfaction with a website relates to 'stickiness' (Holland and Baker, 2001), a quality that refers to the sum of all the website qualities that induce visitors to remain at the website.

Other specifics relate to the fact that a website perceived as attractive can have a positive impact on intention to use a website (Van der Heijden, 2003) or perform a search (Wang et al., 2010), with e-design having a potentially greater impact on e-loyalty and customer retention (Aaker, 1991; De Chernatony and McDonald 1992; Kapferer, 1992) than traditional attributes such as product selection and price (Ibeh et al., 2005). A positive correlation has also been found between positive emotions and intention to purchase (ibid.), with this last study finding design having a stronger influence on the activation of a search than on intention to purchase. It should be pointed out, however, that the methodology in this last study involved eliciting reactions to a random set of commercial websites, and research by the author of the present chapter, described later on, shows how the selection of websites is all important since those designed using a masculine aesthetic (the case of the majority of commercial websites) have less appeal to women than to men. In this way, the methodology used in the 2010 study (ibid.) could have influenced the results and the study would need to be repeated with a non-random selection of websites in order to determine the relative impact of design on propensity to search and propensity to purchase.

The importance of design and e-design in particular are the reasons for the focus on this area here.

3 Using an interactionist approach to understand preferences

Before the dot.com burst in late 2000, few had pondered whether there was a need for increasing corporate profits by customising marketing communications for different segments of Internet users (Kim et al., 2001). However, with the increasing importance of online sales and the growing number of shoppers purchasing from online stores, it is imperative for marketers to develop a better understanding of Internet surfers and shoppers (Donthu and Garcia, 1999). The increasing competition online and the worldwide nature of the market mean that a 'standardised treatment of customers is not the "golden path" of internet marketing' (Barnes et al., 2004).

So, there is increasing recognition of the need to develop values for a new brand that turns on research into consumers' needs (Gordon, 1999).

In the field of e-commerce, however, while lip service is paid to the view that 'a website has to be designed for a targeted customer segment...' (Gommans et al., 2001, p. 51), the emphasis in much of the literature on 'web atmospherics' is on finding universal solutions (Palmer, 2002; Joergensen and Blythe, 2003).

The universalist approaches seek to identify the factors in the attribute that will have universal appeal and this approach stands in stark contrast to so-called Field theory (Lewin, 1936) or interactionism (Mischel, 1977), which assumes that individuals will view physical and social settings differently, producing differences in 'life-space' and consumption behaviour (Gehrt and Yan, 2004). These theories dictate that characteristics of the stimulus object (attributes), characteristics of the individual (demographics, Internet usage), and the situation (situational factors) affect reactions to the stimulus object (format preference). This means that instead of seeking solutions or laws that will apply to *all* situations, we should seek out solutions that work in *particular* instances, thereby shaping products around the 'unique and particular needs' of the customer that are well established (Hammer, 1995).

The precise mechanisms involved in delivering this process to a diversity of online customers has not (prior to work involving the author) been the object of detailed study. So, although as we have seen, there has been an appreciation that 'a website has to be designed for a targeted customer segment' (Gommans et al., 2001, p. 51), there has been a failure to compare and identify the preferences of different market segments. One area that has been overlooked relates to a study of the behaviour of women in targeted activity by the retail sector (Burmaster, 2006) with until recently 'a paucity of information on how men and women react to design elements of a website' (Cyr and Bonanni, 2005, p. 5). A further area of neglect has been the study of the impact of audience age on the Internet, the subject of Chapter 4 in this book.

We have talked of the overarching importance of matching websites to the users' preference, but a key and related question concerns the variables that influence the type of site produced. How do someone's personality imprint on web productions, and analogously how do nationality and gender? These are relatively neglected areas of research, which the author has attempted to correct through research of her own or by inviting work on this topic in a special issue of a journal (Harris, 2007).

The overview in this chapter will fill the gaps identified above, exploring the impact of segmentation variables on web design *productions* and in some cases *preferences*, and exploring the implications of these findings for organisations. Before looking at these in detail, the overview offers a summary concerning the conceptual background to the concept of diversity.

4 Diversity and equal opportunities

Equal opportunities (EO) policies were introduced in the 1960s and 1970s as part of a European initiative to complement anti-discrimination and equal pay legislation (Moss and Daunton, 2006e; Moss, 2010) in an attempt to provide equal opportunities and outcomes in the workplace (Kirton and Greene, 2000; Armstrong, 2001). The emphasis in these policies was on a philosophy of sameness (Gagnon and Cornelius, 2000; Kirton and Greene, 2000) rooted in an assumption regarding the fundamental sameness of individuals (Miller, 1996). Assimilation was perceived as a one-way process with minorities required to adopt the norms and practices of the majority (Nkomo, 1992) and this mindset produced an acceptance that white, non-disabled, heterosexual men's experiences and interpretations of organisational life were valid and universally applicable (Alvesson and Billing, 1997). This led to organisational analyses produced 'through a lens which is primarily white and male' (Cianni and Romberger, 1997, p. 116), producing organisational cultures constructed around a 'white, male norm' (Kirton and Greene, 2000, pp. 288–9).

In the fullness of time, the notion of 'sameness' implied within EO policies was replaced by diversity initiatives, which viewed differences as strengths rather than weaknesses (White, 1995). These diversity initiatives attempted to chart the impact of culturally reproduced and socially constructed group membership on individuals (Nkomo, 1992; Kirton and Green, 2001) and included studies focusing on gender and its relation to organisational culture (Acker, 1992; Gherardi, 1996), leadership style (Rosener, 1990; Alimo-Metcalfe and Alban-Metcalfe, 2003) as well as studies evaluating managers' behaviours (Powell et al., 2004).

Despite the advances made, there was a feeling that discussions of group-based diversity were held back by a fear that the discussion of such differences would be used, as arguably it has in the past, to reassert inferiority and exclusion (Webb, 1997). This reluctance to map group-based differences had, according to Liff (1996), the effect of maintaining the power of dominant groups and, according to Barmes and Ashtiany (2003, p. 291), the effect of 'drastically underestimating the difficulties and obstacles typically encountered by members of disadvantaged groups compared to others'. This neglect heightens the importance of bringing to light the perspective of diverse groups. So, following this brief introduction to the notions of EO and diversity, we can now look at what we know concerning diversity and web design.

5   Diversity and e-design

A website is the product of a long process involving people from a number of functions including web designers graphic designers, brand managers and marketing personnel. The author has categorised the actions of these personnel as having *performance* elements (for example, product design and management tasks such as leadership) and/or *preference* elements, for example, recruitment of designers, selection of designs and selection of logos (Moss, 2007b, 2009a). These *performance* and *preference* elements will be examined in turn.

5.1   Performance elements

According to an Institute of Employment Studies report on measures of organisational performance, *performance* elements can include management as well as innovation elements, with the latter including new product development (NPD) (Page et al., 2006; Moss, 2007b). Both these management and innovation elements will be investigated in the following sections.

5.1.1   *Management*

Management and leadership are overlapping and related activities (Mintzberg, 1973; Whetton and Cameron, 2005) and there is a clear link between leadership and innovation, with studies finding good leadership to be critical to NPD (Brown and Eisenhardt, 1998). The research highlights two factors as critical to greater innovation and the development of products acceptable to the target market (Barczak and Wilemon, 1992), these being (i) the development of a vision (Song and Noh, 2006) and (ii) the use of a participatory style, twin elements of part of the so-called 'transformational' style of leadership. The literature widely reports transformational leadership to be the style of leadership that women prefer to exercise (Rosener, 1990; Nkomo, 1992; Kirton and Greene, 2000; Alimo-Metcalfe and Alban-Metcalfe, 2003) with men more likely to use the transactional style of leadership, a style not credited with a positive impact on innovation.

The observation that men and women manage differently has been widely asserted (White, 1995; Moore, 2000; Bird and Brush, 2002; Vinnicombe and Singh, 2002) and is significant given the tendency (as we shall see later when looking at *preferences*) for people to ascribe higher ratings to leadership styles in others that mirror their own personal way of enacting leadership. This conclusion arises from the finding that men and women have a tendency to use transactional and transformational leadership styles respectively (White, 1995; Bird and Brush, 2002; Vinnicombe and Singh, 2002; Eagly et al., 2003), and that men tend to ascribe higher values to men's leadership skills and women to women's leadership skills (Luthar, 1996).

Given this and the fact that management worldwide tends to be male-dominated, senior management is likely to exercise and appoint leaders whose leadership style is transactional in nature. This is a command and control style of leadership, which may impede the participatory style associated with innovation and the development of products acceptable to the target market (Barczak and Wilemon, 1992). The impact of personality on leadership has also been studied, and a meta-analysis of the link between personality and leadership found a correlation between extroversion, conscientiousness and leadership (Judge et al., 2002). Extrapolating from this, it would appear that extroversion is a characteristic that would help advance this process.

It is worth noting that a further variable, nationality, can also be expected to have an impact on the participatory nature of management. Hofstede famously distinguished the elements that, in his view, distinguished management in different countries (Hofstede, 2001), and a review of his work and of the critiques of it is found in an article by the author comparing French and UK websites (Gunn and Moss, 2006). Moreover, according to Song and Noh (2006), the project team lies at the heart of the product development process, and the author has demonstrated the positive impact on teamwork of a collectivist culture and the negative impact of an individualistic society (Moss et al., 2007c). These factors have not previously been highlighted in discussions of NPD.

5.1.1.1 Brand management. One further aspect of management that will have a bearing on NPD is brand management. Branding has been characterised as the process of creating value through the provision of a compelling offer and customer experience (Aaker, 1991; De Chernatony and McDonald, 1992; Kapferer, 1992), and research shows the extent to which brand values reflect the values of brand managers (De Chernatony et al., 2004). Some argue that it is employees who have most knowledge and experience of the brand (Collins and Porras, 1998; Driscoll and Hoffman, 1999), and although some consider entrusting employees with brand development to be optimal (De Chernatony et al., 2004), this view takes no account of the extent to which segmentation variables (e.g., gender, nationality and personality) affect employees' *productions* and *preferences*. If it is the case that brand values reflect the values of brand managers, then differences between the demographics of brand managers and the target market could produce a mismatch in terms of the relevance of the brand to the end-user. It follows that in order to optimise the brand for a diverse target market, a diverse management base is needed.

5.1.2   Aesthetic productions

A body of research has demonstrated the link between art and its creators, with Tunnelle declaring the artist to be someone who sees things not as they are but as he is (Hammer, 1980). The relationship between art and a number of variables (gender and personality) has been the focus of extensive study, notably in the fields of art therapy and psychology, with extensive evidence of the impact of these independent variables on the dependent variable, fine art productions.

The present author has extended this work into the field of design and has likewise found a strong impact of independent variables (gender and nationality) on design *productions*, including web design. This impact is not surprising given the relatedness of art and design (Moss, 2009a, 2009b) and the original contribution of this work is in revealing the significant and specific impact of these variables. In order to gain an understanding of the wider context of this work, we will examine the aesthetic background, including a discussion of the connectedness of art forms (whether art, graphic design or web design) and an examination of the research linking graphic expression to its creators (Moss, 2008c). The discussion will then focus on web design and the specific way in which gender and designer nationality can influence design elements. This discussion will focus, in the first instance, on the impact of gender and nationality on personal websites and then move to a discussion of their impact on commercial websites.

5.1.2.1   Connectedness of visual forms.   We referred to the issue of the potential interconnectedness of design (including web design) and other forms of graphic expression such as fine art on the basis that a finding of interconnectedness would mean that the literatures from *all* these fields

could be used to inform discussions relating to the imprint of variables (gender, nationality and personality) on graphic expression. A debate on the interrelatedness of various forms of graphic expression has been pursued since antiquity and was revisited in the 1950s in Read's *Art and Industry* (1953). This book argues that a distinction between art and design is the creation of the machine age and that in the pre-Renaissance period, the disciplines now known as architecture, sculpture, painting, music and poetry were not recognised as separate classes of disciplines.

The debate was resumed by Buchanan and Margolin (1995) who, acknowledging Read's earlier contribution, argue that design can be both a cognitive and expressive skill not inherently different from art (Buchanan and Margolin, ibid.). Analogously, Rogoff (Mirzoeff, 1998) argues that images do not stay within discrete disciplinary fields such as 'documentary film' or 'Renaissance painting' since neither the eye nor the psyche operates along or recognises such divisions. He argues that the differences between the functionality and expressiveness of design and fine art, and the extent to which these are produced individually or in teams, can be differences of degree rather than of principle. For example, there have been periods when art objects were produced by a team and designs by individuals, so there is no water-tight definition in terms of practice either (ibid.).

The relatedness of art and design, argued at a theoretical level, is supported by empirical research showing the connections between graphic expression and its creators (Preyer, 1985) and the consistency of different forms of graphic expression (Allport and Vernon, 1933; Moss, 2009a).

5.1.2.2 Aesthetic background: links between graphic productions and their creators. The close correspondence between different forms of graphic expression is attributed to the fact that all forms of expression, whether sketches or models, are directed by motor movements in the brain with such motor acts reflecting 'to a large degree the organisation of the total brain field' (Allport and Vernon, 1933). These psychologists argue that the brain directs the hand of the writer and the artist (this is similar to Preyer's concept of 'brainwriting' (1895; Moss, 2009a)), and that people's graphic output, whether drawings or paintings, reflect aspects of themselves. More on this is described in the next section. In the sections that follow, we explore the links between graphic expression and web design, and the variables of gender and nationality.

5.1.2.3 Aesthetic background: the influence of personality on visual productions. Table 2.3 summarises the links commentators have found between graphic expression and personality (see Moss, 2008c, 2009a).

It can be seen that straight lines are associated in the earlier literature with aggression and rounded forms with non-aggression (Moss, 2008c, 2009a). Concluding from 80 years of research into projective and non-projective assessment of children's drawings, Harris (2007) concluded that 'it is indeed possible for artist characteristics such as intellectual acuity, developmental maturity, personality, values, attitudes, emotions, behaviour and culture of origin to be reflected through children's artistic works'. Moreover, the ability to make these inferences is not restricted to interpretations of children's work. In a recent study of artwork by adult inmates at a therapeutic prison, an art therapist describes the elements in graphic expression that can permit inferences concerning personality (Wylie, 2007). He identifies six elements from which a personality appraisal can be made:

- Use of space – utilisation of surface area of the paper and whether the left, centre, and right-hand side of the page are equally used and the direction in which the narrative is read (e.g., whether the picture can be read from left to right, from past to future). The size of the image relative to the page is also an important consideration (a small drawing in a large space could indicate inhibition or alternatively lack of engagement in the topic, while appealing figures might be exaggerated in size) (Thomas et al., 1989)
- Use of colour – the addition of colour indicates emotional investment. In this way, dark colours are associated with a negative emotion, while bright colours (e.g., yellow or orange) are often associated with positive feelings (Burkitt and Newall, 2005)
- Use of diverse art materials – this indicates desire for clarity in communication
- Realism – the extent to which there is realism in the drawing indicates the capacity for reality confrontation
- Maturity of representation – the more mature the representation, the more it indicates the presence of cognitive resource
- Theme – the extent to which this is followed through on all parts of the page shows the ability to persist with a single theme

In Wylie's study, he was able to predict by looking at people's drawings whether an inmate at the therapeutic prison was ready for group therapy (Wylie, 2007).

Table 2.3 Summary of researchers' views on ways in which aggression and non-aggression are manifested in graphic expression

Personality trait	Manifestation in graphic expression	Author giving this interpretation
Aggressiveness	Straight line	Waehner (1946)
Aggressiveness, outgoing behaviour and assertiveness	"	Alschuler and Hattwick (1969)
Assertiveness	"	Hammer (1980)
N-Ach, non-conforming, energetic	"	Aronson (1958)
Aggressiveness and preoccupation with conflict and power	Violent themes	McNiff (1982)
Creativity, restraint, self-centredness	Rounded forms	Waehner (1946)
Dependence, compliance, affection, fanciful imagination	"	Alschuler and Hattwick (1969)
Femininity	"	Hammer (1980)
Non-aggressiveness, concern with people and animals connected with environment	Life themes	McNiff (1982)

5.1.2.4 Aesthetic background: the influence of personality on web design productions. In an interesting experiment, ten 9–10-year-old children produced 153 drawings using computer software as well as 235 freehand drawings, and teachers viewing these productions were asked to make inferences about the children's learning styles, school subject preferences, behaviour patterns and any other information that occurred. These assumptions were then compared with statements about the children by the children themselves, their parents and their teachers, with the statements being a response to a request to describe the children's most and least favourite school subjects, problem-solving methods, social interaction patterns, personal life philosophies and activity preferences. The statements made by viewing teachers (viewing online and freehand drawings) were found to correlate in 69 per cent and 68 per cent of cases, with statements from interviews demonstrating a high ability to infer personality from online expression (Harris, 2007). This strongly suggests that information about personality is in fact transmitted through online graphic expression as well as through more traditional graphic expression such as freehand drawings.

The influence of nationality and gender on web design is explored in the next section.

5.1.2.5 Aesthetic background: the influence of nationality on visual expression. In terms of nationality, there is recognition of the differences that can divide cultures (Adler, 2008) and a recognition, even by a strong critic of Hofstede's well known analysis of differences in management cultures, McSweeney (2002), that 'Hofstede's dimensions can usefully frame initial discussion about national peculiarities'.

Despite the endorsement of Hofstede's work on nationality and management styles, and some studies relating his concepts to marketing (Kapferer, 1992; Samli, 1995; Schuiling and Kapferer, 2004), there is relatively little research describing the impact of nationality on design productions and preferences (Moss and Vinten, 2001). A comparison of life assurance literature produced in the UK and France (Moss and Vinten, 2001) revealed differences in the use of language and imagery, which conformed with Hofstede's view of France as a high power distance and risk averse culture, and the UK as a lower power distance and uncertainty avoiding culture. The French literature, for example, was more formal and more likely to portray a powerful figure (e.g., a chief executive officer). The UK literature, by contrast, was more informal and avoided the use of worked examples. These conclusions were a useful first step in exploring the impact of national culture on design.

The link between nationality and web design is explored in the next section.

5.1.2.6 Aesthetic background: the influence of nationality on web design productions. We saw earlier the global nature of the Internet population, and one important question relates to the similarity of website productions in different locations. How similar are websites produced in different countries? One study compared the 'look' of websites in Germany, Japan and the US (Cyr and Trevor-Smith, 2004) but used criteria for the websites that were generated by people from industry and the academic community who were asked to suggest characteristics 'that could easily be compared and assessed'. This produced eight criteria (language, layout, symbols, content and structure, navigation, links, multimedia and colours), which are defined in terms that may or may not be priorities in terms of understanding the national style of a website. For example, the variable of language is studied in relation to three visual criteria (headlines, point form and paragraph) rather than, say, in relation to the mental constructs informing the words used. In the same way, the issue of layout and spatial features is studied in relation to page orientation and banner/menu location rather than in relation to the incidence of straight versus circular lines. The lack of external justification for the selection of these criteria unfortunately weakens the methodological validity of this study.

Another study on national differences in website design (Cook and Finlayson, 2005) also suffers from methodological failures, this time rooted in the fact that their assumptions are tested on just two websites and also on commercial websites whose design is subject to commercial constraints. Moreover, even with an improved sample, their model would be difficult to test since its elements are vague (Gunn and Moss, 2006). For example, their model suggests that low masculinity cultures produce 'pleasing visuals', while high uncertainty cultures produce 'redundant cues such as colour and typography' and it is not clear how the presence or absence of these features could be measured and charted.

New research conducted by the author with statistician Dr Rod Gunn (Gunn and Moss, 2006) sought to overcome these limitations. Sixty personal websites produced by students at higher education institutions in the UK and France were rated against twelve criteria used to compare the personal websites of male and female students in the UK (Moss et al., 2006a and see pp. 34–36 below). Of these, twelve showed significant differences between the French and UK websites. Seven of these twelve differences related to factors significantly associated in the UK website study (Moss et al., 2006) with female-produced websites (these instances related to fewer subjects, more pages, less expert language, more rounded lines, greater number of typeface colours, more informal typefaces and greater use of certain colours) and a further three factors significantly more used in the French than the UK websites and weakly associated with the female-produced websites (use of a welcome message, 2D images and colours in the background). Only two other significant differences between the UK and French websites (use of a crest and reference to one's own achievements) were related to factors which were significantly associated in the UK website study with male-produced websites.

This comparison of UK and French websites shows that 83 per cent of the features that differed significantly between the UK and French websites related to features that typified the female-produced websites in the UK-only study (Moss et al., 2006). This might be thought to illustrate the greater femininity of websites in France compared with those in the UK, reflecting in turn the greater femininity of French as compared with British values (Hofstede, 2001). This view is consistent with Samli's hypothesis (1995) that the masculinity/femininity cultural dimension will influence individuals' values across cultures.

In terms of future work, an updating of the values measured by Hofstede, a process recommended by Schaffer and Riordan (2003), would be a helpful step in benchmarking the cultural values reflected in web designs.

5.1.2.7 Aesthetic background: the influence of gender on design productions. Just as there is a literature arguing for the connection between graphic expression and personality, so also is there a literature arguing for a connection with gender. Although some argue against a specific 'feminine sensibility' (Harris and Nochlin, 1976), some agree with Erikson in speaking of a 'profound difference in the sense of space in the two sexes' (1970, p. 100).

Discussing such gender differences today is problematic both because there is a lack of agreement about its relevance and because of a lack of agreement about its meaning (Caterall and Maclaran, 2002). In terms of the latter, interpretations can range from the post-modern view that gender is an unproductive dichotomy (Firat, 1994) and should have no place in consumer research, through the middle position adopted by the so-called liberal feminists who argue that inferred psychological male/female differences can develop out of women's socially allocated roles (Bristor and Fischer, 1993), while a third position is the evolutionary psychological perspective that plays down the influence of sociocultural factors (Jackson, 2001), emphasising instead the role of innate factors (Lupotow et al., 1995). According to recent commentators, this last approach is gaining ground in several disciplines and should not be overlooked even if this approach restricts the possibilities of social and cultural change (Caterall and Maclaran, 2002). So, there is a case for conceiving gender as providing a useful dichotomy and imagining that underlying differences are the result of either or both sociocultural and innate factors.

In exploring the impact of gender on design, it is important to stand outside the patriarchal system in which 'Art by women is judged according to norms and expert constraints that are not their own' (Heide, 1991), acknowledging the strength of a wide range of realities (White, 1995). This approach is philosophically consistent with a diversity approach. Before examining the impact of gender on web design, we will briefly summarise the work which examines the impact of gender on drawings and paintings.

The earliest studies compared the use of both formal (shapes and colours) and thematic features in the drawings and paintings of children and students (summarised in Moss, 2008c and 2009a). Where subject matter is concerned, numerous differences were noted, including the tendency among males and females to draw same-sex figures. This was significantly the case (at the p < 0.05 level) in Majewski's study of 121 children's drawings (1978), and two years later, a study by Levy of a sample of 5,500 adults found that 89 per cent drew their own sex first (Hammer, 1980). Levy's sample included college students, high school students and psychiatric patients, and if the latter group is excluded, a total of 72 per cent drew same-sex figures. Where form is concerned, researchers have consistently observed a male tendency to use straight lines, and females rounded ones (see Table 2.4). Other differences relate to colour, perspective, function and the vertical/horizontal nature of structures:

This overview discusses the manifestations and implications of differences but does not seek to determine underlying factors, arguably a combination of sociocultural and innate factors (Lupotow, et al., 1995; Moss, 2009a).

Table 2.4 The sex with which various graphic features are associated

Graphic characteristic	Sex with which graphic trait is associated	Researchers giving this interpretation
Straight line	Male	Alschuler and Hattwick (1958); Franck and Rosen (1949); Majewski (1978); McNiff (1982); Moss (1995, 1996, 2001)
Rounded line	Female	Waehner (1946); Hammer (1980); Alschuler and Hattwick (1958); Franck and Rosen (1949); Majewski (1978); Moss (1995, 1996, 2001)
Structures built up	Structure is built down low	Franck and Rosen (1949); Erikson (1970)
Angles	Male	Franck and Rosen (1949)
Blunt lines	Female	Franck and Rosen (1949)
Realistic	Male	Kerschensteiner (1905); Ballard (1912); Lippard (1976)
Less realistic	Female	Kerschensteiner (1905); Ballard (1912); Lippard (1976)
Sharp perspective	Male	McCarty (1924); Kerschensteiner (1905); Ballard (1912)

Table 2.4   (Continued)

Graphic characteristic	Sex with which graphic trait is associated	Researchers giving this interpretation
Loose perspective	Female	McCarty (1924); Kerschensteiner (1905); Ballard (1912)
Concern with function	Male	Neubauer (1932); Lark-Horovitz (1967)
Concern with aesthetics	Female	
	Pinks and pastels, warmer use of colours	Alschuler and Hattwick (1958); Lippard (1976); Minamato (1985); Iijima et al. (2001)

5.1.2.8 Aesthetic background: web design productions and gender. Moving now from drawings and painting to web design, there has been a small number of studies in the US (Zahedi et al., 2006) and in the UK (Miller and Arnold, 2000) investigating gender, but the validity of these studies is limited by methodological failures. For example, in respect of the two studies by Miller and Arnold (2000), one used in the authors' words an 'opportunistic and haphazard' sampling of student home pages and the other used an 'opportunistic' sample of web pages but provided no details of the selection or rating method. A second study (Zahedi et al., 2006) classified websites in relation to their audience ('masculine' websites, designed for a male audience with a male focus in design; 'feminine' websites, designed for a female audience with a female focus in design; websites with 'masculine androgyny', designed for a male audience with a female focus in design; and websites with 'female androgyny', designed for a female audience with a male focus in design), but failed to categorise websites according to the gender of their producer.

In order to overcome these weaknesses, the author conducted fresh studies (Moss and Gunn, 2005; Moss et al., 2006a, 2006b, 2008b). In one of these (Moss et al., 2006a), the aim was to identify the range of features used by men and women in websites that they had originated and this was achieved by rating the personal websites of 30 male and 30 female students against 23 criteria. The study focused on personal websites as a medium where 'people tend to ostensibly be...their true selves' (Miller and Arnold, 2003), manifesting the 'virtually real self' even if this consisted, in the act of communication, of multiple identities (ibid.). The fact that the rating criteria could be objectively rated, and that they emerged either from complex rating exercises (Moss, 1995) or from earlier research, thereby minimised the risk of personal bias (Schroeder and Borgerson, 1998).

The three main criteria used derived from research on design or website aesthetics:

- criteria concerning navigation issues;
- criteria concerning language, its register and the amount of self-promotion;
- criteria relating to visual elements.

Where navigation was concerned, the rating features derived from earlier work on gendered preferences (Leong, 1997; Oser, 2003) and included five elements: the number of links on the home page; the number of subjects covered; the use of a site map; the use of a contents page; and the consistency in the pages. Regarding language, the features derived from earlier research on gendered language (Tannen, 1996) with six elements included: the use of a welcome page; self-promotion; formal and expert language; reference to one's own achievements; avoidance of self-denigration; and grammatical abbreviations (all allegedly male features).

Regarding visual features, many of those used derived from research on the gendering of art and design (Moss, 1995, 1999). The thematic elements included five elements: the formality of photos; the gender of images; the use of inanimate/animate themes; self-propelling/stationary objects; and the institution's crest. Where non-thematic elements are concerned, six features were rated: the use of straight/rounded lines; the use of regular or irregular typography; the number and range of colours in the typeface/background; the extent to which design elements appear three dimensional or two dimensional; the presence or absence in the layout of a horizontal line; and finally the type of typeface colours used. Overall, a total of 23 elements were rated, all amenable to objective rating and all researcher-neutral in having been derived from earlier research.

A comparison of the male- and female-produced sites produced by students at a UK university revealed statistically significant differences on 13 (56 per cent) of these 23 elements (Moss et al., 2006a). These were spread across the three areas of navigation, language and visual content. The elements on which there were significant differences related to the number of separate subject areas covered (with men favouring more subjects than women); the character of the language (men favoured formal and expert language, self-promotion and infrequent abbreviations); the thematic features of the images used (men favoured use of own logo, images of men and formal images, and women favoured images of women and informal images); non-thematic visual elements (men favouring the use of straight lines and a conventional layout); and the character of the typography (men favoured formal typography and a smaller number of typeface colours). In terms of navigation, men were more likely to include a site map.

As can be seen, most of the differences occurred in the areas of visual elements and language, with one difference occurring in the area of navigation. The most significant differences (at the $p < 0.001$ level) related to four elements, namely: (i) the use of colours (the use of a variety of text colours was more common among the women's websites); (ii) shape (use of a horizontal layout was more common among the men's websites); (iii) images (men used more formal images); and (iv) language (use of self-denigration and informal language were more common among the women, while the use of expert language was more common among the men). At the lower but still statistically significant level of $p < 0.01$, differences centred on the use of abbreviations, while at the level of $p < 0.05$, differences centred on the use of a male figure, crest, formal typography and straight as against rounded lines (the men's websites were all more likely to contain these features than the women's websites). This strong evidence of difference is suggestive of a plurality of production aesthetics on the part of men and women.

In a second phase of research, the male- and female-produced websites from the UK and French samples were pooled with a similarly sourced Polish sample (Moss et al., 2006d). Across the three samples, statistically

Table 2.5 Factors showing significant differences between the male- and female-produced websites in the UK, France and Poland

Variable tested	Significant
Does it have a site map?	$\chi^2 = 13.891$, df = 1; $p < 0.001$
Denigration of self or task at hand	$\chi^2 = 22.550$; df = 1; $p < 0.001$
The use of expert language	$\chi^2 = 22.848$; df = 1; $p < 0.001$
Reference to own achievements	$\chi^2 = 6.792$; df = 1; $p < 0.05$
Are shapes on page rounded or straight?	$\chi^2 = 26.814$; df = 3; $p < 0.001$
Is there a conventional layout employing horizontal lines across the page?	$\chi^2 = 18.336$; df = 3; $p < 0.001$
The range of colours used in the typeface	$\chi^2 = 24.027$; df = 3; $p < 0.001$

Are the images inanimate or animate?	$\chi^2 = 19.163$; df $= 3$; $p < 0.001$
What gender are the images used?	$\chi^2 = 36.473$; df $= 3$; $p < 0.001$
What tone do the words used display?	$\chi^2 = 24.886$; df $= 3$; $p < 0.001$
What style are the pictures that are used?	$\chi^2 = 18.857$; df $= 3$; $p < 0.001$
What is the style of typeface?	$\chi^2 = 9.423$; df $= 1$; $p < 0.05$
What colour of typeface predominates?	$\chi^2 = 12.323$; df $= 2$; $p < 0.05$

Source: Moss et al. (2006d)

significant differences emerged on 13 features from the 22 features rated. These are shown in Table 2.5.

Those visual elements in respect of which gender differences were noted related to: (i) the relative use of rounded or straight shapes (with men more likely at the 0.001 level to use straight lines than women) and relatedly (ii) the tendency, at the 0.001 level, for men to use a conventional layout with a horizontal line across the page; (iii) the number of colours used in the typeface (with men more likely at the 0.001 level to use a smaller range of colours than women); (iv) the type of colours used (with women more likely at the 0.05 level to employ certain colours than men); (v) the gender of the images displayed (with men more likely at the 0.001 level to have images of males than females, and vice versa for women); (vi) the style of the pictures used (with men more likely at the 0.001 level to use formal rather than informal pictures); (vii) the character of the typeface (with men more likely at the 0.05 level to employ a regular typography than women); (viii) the use of animate images (with women more likely at the 0.001 level to use animate images).

In terms of the elements related to language, the differences related to: (i) denigration of self or task at hand (with men less likely at the 0.001 level to show evidence of this than women) and relatedly (ii) the tendency for men at the 0.05 level to refer to their own achievements; (iii) the tone of the words displayed (with men more likely at the 0.001 level to employ a formal tone in their words than women); (iv) the use of expert language (with men more likely at the 0.001 level to have this than women). In terms of navigation, the main difference related to the use of a site map (with men significantly more likely at the 0.001 level to have a site map.

These differences are sufficiently strong to make a persuasive case for gender differences in web productions across national cultures.

5.1.2.9 Aesthetic background: the influence of age on design productions.
An overview of the literature on age and the Internet is provided in

Chapter 4 of this book. As can be seen there, no research has yet been conducted examining the links between a person's age and the type of websites they produce ('productions').

5.2   Preference elements

Having examined *performance* issues, it is now appropriate to examine a separate but related issue, namely *preferences*. In examining preferences, we will be discussing preferences for visual productions as well as for management style.

5.2.1   Visual productions

To what extent will people's preferences follow the productions associated with them? A disparate body of earlier research on children's drawings and paintings, compared with a separate body of earlier work (again highly dispersed) on visual preferences and personality, allowed the author to hypothesise that visual preferences correlated with a mirroring between the personality of the producer and the beholder (Moss, 2008c, 2009a, 2010). In the section that follows, we look at the studies that generated this hypothesis and then examine empirical work by the author with graphic and web design to test for the presence of the mirroring effect in relation to gender.

5.2.2   Personality and preferences for fine art

Earlier research had not directly addressed the question of whether people of one personality type are drawn to fine art produced by people of similar personality, but inferences could be made based on theoretical work as well as empirical work not directly addressing this issue (Moss, 2009a).

Where theory is concerned, the scholar and art critic Joan Evans expressed the view (1939) that:

> men of each psychological type tend to admire the art produced by artists of the same type. ... A man will always tend to have a primary attraction towards the art produced by men of like temperament with himself. (p. 64)

In terms of empirical research, hypotheses as to the nature of the interaction between a creator's and observer's personality can be inferred from a number of studies where this question is not an object of study but an incidental finding across studies (Moss, 2009a). The first of these studies (Welsh, 1949) found conservative and conventional personalities to have a preference for simple and symmetrical objects, with anti-social/dissident personalities having a preference for complex, asymmetrical pictures. Since an earlier study by Waehner (1946) associated symmetrical drawing with conventional characteristics on the part of the artist, the preference that Welsh associates with conservative types (a preference for symmetrical objects) constitutes an instance of a mirroring effect of personality types in preference.

In a further study, Barron (1963) explored the painterly preferences of two personality types (see Table 2.6).

Table 2.6 Preferences associated with particular kinds of personality (Barron, 1963)

Personality characteristics of beholders	Type of paintings they prefer
Conservative, serious, deliberate, responsible	Portraits, landscapes and traditional themes
More emotional, temperamental and pessimistic	Experimental, sensual and primitive work

Since Waehner (1946) interpreted landscape painting and paintings whose content reflected the environment as a sign of conventionality on the part of the artist, and since Barron's findings show that these are the very types of painting preferred by those with 'conservative' personalities, there appears once again to be a mirroring between the personality of the beholder and that of the painter whose work is liked.

Contemporary with Barron's study was one by Knapp and Wolff (1963) showing how preferences for abstract art were associated with intuitive types, and preferences for representational art with sensing types. Given that a detailed quantitative study by Burt (1968) associated abstract art with the intuitive artist, and representational art with the sensing artist, these results appear to offer a further instance of the mirroring of personality in preferences. Moreover, Jacoby and Jacobs (1969) found that 'cautious and conservative' individuals favoured small cars, while large cars were preferred by 'confident explorers'. Hammer (1980) claimed that large objects were produced by aggressive, confident personalities and small objects by those with less confidence, and if this view is correct, then the 1969 study also illustrates the interactive effect of personality in productions and preferences.

It is worth noting, finally, that the colour expert Birren (1973), basing his conclusions on 'many years of observation', matched observers' colour preferences with particular personality types in accordance with the following principles:

- Those who dislike colour will not have an agreeable rapport with the outside world and will be introspective and inhibited.
- Those who like colour will have an agreeable rapport with the outside world and will have outward-directed interests and be emotionally responsive.
- Softer illumination and cool colours (e.g., the blue end of the colour spectrum) represent a withdrawal from the outside world.

Given that earlier research (Alschuler and Hattwick, 1969) exploring painterly tendencies associated a delight in the use of colour with emotional tendencies, and a use of blue or black as indicative of self-control and the repression of emotion, Birren's opinions could also be seen as a further case of the mirroring effect of personality and preferences.

5.2.3   *Personality and preferences for web design*

A paper in 2007 (Cunningham et al.) describes the way websites can be modified to appeal to the 16 Myers-Briggs personality types. Unfortunately, the validity of the predictive models presented here is not put to the test and the suggestions as to how websites can be modified to appeal to different types are presented at a hypothetical level only. The evidence presented in Chapter 5 of this book, examining how the text on a website was modified to suit the presumptive personality type of the end-users, provides persuasive evidence, however, as to the efficacy of this approach since the modified site attracted a 27 per cent higher click-through rate.

5.2.4   *Gender and preferences for graphic design*

In order to test the extent to which there was, likewise, a mirroring effect of gender, 65 subjects (30 male and 35 females) were asked to express preferences between four Christmas cards, two of which were designed by men and two by women. The study was written by the author and co-authored by Andrew Colman, Professor of Psychology at Leicester University (Moss and Colman, 2001). The study revealed a significant tendency for respondents to prefer cards designed by people of their own gender (see Table 2.7), confirming a highly significant tendency towards same-sex preferences (Moss and Colman, 2001).

Table 2.7 Male and female preferences between male- and female-produced Christmas cards

	Respondents' preferences	
	Female respondents	**Male respondents**
Female designer	24	7
Male designer	11	23

The following section examines whether a similar mirroring was found in men and women's ratings of male- and female-designed websites.

5.2.5 Gender and preferences for web design

A study by Flanagan and Metzger (2003) into the impact of gender on evaluations of site credibility was based on the evaluation of two websites. Unfortunately, this was an unrepresentative sample of websites and one in which the gender of the producer(s) of the websites was not specified. Despite these methodological drawbacks, the study had the merit of distinguishing website *production* and *preference* aesthetics.

A second study of reactions (Cyr and Bonanni, 2005), comparing the preferences of 76 Canadian students for a single Sony website, found that women systematically reported lower preference values than men. The study also found that: (i) more men than women reported the site to be better organised; (ii) more men than women had favourable impressions of the way product information was presented; (iii) more men than women were satisfied with the navigation design; (iv) significantly more women than men questioned the value of animations; and (v) women were more attracted by the colours on the site, and men by the interactive and 'flashy' aspects of the site.

While this study is welcome in having investigated web design preferences, the study has serious methodological weaknesses. First, it used only a single-stimulus website and even then made no attempt to categorise it in terms of its place on a visual aesthetic continuum. Had the authors done this, or better still elicited responses to a range of websites from across a notional visual aesthetic continuum, the study would have had greater validity. A third study (Zahedi et al., 2006) advocated that websites be produced 'in line with the audience's culture', but although websites were grouped into four types no empirical evidence was offered in support of this categorisation.

Given the methodological shortcomings of these studies, the author initiated a new study (Moss, 2008a, 2009a, 2010) in which students (38 males and 26 females) were asked to rate six of the student websites that were found in the earlier study (Moss, 2006a) to be typical of male- and female-produced websites. The results of these preference tests showed a statistically highly significant tendency by men and women to ascribe higher ratings to sites exemplifying the production aesthetic typical of their own gender (and produced by people of their own gender) than of the other gender. Surprisingly, as the following results (see Table 2.8) reveal, the female respondents showed a significant tendency to prefer the female-produced websites on all measures, while the men could tolerate the female websites when it came to pictures and were indifferent between the male and female websites when it came to shapes.

Table 2.8 Preference test results: the significance levels show the extent to which each gender prefers websites (or elements of the websites) produced using the production of their own gender (Moss and Gunn, 2008)

Elements measured	Male preferences for websites showing the male production aesthetic	Female preferences for websites showing the female production aesthetic
Overall preference for the website	0.01	0.01
Language	0.01	0.01
Pictures	Prefer the female production aesthetic	0.01
Shapes	No significant preference	0.01
Layout	0.01	0.01
Typography colours	0.01	0.01

These results (ibid.) exemplify the tendency for preferences to mirror productions and they support the case for developing websites with elements of the male and/or female aesthetic rather than websites displaying male androgyny or female androgyny (Zahedi et al., 2006).

5.2.6 *Commercial websites*

We have seen how men and women's website preferences match their own production aesthetic and so it is interesting to explore whether these preferences are mirrored in commercial websites. To do this, the presence/absence of the 13 factors found that distinguished sites produced in the formative study of the male and female web *production* aesthetic (Moss et al., 2006a) was measured in a sample of websites from three industries. The three industries consisted of the angling and beauty industries (Moss et al., 2006b), industries with a predominantly male and female market respectively, as well as higher education (Moss and Gunn, 2005), a sector attracting equal proportions of male and female customers (see Table 2.9).

In the case of angling, an industry with a predominantly male market, an optimally designed website would (based on the findings of our preference tests) contain a high proportion of features from the male *production* aesthetic. Given their minority status as customers, one could reasonably expect women visiting the site to adapt to the male aesthetic displayed there. On the other hand, in the case of websites targeting a predominantly female market (the case of the beauty industry), one could expect optimally designed websites to contain features from the female *production* aesthetic. In the case of higher education (HE), a sector with a less skewed demographic, one might expect an optimally designed website to contain a mixture of features from the male and female *production* aesthetic.

In order to measure the aesthetics used in the websites of these three sectors, a randomly selected sample of 30 websites was analysed in each industry. These sites were rated against the factors that distinguished the male from the female *production* aesthetic, thereby eliciting the extent to which these industry sites employed a male or female design production aesthetic. In a further stage, the resulting 'gender production coefficient' was compared with men and women's preferences (Moss and Gunn, 2005) to establish the probability of an aesthetic match.

The results showed that a likely match between website aesthetic and preference aesthetic of the target market existed only in the case of websites from the angling industry since these display a predominantly male production aesthetic (with an overall male gender coefficient of 0.66) and the market consists largely of men (Moss et al., 2006b). Such a good match between *production* and *preference* aesthetics was not found in the websites created for the non-male-dominated beauty and HE sectors (Moss and Gunn, 2005; Moss et al., 2006b) since these evinced

Table 2.9 UK HEIs, full-time undergraduate students by gender, 1995–2003

	1995/ 1996	1996/ 1997	1998/ 1999	1999/ 2000	2000/ 2001	2001/ 2002	2002/ 2003
Female	50%	53%	52%	53%	53%	53%	53%
Male	50%	47%	48%	47%	47%	47%	47%

Source: HESA online statistics.

a predominantly male design aesthetic, with male gender coefficients of 0.68 and 0.72 respectively. Since the markets of these industries is made up greatly or largely of women, the predominantly male *production* aesthetic employed in these industry websites is not likely to match the *preferences* of the target market.

In order to discover the gender of those involved in the design of the websites in these three industries, telephone interviews were conducted with personnel in the three industries concerned (Moss et al., 2008b). The interviews revealed that the majority of those involved in the design of the websites in the three sectors were men (see Table 2.10), a finding consistent with statistics regarding the high proportion of men in the information technology (IT) sector (Baroudi and Igbaria, 1994; Igbaria and Parasuraman, 1997; Equal Opportunities Commission, 2002).

The telephone interviews also offered insights into the division of labour between web designers and business personnel since they showed that in the angling industry, exclusive reliance was placed on the design and creative input of the male web designers. In the beauty salons, by contrast, the personnel in the business provided a range of creative inputs to the website designs even where a designer had been employed to produce the website. This additional input applied to 73 per cent of the sample surveyed (i.e., 16 respondents) and was provided exclusively by women working in those businesses. However, the interviews revealed that fewer than one-quarter of the beauty salon businesses had an extensive input into the design of the website, with just over half providing little input. It can be inferred, from these results, that the majority of those working on web design in all three of these industries were men.

One might reasonably ask how representative this picture is for the Web design industry as a whole. Unfortunately, there is very little published research on the demographics of the Web design industry. There is a study examining the use of websites in small businesses (Thelwall, 2000) and claims that Internet design is male dominated (Simon and

Table 2.10   The design history of the angling, beauty salon and higher education (HE) websites, with data deriving from telephone interviews

Gender of person(s) who undertook the design of the company's website	Angling websites % (no.)	Beauty salon websites % (no.)	HE websites % (no.)
One or more men	77 (34)	78 (37)	74 (38)
One or more women	8 (3)	18 (9)	7 (5)
A man and a woman	7 (3)	4 (2)	19 (11)
Interview responses	73 (44)	73 (44)	84 (54)

Peppas, 2005) but, beyond that, there is little research on the demographics and modus operandi of this relatively new industry. One way of verifying the reliability of the data obtained from the study of these three industries is by ascertaining the skills base of those working in web design (e.g., IT or graphics) and mapping the demographics of these skill areas.

A first step involved telephone interviews with companies listed in the New Media Age's list of the top ten interactive agencies (New Media Age data). Discussions with project and HR managers in six of the ten companies approached revealed that the background of web designers lay in computing/IT, graphic design or another area. Respondents indicated that the majority of web designers came from the first two areas (in equal proportions) with a much smaller number from the third category. Four of the six companies referred to the existence of two principal departments (i) 'Design' and (ii) a 'Technical' department, the latter staffed largely by people with a computer science background and the former by 'creative people' (the words of one respondent), typically those with graphic design qualifications from art and design schools. The remaining two companies had an 'Information Architecture' department staffed by usability experts familiar with 'user centred design'. A high proportion of these had a 'human computer interaction' background based in IT or in graphic design (Moss et al., 2008b).

These interviews revealed that the professional background of web designers lay in IT and graphics: the gender demographics of these two industries in turn provide pointers as to the gender of those in the Web design industry. Where graphic design is concerned, although there is a view that the paradigms taught in graphic design derive from modernism and have a patriarchal origin, there is little published material on gender demographics in this industry. In terms of unpublished material, membership data from the professional body representing designers in the UK, the Chartered Society of Designers provides a gender breakdown by specialism and grade of membership, and in 2006 figures for graphic design reveal that women constitute 56 per cent of graduate members, 21 per cent of members and 12 per cent of fellows. Membership grade does not necessarily correlate with job seniority but if a correlation is assumed, then the implication is that the majority of middle and senior ranks of graphic designers are male, with a majority of women in junior positions. A tentative conclusion might be that graphic design, a feeder for web design, is a profession in which men and women are equal numerically at entry levels but horizontally segregated at levels above this (Moss, 2009a, 2010; Moss et al., 2008b).

As for IT, there is a large literature on gender demographics show-ing higher male than female participation rates. Women in the 1990s accounted for 19–22 per cent of personnel, with men dominating at all levels across the three fields of information systems, information tech-nology and computer science (Robertson et al., 2001). The picture varies by geography, time and IT specialism, and in the US the proportion of women among computer professionals fell in the 1990s from 35.4 per cent to 29.1 per cent; in the UK, in 1994, women made up 30 per cent of computer scientists, 32 per cent of systems analysts, 35 per cent of computer programmers, 10 per cent of information system services (ISS) directors, 18 per cent of project leaders and 14 per cent of applications development managers (Baroudi and Igbaria, 1994/1995).

The trend for female participation in IT is downwards. The 1980s saw an influx of women into IT, with a fourfold increase between 1980 and 1986 in the number of women awarded bachelor's degrees in computer science, and a threefold increase in the number of women awarded mas-ter's degrees (Igbaria et al., 1997). Recent years, however, have seen a sharp decline in the number of women pursuing degrees in computer-related fields, together with a reduction in the numbers of women taking advanced-degree programmes (ibid.). Table 2.11 indicates the percentage of male and female employees reported for the IT profession in 2002 (Equal Opportunities Commission, 2002), showing the horizontal and vertical segregation discussed by Robertson et al. (2001).

Table 2.11   Percentage of men and women in the IT profession from *Facts about Women and Men in Great Britain* (Equal Opportunities Commission, 2002)

Occupation	% Males	% Females
Software professionals	84	16
ICT managers	83	17
IT operations, technicians	71	29

Research has identified one of the effects of the vertical and hori-zontal male domination of the IT profession to be the creation of a 'masculine computer culture' producing a 'masculine discourse' and a prioritisation of technical issues (Robertson et al., 2001), both of which deter women from entering the field (ibid.). The authors suggest that it is only by including a 'broader set of skills and discursive practices' that a more diverse group of people can be attracted into the profes-sion (including a critical mass of women) and the masculine culture impacted.

So, an examination of the demographics of both the graphics and IT sectors, sectors feeding the Web design sector, reveals sectors that are horizontally and vertically segregated by gender. Given what we have seen concerning the production and preference aesthetic, one could reasonably expect this male dominance to reflect itself in the Web productions and preferences of staff within this sector.

5.2.7 Management

What about management's preferences for different styles of management? We reported earlier on the research finding that men and women exercise different styles of leadership. The gender differences appear to relate not just to the way that men and women enact leadership (that is, their management *performance* styles) but also to their evaluations of leadership styles (i.e., their management *preferences*). One study, for example (Luthar, 1996), asked men and women to evaluate the leadership skills of other men and women and found that men ascribed higher values to men's skills than women's, and vice versa for women. Moreover, another study (Moss and Daunton, 2006) showed the extent to which a sample of male recruiters unconsciously substituted transactional leadership criteria for the transformational criteria in the job specification. Although the sample was small, this behaviour matched Luthar's conclusions as to men's higher rating of transactional over transformational leadership.

Preference elements extend to appraisals of professional competence and there is a large body of research demonstrating the natural bias individuals have in favour of others who are similar. This is the 'similarity-attraction' paradigm (Byrne, 1971; Byrne and Newman, 1992) and studies have demonstrated the extent to which it influences the recruitment selection and attrition cycle (Schneider, 1987; Stockdale and Crosby, 2004). Schneider's model shows organisations becoming increasingly homogeneous, not only because individuals are attracted to join and remain with organisations in which they perceive that they 'fit in', but also since organisational members are likely to feel comfortable with applicants who are similar.

Since the type of design and marketing staff employed will be a function of the type of staff recruited, a process influenced by the 'similarity-attraction' paradigm, so also will the recruitment process influence the kind of products and advertising produced. As a consequence, if an organisation has a senior management consisting predominantly of men, they will tend to appoint other men, and these men, if assuming the role of designers or brand managers, are likely to produce designs and brands that are at the masculine end of the production aesthetic continuum. In this situation, achieving congruity with a predominantly female customer base may present challenges and may deprive the organisation of the benefits of congruity (Brock, 1965; Crozier and Greenhalgh, 1992; Hammer, 1995; Karande et al., 1997; De Chernatoney et al., 2004). These benefits include enhanced customer pleasure and purchasing (Groppel, 1993; Donovan et al., 1994; Yahomoto and Lambert, 1994), benefits which are too important for organisations to ignore (Moss et al., 2008b; Moss, 2009a).

The link between the outside processes of competition and the internal processes of creating and sustaining change is described as the 'inside-out' and 'outside-in' perspective (Baden-Fuller, 1995) and links with the view that 'customer service and products can be more effectively provided if an organisation's workforce mirrors its customers' (Loden and Rosener, 1991). How can recruitment achieve this situation? There is a recognition that status quo recruitment is 'conservative', involving recruitment 'from the same social strata and age groups' (Boxall and Purcell, 2003: p. 141) and that 'highly masculinised' organisations are often 'hostile to transformational approaches' (Marshall, 2008). The benefits of a less homogeneous managerial workforce in an increasingly competitive environment are stressed by Kramar (1998) and Marshall who describe how 'innovative firms... attempt to recruit talented people who can help them develop a stream of new products and processes. They therefore use all possible channels to generate a heterogenous group of applicants' (Marshall, 2008). How easy is this likely to be?

Where web designer recruitment is concerned, the subtle interplay between *productions* and *preferences* has been demonstrated in respect of gender (Moss, 2007b, 2008a, 2008b, 2009a), personality (Moss, 2010), age and nationality (Moss, 2007a), showing how problematic is the process of recruiting web designers to design for a market whose preferences may not mirror those of senior management or the Web designers themselves.

Previous literature had alluded, in general terms, to the difficulty of merging different cognitive styles, attitudes and values (Ancona and Caldwell, 1992) but the complexities in operationalising the mirroring principle across a number of design disciplines, including web design, have only recently been exposed by the present author (Moss, 2009a; Moss and Gunn, 2007b, 2008a, 2008b). Factors that render this process problematic include a mismatch between the demographics of the organisation and those of the customer base, resulting in a mismatch between the *preferences* of an organisation's internal and external stakeholders (Loden and Rosener, 1991; Karpin, 1995). Such a mismatch is likely to be common in the male-dominated web design industry (Moss, 2007b, 2009a; Moss and Gunn, 2008a, 2008b) insofar as its workforce is male dominated (Moss et al., 2006b, 2007b; Moss and Gunn, 2008a, 2008b) but its customer base a mixture of both genders. The same is true, to a lesser extent, of the graphic design industry.

Research has discussed the possible role of training in alleviating this mismatch, for example training producers in the preferences of the target market, but the efficacy of training as a means of influencing and transforming *productions* and *preferences* remains uncharted except where efforts at leadership training are concerned (Moss et al., 2006c). One could conceive that such training might encounter difficulties, for example overcoming the impact of socialised or biologically determined differences on design *productions* and *preferences* (Moss, 2010), but research is needed to explore the practical outcomes and issues here.

6 Conclusions

The mirroring principle holds that the efficacy of messages can be maximised if they contain features that mirror the preferences of the target market (Hammer, 1980; Janz and Prasarnphanich, 2003). We have seen how, where *productions* are concerned, designs and products can reflect aspects of their creators, whether personality, nationality or gender. We have also seen how these factors can be reflected in management style. On the other hand, where *preferences* are concerned, we have seen how these tend to parallel and mirror *production* tendencies. In this way, segmentation variables appear to act on *preferences* in an analogous way to the way they act on *performances*.

The parallels between the psychology of *performance* and the psychology of *preference* suggest that congruence can best be achieved by ensuring that those personnel creating products match the demographics of those consuming products. In other words, the creatives employed by firms should have the personal characteristics (personality, gender and nationality) of those in the target market. Unfortunately, considerable difficulties stand in the way of selecting staff whose values are not congruent with those of the recruiters (Moss and Daunton, 2006) although some notions of how leaders with non-congruent styles could be recruited have been charted, including training and reinforcement of leadership values (Moss et al., 2006c). Unfortunately, details of the processes needed to encourage the recruitment of designers with non-congruent styles have yet to be charted.

The extent to which people are unwittingly subject to the influence of segmentation variables (whether personality, gender or nationality) can lead organisations, unbeknown to themselves, to recruit people like themselves (Lewis, 2006), employing creatives whose values match those of senior staff rather than those of the end-user or purchaser. Such a mismatch between internal organisational values and external customer values can present obstacles to achieving congruity between internal *productions* and external customer *preferences*. A model is presented in Figure 2.1 that sets out the issues for achieving congruence between products and markets in the Web design industry.

The complexity of the model shows the difficulties that need to be overcome in order to achieve congruence and enable organisations genuinely to profit from diversity. These difficulties have implications for both marketing and human resource processes, highlighting the extent to which the achievement of congruence needs to take account of leadership style, recruitment processes, and the influence of nationality, personality and gender inside and outside the organisation. The complexity of considering the match of skills needed to create a product with appeal to a mixed market throws up issues that are as complex as those of a product with a more homogeneous market.

In terms of research, areas for future work could profitably focus on exploring the solutions proposed in this model across a number of segmentation variables and detailing ways in which the obstacles highlighted by this model can be overcome. In this respect, it may be possible to educate designers away from their initial *productions* and *preferences*

PROVISION OF PRODUCTS		PREFERENCES
Products supplied: these- - -> are a function of the P, G and N of the producer	Congruence needed<- - - to create increased attention and increased purchasing	External customer preferences: these are a function of the P, G and N of consumers. Likewise with internal customers. Potential for conflict between the two
Provision of leadership: this is a function of the G of the recruiters	Need TfTc leadership for NPD	Internal customers: Their leadership style preferences are a function of their G
Ability to engage in teamwork: this is a function of the N of the team members	KM relies on teamwork	Teamworking preferences of internal customers are a function of their N

Figure 2.1 Congruence needed between products and preferences
P = personality; N = nationality; G = gender; KM = knowledge management; TfTc = Transformational leadership plus contingent reward; NPD = new product development.

through a campaign of educating organisational internal stakeholders in alternative values (Moss, 2009a), but these processes need to be thoroughly researched and evaluated.

References

Aaker, D. (1991), *Managing Brand Equity: Capitalising on the Value of a Brand Name* (New York: Free Press).

Acker, J. (1992), 'Gendering organizational theory', in Mills, A. and Tancred, P. (eds), *Gendering Organizational Analysis* (London: Sage).

Adler, N. and Gunderson, A. (2008), *International Dimensions of Organisational Behaviour*, 5th edition (Mason, Ohio: Thomson South Western).

Alimo-Metcalfe, B. and Alban-Metcalfe, J. (2003), 'Gender & leadership: a masculine past, but a feminine future?' *Proceedings of the BPS Annual Occupational Psychology Conference*, Brighton, 8–10 January, 67–70.

Allen, D. (2001), 'eMarketer: women on the Web, ebusinessforum.com', available at http://www.ebusinessforum.com (accessed April 2005).

Allport, G. W. and Vernon, P. E. (1933), *Studies in Expressive Movement* (New York: Macmillan).

All about market research, billion http://www.allaboutmarketresearch.com/internet.htm, accessed 22 November 2011.

Alschuler, R. H. and Hattwick, W. (1969), *Painting and Personality* (Chicago: University of Chicago Press).

Alvesson, M. and Billing, Y. (1997), *Understanding Gender and Organizations* (London: Sage).

Ancona, D. G. and Caldwell, D. F. (1992), 'Demography and design: predictors of new product team performance', *Organization Science*, 3, 321–41.

Armstrong, M. (2001), *Handbook of Human Resource Management Practice* (London: Kogan Page).

Aronson, E. (1958), 'The need for achievement as measured by graphic expression', in Atkinson, J. W. (ed.), *Motives in Fantasy, Action and Society* (Princeton: Van Nostrand Press).

Baden-Fuller, C. (1995), 'Strategic innovation, corporate entrepreneurship and matching outside-in to inside-out approaches to strategy research', *British Journal of Management*, 6 (Special issue), 3–16.

Ballard, P. B. (1912), 'What London children like to draw', *Journal of Experimental Paediatrics*, 1, 185–97.

Barczak, G. and Wilemon, D. (1992), 'Successful new product team leaders', *Industrial Marketing Management*, 21 (1), 61–8.

Barletta, M. (2006), *Marketing to Women: How to Increase your Share of the World's Largest Market* (New York: Kaplan Publishing).

Barmes, L. and Ashtiany, S. (2003), 'The diversity approach to achieving equality: Potential and pitfalls', *Industrial Law Journal*, 32 (4), 274–96.

Barnes, B., Fox, M., and Morris, D. (2004), 'Exploring the linkage between internal marketing, relationship marketing and service quality: a case study of a consulting organisation', *Total Quality Management and Business Excellence*, 15 (5/6), 593–601.

Barnes, S., Bauer H., Neumann, M., and Huber, F. (2007), 'Segmenting cyberspace: a customer typology for the Internet', *European Journal of Marketing*, 41 (1/2), 71–93.

Baroudi, J. J. and Igbaria, M. (1994/5), 'An examination of gender effects on career success of information system employees', *Journal of Management Information Systems*, 11 (3), 181–201.

Barron, F. (1963), *Creativity and Psychological Health* (Princeton, NJ: Van Nostrand Press).

Bass, B. (1998), 'Current developments in transformational leadership: research and applications', invited address to the American Psychological Association, San Francisco, August.

Baum, J. J. (1996), 'Organisational ecology', in Clegg, S. R., Hardy, C. and Nords, W. R. (eds), *Handbook of Organization Studies* (London: Sage).

Bennett, O. (1998), 'Warrior or Madonna: which will you be?', *The Guardian*, 28 December, pp. 8–9.

Berliner, W. (2004), 'Where have all the young men gone?', *The Guardian*, 18 May.

Berry, L. (2000), 'Cultivating service brand equity', *Journal of the Academy of Marketing Science*, 28 (1), 129–37.

Berscied, E. and Walster, E. (1978), *Interpersonal Attraction* (Cambridge: Addison-Wesley).

Bimber, B. (2000), 'Measuring the gender gap on the Internet', *Social Science Quarterly*, 81, 868–76.

Bird, B. and Brush, C. (2002), 'A gendered perspective on organizational creation', *Entrepreneurship: Theory & Practice*, 26 (3), 41–59.

Birren, F. (1973), 'Colour preference as a clu.

Bloch, P. H. (1995), 'Seeking the ideal form: product design and consumer response', *Journal of Marketing*, 59, 16–29.

Bloch, P. H., Brunel, F. and Arnold, T. (2003), 'Individual differences in the centrality of visual product aesthetics: Concept and measurement', *Journal of Personality and Social Psychology*, 71, 665–79.

Boxall, P. and Purcell, J. (2003), *Strategy and Human Resource Management* (Hampshire: Palgrave Macmillan).

Bristor, J. and Fischer, E. (1993), 'Feminist theory and consumer research', *Journal of Consumer Research*, 19 (4), 518–36.

Brock, T. C. (1965), 'Communicator-recipient similarity and decision change', *Journal of Personality and Social Psychology*, 1, 650–54.

Brown, S. and Eisenhardt, K. (1998), *Competing on the Edge: Strategy as Structured Chaos* (Boston: Harvard Business School Press).

Buchanan, R. (1995), 'Rhetoric, humanism and design', in Buchanan, R. and Margolin, V. (eds), *Discovering Design* (Chicago: University of Chicago Press).

Buchanan, R. and Margolin, V. (eds) (1995), *Discovering Design* (Chicago: University of Chicago Press).

Burkitt, E. and Newall, T. (2005), 'Effects of human figure on children's use of colour to depict sadness and happiness', *International Journal of Art Therapy*, 10 (1), 15–22.

Burmaster, A. (2006), 'E-tailers will pay if they ignore female shoppers', *New Media Age*, 21 December, p. 7.

Burt, R. B. (1968), *An Exploratory Study of Personality Manifestations in Paintings*, doctoral dissertation, Duke University (Dissertation abstracts International 29, 1493-B (Order number 68-14, 298)).

Butler, J. (1990), *Gender Trouble: Feminism and the Subversion of Identity* (New York and London: Routledge).

Byrne, D. and Neuman, J. (1992), 'The implications of attraction research for organizational issues', in Kelley, K. (ed.), *Issues, Theory and Research in Industrial and Organizational Psychology* (New York: Elsevier).

Byrne, F. (1971), *The Attraction Paradigm* (New York: Academic Press).

Caterall, M. and Maclaran, P. (2002), 'Gender perspectives in consumer behaviour: an overview of future directions', *Marketing Review*, 2 (4), 405–25.

Chau, P., Au, G. and Tam, K. (2000), 'Impact of information presentation modes on online shopping: an empirical evaluation of a broadband interactive shopping service', *Journal of Organizational Computing Electronic Commerce*, 10 (1), 1–22.

Chen, S. C. and Dhillon, G. S. (2002), 'Interpreting dimensions of consumer trust in e-commerce', *Information Management and Technology*, 4, 303–18.

Church, A., Ravenscroft, N., Curry, N., Burnside, N., Fish, P., Joyce, C., Hill, D., Smith, T., Scott, P., Markwell, S., Mobbs, B. and Grover, S. (2001), *Water-based Sport and Recreation: The Facts*. Project Report. DEFRA, London.

Cianni, M. and Romberger, B. (1997), 'Life in the corporation: a multi-method study of the experiences of male and female Asian, black Hispanic and white employees', *Gender, Work and Organization*, 4 (2), 116–27.

Collins, J. and Porras, J. (1998), *Built to Last* (London: Random House).

Cook, J. and Finlayson, M. (2005), 'The impact of cultural diversity on website design', *Advanced Management Journal*, 70(3), 15–23.

Crozier, W. and Greenhalgh, P. (1992), 'The empathy principle: towards a model for the psychology of art', *Journal for the Theory of Social Behaviour*, 22, 63–79.

Cyr, D. and Bonanni, C. (2005), 'Gender and website design in e-business', *International Journal of Electronic Business*, 3 (6), 565–82.

Cyr, D. and Trevor-Smith, H. (2004), 'Localization of web design: a comparison of German, Japanese, and U.S. website characteristics', *Journal of the American Society for Information Science and Technology*, 55 (13), 1–10.

De Chernatony, L. and McDonald, M. (1992), *Creating Powerful Brands: The Strategic Route to Success in Consumer, Industrial and Service Markets* (Oxford: Butterworth-Heinemann).

De Chernatony, L., Drury, S. and Segal-Horn, S. (2004), 'Identifying and sustaining services brands' values', *Journal of Marketing Communications*, 10 (2), 73–94.

Dholakia, R. and Uusitado, O. (2002), 'Switching to electronic stores: consumer characteristics and the perception of shopping benefits', *International Journal of Retail and Distribution Management*, 30 (10), 459–70.

Dittmar, H., Long, K. and Meek, R. (2004), 'Buying on the Internet: gender difference in on-line and conventional buying motivations', *Sex Roles*, 50 (5–6), 423–44.

Donovan, R. J., Rossiter, J. R., Marcoolyn, G. and Nesdale, A. (1994), 'Store atmosphere and purchasing behaviour', *Journal of Retailing*, 70 (3), 283–94.

Donthu, N. and Garcia, A. (1999), 'The Internet shopper', *Journal of Advertising Research*, 39 (3), 52–8.

Driscoll, D.-M. and Hoffman, M. W. (1999), 'Gaining the ethical edge: procedures for delivering values-driven management', *Long Range Planning*, 32 (2), 179–89.

Durndell, A. and Haag, Z. (2002), 'Computer self efficacy, computer anxiety, attitudes towards the Internet and reported experience with the Internet, by gender, in an East European sample', *Computers in Human Behaviour*, 18 (5), 521–35.

Eagly, A., Johannesen-Schmidt, M. and van Engen, M. (2003), 'Transformational, transactional, and laissez-faire leadership styles: a meta-analysis comparing women and men', *Psychological Bulletin*, 129 (4), 569–92.

Economist, Technology Quarterly, The Internet:predictions that an "exaflood" of traffic will overload the internet have been doing the rounds. But will it really happen?, http://www.economist.com/node/12673221, accessed 22 November. 2011.

Eurostat (2010), http://www.prweb.com/releases/age-uk/myfriends-online-week 2011/prweb5207074.htm, accessed on 22 November 2011.

Equal Opportunities Commission (2002), *Facts About Women and Men in Great Britain* (Manchester: Equal Opportunities Commission).

Erikson, E. H. (1970), *Childhood and Society* (Penguin: Harmondsworth).

Eroglu, S., Machleit, K. and Davis, L. (2003), 'Empirical testing of a model of online store atmospherics and shopper responses', *Psychology and Marketing*, 20 (2), 139–50.

Evans, J. (1939), *Taste and Temperament* (London: Jonathan Cape).

Firat, F. A. (1994), 'Gender and consumption: transcending the feminine?', in Costa, J. (ed.), *Gender Issues and Consumer Behaviour*, Thousand Oaks: Sage, pp. 205–28.

Flanagin, A. and Metzger, M. (2003), 'The perceived credibility of personal web page information as influenced by the sex of the source', *Computers in Human Behaviour*, 19, 683–701.

Fogg, B., Soohoo, C. and Danielson, D. (2002), 'How do people evaluate a web site's credibility? Results from a large study', Persuasive Technology Lab, Stanford University.

Franck, K. and Rosen E. (1949), 'A projective test of masculinity–femininity', *Journal of Consulting Psychology*, 247–56.

Gagnon, S. and Cornelius, N. (2000), 'Re-examining workplace equality: the capabilities approach', *Human Resource Management Journal*, 10 (4), 68–87.

Garbarino, E. and Strahilevitz, M. (2004), 'Gender differences in the perceived risk of buying online and the effects of receiving a site recommendation', *Journal of Business Research*, 57, 768–75.

Gehrt, K. C. and Yan, R.-N. (2004), 'Situational, consumer, and retailer factors affecting internet catalog, and store shopping', *International Journal of Retail and Distribution Management*, 32 (1), 5–18.

Gherardi, S. (1996), 'Gendered organisational cultures: narratives of women travellers in a male world', *Gender, Work and Organization*, 3 (4), 187–201.

Global Internet Advisors (2008), http://asiafinanceblog.blogs.com/, accessed on 22 November 2011.

Gommans, M., Krishnan, K. S. and Scheffold, K. B. (2001), 'From brand loyalty to e-loyalty: a conceptual framework', *Journal of Economic and Social Research*, Amsterdam: Association for Consumer Research, 43–58.

Gordon, I. (1999), *Relationship Marketing: New Strategies, Techniques and Technologies to Win the Customers You Want and Keep Them Forever*, John Wiley and Sons Publishers, p. 336.

Groppel, A. (1993), 'Store design and experience orientated consumers in retailing: comparison between the United States and Germany', in Raaij, W. F. and Bamossy, G. J. (eds), *European Advances in Consumer Research*, pp. 99–109.

Grover, V. and Saeed, K. A. (2004), 'Strategic orientation and performance of internet-based businesses', *Information Systems Journal*, 14 (1), 23–42.

Gunn, R. and Moss, G. (2006), 'An interactive aesthetic for French and UK e-commerce', *International Journal of Technology, Knowledge and Society*, avaliable at http://ijt.cgpublisher.com/home.html.

Gunn, R., Moss, G., Sanders, G. and Gasper, R. (2007), 'Are nursing and police websites adapted for their target markets?', CITSA, Florida, 13–15 July.

Hammer, E. F. (1980), *The Clinical Application of Projective Drawings*, Springfield: Charles C. Thom.

Hammer, M. (1995), *Reengineering the Corporation*, London: Nicholas Brealey Corporation.

Hammitt, W. E., Backlund, E. A. and Bixler, R. D. (2004), 'Experience use history, place bonding and resource substitution of trout anglers during recreation engagements', *Journal of Leisure Research*, 36 (3), 256–378.

Harris, A. and Nochlin, L. (1976), *Women Artists*, California: Los Angeles County Museum of Art.

Harris, J. (2007), 'Personal projections in artists' work: implications for branding', *Journal of Brand Management*, 14 (4), 296–313.

Hartline, M., Maxham, J. and McKee, D. (2000), 'Corridors of influence in the dissemination of customer-oriented strategy to customer contact service employees', *Journal of Marketing*, 64 (2), 35–50.

Hassenzahl, M. (2007), 'Aesthetics in interactive products: correlates and consequences of beauty', in Schifferstein, H. N. J. and Hekkert, P. (eds), *Product Experience*, Amsterdam: Elsevier.

Heide, G.A. (1991), *The Dancing Goddess: Principles of a Matriarchal Aesthetic*.

Hofstede, G. (2001), *Culture's Consequences: Comparing Values, Behaviors, Institutions, and Organizations across Nations*, New York: Sage.

Holland, J. and Baker, S. (2001), 'Customer participation in creating site brand loyalty', *Journal of Interactive Marketing*, 15 (4), 34–45.

Ibeh, K., Luo, Y. and Dinnie, K. (2005), 'E-branding strategies of internet companies: some preliminary insights from the UK', *Journal of Brand Management*, 12 (5), 355–73.

Igbaria, M. and Parasuraman, S. (1997), 'Status report on women and men in the IT workplace', *Information Systems Management*, 14 (3), 44–54.

Iijima, M., Arisaka, O., Minamoto, F. and Arais, Y. (2001), 'Sex differences in children's free drawings: a study on girls with congenital adrenal hyperplasia', *Hormones and Behavior*, 40, 99–104.

IITA: Electronic commerce and the NII (1994), Information Infrastructure Technology and Applications Task Group, National Coordination Office for High Performance Computing and Communications, 13–14 February.

Jackson, C. and Hirsch, W. (1991), 'Women managers and career progression: the British experience', *Women in Management Review and Abstracts*, 6 (2), 10–16.

Jackson, S. (2001), 'Why a materialist feminism is (still) possible – and necessary', *Women's Studies International Forum*, 24 (3/4), 283–93.

Jacoby and Jacobs (1969), 'Personality and consumer behaviour, how not to find relationships', *Purdue Papers in Consumer Psychology*, No. 102.

Janz, B. D. and Prasarnphanich, P. (2003), 'Understanding the antecedents of effective knowledge management: the importance of a knowledge-centred culture', *Decision Sciences*, 34 (2), 351–84.

Joergensen, J. and Blythe, J. (2003), 'A guide to a more effective World Wide Web', *Journal of Marketing Communications*, 9, 45–58.

Jordan, P. W. (1998), 'Human factors for pleasure in product use', *Applied Ergonomics*, 29, 25–33.

Judge, T. A., Bono, J. E., Ilies, R. and Gerhardt, M. W. (2002), 'Personality and leadership: a qualitative and quantitative review', *Journal of Applied Psychology*, 87 (4), 765–80.

Jupiter Communications (2004), 'Portrait of the European online population through 2009', market forecast report available at http://www.jupiterresearch.com/bin/item.pl/research:vision/jup/id595079.

Kant, E. (1978), *Critique of Judgement*, translated by Meredith, J. C., Oxford: Clarendon Press.

Kapferer, J. (1992), *Strategic Brand Management*, New York: Free Press.

Karande, K., Zinkhan, G. M. and Lum, A. B. (1997), 'Brand personality and self concept: a replication and extension', *American Marketing Association, Summer Conference*, 165–71.

Karpin, D. (Chair) *Report of the Industry Task Force on Leadership and Management Skills* (April 1995) Executive Summary: Enterprising Nation: renewing Australia's managers to meet the challenge of the Asia-Pacific Century. Canberra: AGPS.

Katz, J. E., Rice, R. and Aspden, P. (2001), 'The Internet 1995–2000', *American Behavioural Scientist*, 45, 405–19.

Kim, J. W., Lee, B. H., Shaw, M. J., Chang, H. L. and Nelson, M. (2001), 'Application of decision-free induction techniques to personalised advertisements on Internet storefronts', *International Journal of Electronic commerce*, 5 (3), 45–62.

Kirton, G. and Greene, A. (2000), *The Dynamics of Managing Diversity*, Oxford: Butterworth Heinemann.

Knapp, R. H. and Wolff, A. (1963), 'Preferences for abstract and representational art', *Journal of Social Psychology*, 60, 255–62.

Kotler, P. (1973–4), 'Atmospherics as a marketing tool', *Journal of Retailing*, 49 (Winter), 48–63.

Kramar, R. (1998), 'Managing diversity: beyond affirmative action in Australia', *Women in Management Review*, 13 (4), 133–42.

Kyle, G., Bricker, K., Graefe, A. and Wickham, T. (2004), 'An examination of recreationists' relationships with activities and settings', *Leisure Sciences*, 126, 123–42.

Lavie, T. and Tractinsky, N. (2004), 'Assessing dimensions of perceived visual aesthetics of web sites', *Journal of Human-Computer Studies*, 60, 269–98.

Leong, K. (1997), 'Women gaining clout online', *Internetweek*, 686, 107.

Levine, K. J., Miller, V. D., Kamrin, M. A. and Dearing, J. W. (1999), 'Anglers' attitudes, beliefs, and behaviours as impacted by the Michigan Fish Consumption Advisory', *Journal of Public Health Management Practice*, 5 (6), 18–28.

Lewin, K. (1936) *Principles of Topological Psychology*. New York: McGraw-Hill.

Lewis, C. (2006), 'Is the test relevant?', *The Times*, Career section, 30 November, p. 8.

Liff, S. (1996), 'Two routes to managing diversity: individual differences or social group characteristics', *Employee Relations*, 19 (1), 11–26.

Loden, M. and Rosener, J. (1991), *Workforce America! Managing Employee Diversity as a Vital Resource*, Homewood, IL: Business One Irwin.

Lupotow, L., Garovich, L. and Lupetow, M. (1995), 'The persistence of gender stereotypes in the face of changing sex roles: evidence contrary to the sociocultural model', *Ethology and Sociobiology*, 16, 509–30.

Luthar, H. (1996), 'Gender differences in evaluation of performance and leadership ability: autocratic vs. democratic managers', *Sex Roles*, 35 (5–6), 337–61.

Majewski, M. (1978), *The Relationship between the Drawing Characteristics of Children and their Sex*, unpublished doctoral dissertation, Illinois State University.

Marshall, J. (2008), 'Women and leadership: transforming visions and diverse voices', *Times Higher Education*, 12 June, http://www.timeshighereducation. co.uk/story.asp?storyCode=402345&sectioncode=26>, accessed 23 December 2008.

Maughan, L., Gutnikov, S. and Stevens, R. (2007), 'Like more, look more: look more, like more: the evidence from eye-tracking', *Journal of Brand Management*, 14 (4), 336–48.

McNiff, K. (1982), 'Sex differences in children's art', *Journal of Education*, 164, 271–89.

McSweeney, B. (2002), 'Hofstede's model of national cultural differences and consequences: a triumph of faith – a failure of analysis, *Human Relations*, 55 (1), 89–118.

Miller, D. (1996), 'Equality management: towards a materialist approach', *Gender, Work and Organisation*, 3 (4), 202–14.

Miller, H. and Arnold, J. (2000), 'Gender and home pages', *Computers and Education*, 34 (3–4), 335–9.

Miller, H. and Arnold, J. (2003), 'Self in Web home pages: gender, identity and power in cyberspace', in Riva, G. and Galimberti, C. (eds), *Towards Cyber Psychology: Mind, Cognitions and Society in the Internet Age*, Amsterdam: IOS Press.

Minamato, F. (1985), *Male-Female Differences in Pictures* (Tokyo: Shoseki).

Mintel (2005), 'Health and beauty treatments – UK', March, www.mintel.co.uk

Mintzberg, H. (1973), *The Nature of Managerial Work*, New York: Harper & Row.

Mirzoeff, N. (ed.) (l998), *The Visual Culture Reader*, London: Routledge.

Mischel, W. (1997), 'The interaction of person and situation', in Magnusson, D. and Endler, N. S. (eds.), *Personality at the Crossroads: Current Issues in Interactional Psychology*, Hillsdale, NJ: Erlabum, pp. 333–52.

Mitchell, V.-W. and Walsh, G. (2004), 'Gender differences in German consumer decision-making styles', *Journal of Consumer Behaviour*, 3 (4), 331–47.

Moore, D. (2000), *Careerpreneurs – Lessons from Leading Women Entrepreneurs on Building a Career without Boundaries*, Palo Alto, CA: Davies-Black Publishing.

Moss, G. (1995), 'Differences in the design aesthetic of men and women: implications for product branding', *Journal of Brand Management*, 3 (3), 51–61.

Moss, G. (1999), 'Gender and consumer behaviour: further explorations', *Journal of Brand Management*, 7 (2), 88–100.

Moss, G. (2000), 'Design with a difference', *Designing*, Spring, 22.

Moss, G. and Colman, A. (2001), 'Choices and preferences: experiments on gender differences', *Journal of Brand Management*, 9 (2), 89–98.

Moss, G. and Vinten, G. (2001), 'Choices and preferences: the effects of nationality', *Journal of Consumer Behaviour*, 1 (2), 198–207.

Moss, G. (2003), 'The implications of the male and female design aesthetic for public services', *Innovation Journal*, 8 (4).

Moss, G. and Gunn, R. (2005), 'Websites and services branding: implications of universities' websites for internal and external communication', 4th International Critical Management Studies Conference, Cambridge, 4–6 July.

Moss, G., Gunn, R. and Heller, J. (2006a), 'Some men like it black, some women like it pink: consumer implications of differences in male and female website design', *Journal of Consumer Behaviour*, 5, 328–41.

Moss, G., Gunn, R. and Kubacki, K. (2006b), 'Successes and failures of the mirroring principle: the case of angling and beauty websites', *International Journal of Consumer Studies*, 30, 1–10.

Moss, G. and Gunn, R. (2006c), 'Gendered subjectivities in website design: an exploration of weblog views', Women into IT (WINIT), Salford University, 21 March.

Moss, G., Gunn, R. and Kubacki, K. (2006d), 'Optimising web site design in Europe: gender implications from an interactionist perspective', *International Journal of Applied Marketing*, 2 (1).

Moss, G. and Daunton, L. (2006e), 'The discriminatory impact of deviations from selection criteria in Higher Education selection', *Career Development International*, 11 (6), 504–21.

Moss, G., Daunton, L. and Gasper (2006f), 'The impact of leadership selection on High Performance Working', *CIPD Professional Standards Conference*, 26–28 June, Keele University.

Moss, G. (2007a), 'The impact of personality and gender on branding decisions', *Journal of Brand Management*, 14 (4), 277–83.

Moss, G. (2007b), 'The psychology of performance and preference: advantages, disadvantages, drivers and obstacles to the achievement of congruence', *Journal of Brand Management*, 14 (4), 343–58.

Moss, G., Kubacki, K., Hersh, M. and Gunn, R. (2007c), 'Knowledge management in Higher Education: a comparison between individualistic and collectivist cultures', *European Journal of Education*, 43 (3), 377–94.

Moss, G. and Gunn, R. (2008a), 'Gender differences in website production and preference aesthetics: preliminary implications for ICT in education and beyond', *Behaviour and Information Technology*, DOI: 10.1080/0144929080.

Moss, G., Gunn, R. and Kubacki, K. (2008b), 'Gender and web design: the implications of the mirroring principle for the services branding model', *Journal of Marketing Communications*, 14 (1), 37–57.

Moss, G. (2008c), 'The implications of diversity in e-commerce', in Nescott, B. K. (ed.), *E-commerce Coming into its Own*, USA: Nova Publications.

Moss, G. (2009a), *Gender, Design and Marketing*, Surrey: Gower.

Moss, G. (2009b), 'The implications of diversity in e-commerce', in Nescott, B. K. (ed.), *E-commerce Coming into its Own*, USA: Nova Publications.

Moss, G. (ed.) (2010), *Profiting from Diversity*, Basingstoke: Palgrave Macmillan.

New Media Age, http://www.nmatop100.co.uk/Top100/default.aspx, accessed 1 September 2007.

Nielsen Wire (2010), Users 50 and over dirve half of latest UK web surge, http://blog.nielsen.com/nielsenwire/global/users-50-and-older-drive-half-of-latest-u-k-web-surge/ accessed on 22 November 2011.

Nkomo, S. (1992), 'The emperor has no clothes: rewriting race in organizations', *Academy of Management Review*, 17 (3), 487–513.

Odlyzco, A. (2011), http://arstechnica.com/old/content/2008/04/exaflood-not-happening.ars, accessed on 6 May 2011.

Ono, H. and Zavodny, M. (2003), 'Gender and the Internet', *Social Science Quarterly*, 84 (1), 111–21.

Oser, K. (2003), 'Marketing well to women pays off', *Direct*, December.

Page, R., Jagger, N., Tamkin, P. and Henwood, N. (2006), 'The measurement of organisational performance', Institute of Manpower Studies, available at the following website, accessed on 3 December 2006, http://64.233.83.104/ search?q=cache:p51_Vjw:www.sda.org.uk/pdf/Final%e%2520Measurement %2520of%2520Organisational%2529Performance.pdf+%27there+are+a+ range+of+performance+measures+that+are+believed+to+be+related+to+ the+bottom+line%27&hl=en&gl=uk&ct=clnk&cd=1.

Palmer, J. (2002), Web site usability, design and performance metrics, *Information Systems Research*, 13 (2), 151–67.

Porteous, J. D. (1996), *Environmental Aesthetics: Ideas, Politics and Planning*, London: Routledge.

Potter, E. (1994), 'Commercialisation of the World Wide Web', WELL topic in the Internet conference on the WELL, 16 November.

Powell, G., Butterfield, A., Alves, J. and Bartol, K. (2004), 'Sex effects of evaluations of transformational and transactional leaders', Academy of Management, Best Conference Paper.

Preyer, W. (1895), *On the Physiology of Handwriting*, Hamburg.

Read, H. (1953), *Art and Industry*, London: Faber and Faber.

Robertson, M., Newell, S., Swan, J., Mathiassen, L. and Bjerknes, G. (2001), 'The issue of gender within computing: reflections from the UK and Scandinavia', *Information Systems Journal*, 11, 111–26.

Rodgers, S. and Harris, M. A. (2003), 'Gender and e-commerce: an exploratory study', *Journal of Advertising Research*, September, 322–9.

Rosener, J. (1990), 'Ways women lead', *Harvard Business Review*, November/ December, 119–25.

Roy, R. and Wield, D. (1989), *Product Design and Technological Innovation* (Philadelphia: Open University/Taylor and Francis).

Samli, C. (1995), *International Consumer Behavior: Its Impact on Marketing Strategy Development*, Westport: Quorum Books.

Schaffer, B. and Riordan, C. (2003), 'Review of cross-cultural methodologies for organisational research: a best practice approach', *Organizational Research Methods*, 6 (2), 169–215.

Schenkman, N. and Jonsson, F. (2000), 'Aesthetics and preferences of web pages', *Behaviour and Information Technology*, 19 (5), 367–77.

Schneider, R. (2001), 'Variety performance', *People Management*, 7 (9), 27–31.

Schroeder, J. and Borgerson, J. (1998), 'Marketing images of gender: a visual analysis', *Consumption, Markets and Culture*, 2 (2), 105–231.

Schuiling, I. and Kapferer, J.-N. (2004), 'Real differences between local and international brands: strategic implications for international marketers', *Journal of International Marketing*, 12 (4), 97–112.

Simon, J. and Peppas, S. (2005), 'Attitudes towards product website design: a study of the effects of gender', *Journal of Marketing Communications*, 11 (2), 129–44.

Song, M. and Noh, J. (2006), 'Best new product development and management practices in the Korean Hightech Industry', *Industrial Marketing Management*, 35 (3), 262–78.

Stockdale, M. and Crosby, F. (2004), *The Psychology and Managements of Workplace Diversity*, Oxford: Blackwell.

Tannen, D. (1990), *You Just Don't Understand Me*, New York: Harper Collins.

Thelwall, M. (2000), 'Effective websites for small and medium-sized enterprises', *Journal of Small Business and Enterprise Development*, 7, 150–9.

Thomas, G., Chaigne, E. and Fox, T. (1989), 'Children's drawings of topics differing in significance: effects on size of drawing', *British Journal of Developmental Psychology*, 7, 321–31.

Van der Heijden, H. (2003), 'Factors influencing the usage of websites: the case of a generic portal in the Netherlands', *Information Management*, 40 (6).

Van Iwaarden, J., van der Wiele, T., Ball, L. and Millen, R. (2004), 'Perceptions about the quality of web sites: a survey amongst students at Northeasten University and Erasmus University', *Information and Management*, 41 (8), 947–59.

Van Slyke, C., Comunale, C. and Belanger, F. (2002), 'Gender differences in perceptions of web-based shopping', *Communications of the ACM*, 45 (7), 82–6.

Vinnicombe, S. and Singh, V. (2002), 'Developing tomorrow's women business leaders', in Burke, R. and Nelson, D. (eds), *Advancing Women's Careers*, Oxford: Blackwell.

Waehner, T. S. (1946), 'Interpretations of spontaneous drawings and paintings', *Genetic Psychology Monograph*, 33, 3–70.

Wang, Y., Hong, S. and Lou, H. (2010), 'Beautiful beyond useful? The role of web aesthetics,' *Journal of Computer Information Systems (JCIS)*, 50 (3), 121–9.

Webb, J. (1997), 'The politics of equal opportunity', *Gender, Work and Organization*, 4 (3), 159–67.

Welsh, G. S. (1949), 'A projective test for diagnosis of psychopathology', unpublished PhD thesis, University of Minnesota, avaliable at http://www.defra.gov.uk/wildlife-countryside/resprog/findings/2001dec.htm.

Whetten, David, A. and Cameron, Kim, S. (2005) *Developing Management Skills*. 6th edition, Prentice Hall.

White, J. (1995), 'Leading in their own ways: women chief executives in local government', in Itzin, C. and Newman, J. (eds), *Gender, Culture and Organizational Change*, London: Routledge.

Wilson, M. (2004), 'A conceptual framework for studying gender in information systems research', *Journal of Information Technology*, 19 (1), 81–92.

Wylie, B. (2007), 'Self and social function: art therapy in a therapeutic community prison', *Journal of Brand Management*, 14 (4), 324–34.

Yahomoto, M. and Lambert, D. R. (1994), 'The impact of product aesthetics on the evaluation of industrial products,' *Journal of Product Innovation Management*, 11, 309–24.

Zahedi, F., van Pelt, W. V. and Srite, M. (2006), 'Web documents' cultural masculinity and femininity', *Journal of Management and Information Systems*, 23 (1), 87–128.

Zhang, P. and von Dran, G. M. (2000), 'Satisfiers and dissatisfiers: a two-factor model for website design and evaluation', *Journal of American Association for Information Science (JASIS)*, 51 (14), 1253–68.

Section B
Segmenting Diversity

Age

3
Digital Communications and Older Groups: An Anglo-French Comparison

Hilary Mullen, Gloria Moss and Catharina Wulf

1 Fifty+ generations: a growing demographic

While, in general, birth rates decline across most developing nations, an important statistic is an increase in life expectancy. According to UK statistics, by 2007 the number of Britons aged over 65 exceeded the number of those aged under 16 for the first time, and it is estimated that by 2015 half of the adult UK population will be aged over 50 (Young, 2002/3). It is also estimated that nearly one in five people currently in the UK will live to see their 100th birthday, according to the UK's Department for Work and Pensions. This would mean 10 million people – 17 per cent of the population – becoming centenarians (BBC, 2010).

In France the situation is quite similar. In 2009, the 50+ population represented one-third of the French population, with youngsters below 20 accounting for just a quarter of the population. It is projected that by 2030 one in two French people will be older than 50 (Guérin, 2009, p. 32), by 2040 the number of people over 75 will double, and that by 2050 the number of those who are over 85 will increase from 1.1 million (the figure in 2009) to almost 5 million (Guérin, 2008, p. 19).

Most of the public debates about older people and ageing societies have set a rather pessimistic tone, stressing the problem of providing future pension plans and the potentially negative impact on welfare and care services. Instead of contributing to this pessimistic debate, the authors of this chapter focus on the potential business opportunities generated by the 50+ generations because of their utilisation of digital communications media, and the focus here will be on their use of the Internet and mobile phones. This is a group which is characterised by a relatively high level of disposable income, with a recent survey by Henley Management College in the UK finding that seven out of ten people who will retire in the next five years expect to use some or all of their capital to ensure that they have a comfortable and enjoyable retirement (Demos, 2004). The soon-to-be-retirees, according to the report, plan to treat themselves to holidays, cars and hobbies as well as paying for 'the basics' rather than save up a nest egg for their children (ibid., p. 47). The fact that, according to the Henley survey, 70 per cent of retirees will use their capital to spend during their retirement shows how important a consumer group the 50+ population is.

Before going any further, some clarification of terminology is necessary. The focus in this article is on those over 50 years of age, and therefore on chronological age as against functional age (appearance, activity, body functions), historical age (a person's relation to a specific cultural event), social age (which accounts for a society's rites of passage), or societal age (which investigates the culture's specific perception of ageing) (Lippincott, 2004). Within this focus on chronological age, the lower threshold of 50 is the age referred to in the French decree (number 2009-560 of 20 May 2009) regulating the employment of older people in organisations. The elastic nature of the term 'seniors', extending up to retirees and those with pensions, means that it overlaps with the twin age bands of 'boomer' and 'veteran' discussed in the Chartered Institute of Personnel and Development (CIPD's) report on generational employment (CIPD, 2008). It overlaps, furthermore, with several other categories, and those used in French and UK literature are summarised in Table 3.1.

Table 3.1 Summary of the sub-categories used in French and UK literature on 50+ consumers

Commentator	Age bands used		
	50–60	60–70	80+
UK studies/initiatives			
CIPD (2008)	Boomers born 1948–63	Veterans born 1939–47	
Sudbury and Simcock (2009)	'Positive pioneers' – average age 56	'Solitary sceptics' – average age 66	
	'Cautious comfortables' – average age 58	'Bargain-hunting belongers' – average age 70	
	'Self-assured sociables' – average age 59		

French studies/initiatives

French Napoleonic Code	Decree number 2009–560 of 20 May 2009 specifies 50 as a target recruitment age		
Pleine Vie (2007)	50–59	60–69	
Guérin (2008)	BooBos (50–70)	SeTra (60+)	SeFra (75+)
Tréguer (2002)	Masters (50–59)	Liberated (60–74)	Peaceful (75–84)

Age has been said to correlate very often with intention and usage of mobile technology, with the finding that age is the only significant predictor for use of mobile services (Carlsson et al., 2005). It has been found that older people adopt new technologies when they are suitable and easy enough to use (Gilly and Zeithmal, 1987). Other commentators have highlighted the role of positive attitude in embracing new technology (Smither and Braun, 1994), the importance of safety, usefulness, convenience and complexity, and the positive influence of socialisation agents such as children or grandchildren. The older the person is, the more difficult the adoption of technology is likely to be (ibid.), which in turn increases the role of help from family members.

Before we move on with comparing the 50+ generations' use of digital technologies in the UK and France, let us briefly examine the rationale for a comparison of these two countries as well as a brief overview of Internet and mobile phone usage and the reason for adopting an interactionist approach in this chapter.

2 UK and France comparison

The reason for the comparison of the UK and France is the economic importance of Anglo-French trade. France is the UK's third largest export market (British Government statistics: the 'Overseas Trade Statistics (OTS) of the UK' and the 'UK Regional Trade Statistics (RTS)'. The OTS are published monthly, providing detailed data for over 9,000 commodities and 200 partner countries. The RTS are published quarterly showing trade at summary product and country level, split by UK regions. www.HMRevenue and Customs UK trade information/home.). It accounts for 10 per cent of total UK exports worldwide and 20 per cent of European exports. If we consider the export of services alone to France, we are looking at sales of £5.4 billion. While the proportion of computer and information services is unknown, UK Government statistics show, nonetheless, over the period 2002–3, an increase worldwide in UK exports of computer and information services of 35 per cent. With respect to France, the UK is its fourth largest export market, making up for 9.3 per cent of total French exports in January–June 2004.

We will now turn our attention to an overview of usage relating to the Internet and mobile phones.

3   The Internet

Today the World Wide Web is acknowledged to be an integral part of the marketing mix (Strauss and Frost, 1999) with a 'powerful' role to play in product promotion, sales and distribution (Melewar and Smith, 2003). Since 1998, Internet usage has grown at a rate of 20 per cent per year (Van Iwaarden et al., 2004) and by June 2010 the world Internet user population reached 1.9 billion (All about market research). It has 'transform[ed] the way business is conducted' (Grover and Saeed, 2004) since it is generally believed that the Internet is more than just another selling channel, especially when considering its practical side: consumers can manage their purchases from home and they can take more time to peruse the products and services offered online. Above all, from a marketer's point of view, online communication is less expensive than classical advertising on television or in the printed press. It is estimated, for example, that the Internet helps 'to produce ten times as many units [sold] with one tenth of the advertising budget' (Potter, 1994), to ease customer retention (Van Iwaarden et al., 2004) and to facilitate flexible response, an advantage with shrinking product life cycles (IITA, 1994). Given the competition for the user's attention, the shift to consumer-controlled interaction (Wedende et al., 2001) and the role of national variables in influencing reactions (Samli, 1995), there is a 'pressing need' (Clarke and Doherty, 2004), to understand the factors that can assist in creating websites that successfully target this large consumer group.

4   Mobile telephones

According to the International Telecommunications Union, developments in the mobile sector have been able to change the ICT landscape. By the end of 2007, almost one in two people had a mobile phone. More than one in four Africans and one in three Asians had a mobile phone. By the end of 2010, there were 5.3 billion mobile subscriptions (International Telecommunication Union, 2010), which is equivalent to 77 per cent of the world population. That is a huge increase from 4.6 billion

(International Telecommunications Union, 2010) mobile subscriptions at the end of 2009. Research suggests that older users use mobile phones only for simple functions such as calling or sending messages (Koo and Cheok, 2006).

The focus on the study of a market segment and the way it responds to digital technologies is linked to an interactionist approach to the study of e-marketing and insight into the interactionist paradigm is provided in the next section.

5   An interactionist framework

Where products are concerned, it is commonly accepted that the development of values for a new brand in the goods sector involves research into consumers' needs (Gordon, 1999). In the field of e-commerce, however, while lip service is paid to the view that 'a website has to be designed for a targeted customer segment...' (Gommans et al., 2001, p. 51), the emphasis in much of the literature on 'web atmospherics' is on finding universal solutions (Palmer, 2002; Joergensen and Blythe, 2003).

Universalist approaches seek to identify the factors in the attribute that will have universal appeal and this approach stands in stark contrast to so-called Field theory (Lewin, 1936) or interactionism (Mischel, 1977), which assumes that individuals will view physical and social settings differently, producing differences in 'life-space' and consumption behaviour (Gehrt and Yan, 2004). These theories dictate that characteristics of the stimulus object (attributes), characteristics of the individual (demographics, Internet usage), and the situation (situational factors) affect reactions to the stimulus object (format preference). This means that instead of seeking solutions or laws that will apply to *all* situations, we should seek out solutions that work in *particular* instances, an approach to problem-solving known in the field of human resources as a 'contingency approach'.

More precisely, the interactionist approach is against a 'one-size-fits-all approach to digital marketing, arguing that since the Web is not composed of a monolithic user type, there is no "one best way" for a company to tap into the power of the Internet' (Smith and Whitlark, 2001, quoted in Moss et al., 2008, p. 42). Interactionist research underlines, then, that aesthetic preferences differ according to the people who are targeted, seeking to understand the reactions of segmentation variables. Moreover, the interactionist paradigm places the 'empathy principle at its core, according to which aesthetic value is not inherent in objects, but is the product of empathy between object, perceiver and artist' (Crozier and Greenhalgh, 1992, quoted in Moss, 2009, p. 141). In the light of the demographic importance of senior populations, it would certainly be worthwhile to apply the interactionist approach to the latter, taking into consideration that seniors, just like any other segment, cannot be conceived as a homogeneous group. However, there is an extreme paucity of research where studying differing 50+ segments as a variable are concerned.

In fact, the interactionist approach is consistent with the directive of the business guru Michael Hammer, father of the concept of Business Reengineering, who spoke of the importance for products to be shaped around the 'unique and particular needs' of the customer (Hammer 1995, p. 21), and for products and services to be 'configured to' the needs of customers (ibid., p. 21). In the field of branding, Karande has expressed the view that there should be congruence between the brand personality and the consumer's self-concept on the basis that purchases are thought to offer a vehicle for self-expression (Karande et al., 1997).

An article on e-commerce discusses the importance – in terms of online success – of responding to consumer needs (Palmer, 2002), and developing sites that are responsive to user needs is deemed to be 'critical for all site designers and managers' (Palmer, 2002, p. 1). Important factors are thought to relate to technical issues, such as the speed of loading content (Joergensen and Blythe, 2003), as well as to design and forms (Schenkman and Jonsson, 2000; Palmer, 2002; Lavie and Tractinsky, 2004). This explains how graphics are listed as one of the ten factors causing dissatisfaction with users in the US and the Netherlands (Van Iwaarden et al., 2004). The impact of design on user experience leads 'human computer interaction' specialists to attempt to understand the elements (visual and content) in web design that are valued and those that currently produce a deficit between expectations and experience.

The search for these factors is a prize worth fighting for. Positive online experience is credited with having a greater role in 'customer' loyalty (Kapferer, 1992) than traditional attributes such as product selection and price (Ibeh et al., 2005). The role that websites can play in aiding communications and establishing added value with the user is, therefore, well understood. A detailed understanding, however, of how best to communicate to a variety of audiences online – what we might term 'web atmospherics' – is not as highly developed as product and store atmospherics.

We gather below a survey of the literature on the reactions to the Internet of a growing subset of the population, namely that of people aged 50+. We begin by looking at the Internet usage in this group in the

UK and France (i.e., situational factors) and then go on to look at what we know about individual characteristics such as gender.

6 Access to the Internet by the 50+

6.1 In the UK

Where the Internet is concerned, the picture in the UK is largely one of growth. David Noble, founder of the Web portal wanobe.com, declared in a recent interview that 'One 55-year-old in two goes online on a daily basis' (http://www.marketinguk.co.uk/Web-Sites). Although the Office of National Statistics in the UK (2004) puts usage of the Internet by older users at no more than 15 per cent, this represents a rise of 6 per cent on the previous year. Surveys by the Claritas UK consumer research group (Jeffery, 2003) and Morris et al. (2007) show a growth in the proportion of the over 60s who are online in the UK.

In fact, according to recent research (2011) by UKOM (the UK Online Measurement Company powered by Nielsen), people aged 50+ were responsible for the majority of the increase in UK Internet usage over the period 2009–10. The size of the UK Internet audience grew by 5 per cent from 36.9 million people in May 2009 to 38.8 million people in May 2010 and, according to UKOM, of these 1.9 million new Internet users, 1 million (53 per cent) were at least 50 years old. Of this increase in Internet usage by the 50+, men over 50 were primarily responsible for this growth, accounting for 722,000 (38 per cent) new British Internet users, followed by women over 50 who accounted for 284,000 (15 per cent) new users. This increase in usage by the 50+ population in the UK has produced a situation in which one in four Britons using the Internet today is 50 to 64 years of age. Moreover, where frequency of usage and not just numbers using the Web is concerned, 43 per cent of people aged 55–74 in the UK use the Internet frequently, compared to an EU average of 28 per cent (Eurostat, 2010). The UK tops European heavyweights Germany and France, where 33 per cent and 40 per cent respectively of that age group regularly use the Internet. The Office of National Statistics figure of 15 per cent usage by older users is equivalent to the proportions noted in the US, with only 15 per cent of Americans over the age of 65 having access to the Internet, and 56 per cent over 65 saying they will definitely not go online (Thayer and Ray, 2006). However, we are still behind Scandinavian countries such as Denmark, Norway and Sweden, where over half of 55–74s regularly surf the Web.

At least two factors are thought to account for this rise. First, the influence of workplace habits on those who are below retirement age, and secondly, the additional time available with retirement, as well as the money and growing confidence to explore old and new hobbies. As Emma Reid, Head of Customer Information for the Saga Group writes, 'the Internet makes information accessible at the click of a button' (Demos, 2004, p. 63). Where money is concerned, many belonging to the 50+ generation are currently at the peak of their earning careers and many have recently benefited from, or are about to benefit from, inheritances from their wealthy parents.

The importance of this segment is well illustrated in Figure 3.1, taken from the Nielsen report.

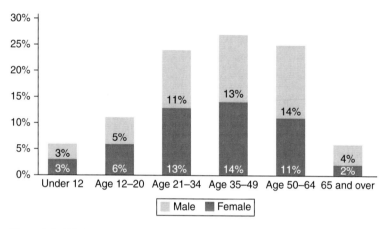

Figure 3.1   UK Internet audience composition (May 2010, Nielsen)

The figure shows usage dropping at the extreme ends of the age spectrum, but it should be pointed out that inequality of access to the Internet correlates not only with the age of the user but also with their level of income and education attainment. This is frequently referred to as the 'digital divide' (Loges and Joo-Young , 2001; Millward, 2003; Timms, 2003; Dutton et al., 2005). In the case of older age groups this trend is sometimes described in terms of a 'grey digital divide' (Millward, 2003). According to the 'Digital Britain' report by the Department of Business Innovation and Skills (2009), older groups are more likely to be excluded from using digital technologies than younger groups. The report recognises that although reasons for digital exclusion vary, some of the most common causes are the expense of digital products, the capabilities of users to interact with them and the availability of support for digital products and services.

This divide may not come as a surprise considering that older people have lived the majority of their lives without the Internet (Loges and Joo-Young, 2001, p. 542), which came into existence and achieved prominence only in the 1990s. On the one hand, it is possible that this 'grey digital divide' is simply a generational phenomenon that will disappear over time as the next generation of 50+ age groups spend more of their working lives surrounded by computers. On the other hand, Loges and Joo-Young warn that older people may continue to be keen to preserve their privacy and finances, thereby reducing their propensity, relative to younger people, to purchase products or services online (Loges and Joo-Young, 2001, p. 559). According to research conducted by the Office for National Statistics (2008), more than 64 per cent of people over 65 have never used the Internet. Moreover, research from the Institute for Financial Studies commissioned by Age UK (2009) shows that non-pensioners increased their spending on communications technology at two and a half times the rate of pensioners in the past 12 years.

This lag between the computer usage of pensioners and non-pensioners explains why Timms (2003) predicted that the digital divide could worsen in the UK before it improves. These conclusions are supported by the results of a survey conducted by the Library and Information Commission in 1999, underlining a lack of access to computers and the Internet as principal barriers to the adoption of the Internet among older people (Flatten et al., 2000, p. 11). However, a British Government initiative created over 6,000 UK online centres across the country, one of the consequences of which is that all public libraries can offer Internet access for their members (Museums Libraries and Archives Council, 2004). Even if older age groups are overall less inclined to use the Internet, the availability of the Internet in libraries might lead more people to accept the possibilities afforded by virtual space.

6.2 In France

In 2002, Tréguer wrote that compared to the US, where about 25 per cent of Internet users belong to the 50+ age group, in Sweden they constitute 22 per cent, followed by Germany and the UK with 20 per cent. For France, Italy and Spain the figure is around 15–17 per cent (Tréguer, 2002, p. 99). Although the three latter countries, which are clearly lagging behind, include France, Tréguer embraces all of them in his optimistic statement: 'Grey power is gradually taking over the Net!' (ibid., 2002, p. 99). He goes on to ask: 'How can we avoid saying something about the spectacular passion of the over 50s for multimedia computing and the Internet? They are greatly fascinated by this technology. By switching on their PC, they are connecting with "modernity" and thus remain in the know' (ibid., 2002, p. 97). Indeed, where France is concerned, a more recent market study reflects the growing trend of the Internet, showing that those aged between 50 and 64 represent 20 per cent of Internet users (Pleine Vie, 2007; George-Hoyau, 2008). Moreover, 46 per cent of French households aged between 50 and 69 have an Internet connection (Pleine Vie, 2007) and it has been suggested that the use of Minitel by this generation in 1982 will have boosted enthusiasm for the Internet (Brousseau, 2003), even if the latter did not offer any interactive features but was mostly used as an electronic telephone book or to reserve train or plane tickets.

In conclusion, it appears that the rate of Net users is on the increase, particularly if we consider that 40 per cent of those aged 60–69 in 2008 owned a computer with Internet connection compared to half of this figure in 2007 (*La Tribune*, 2008). And let us not forget that for those aged 60–69 and still working, having access to the Internet is indispensable (Pleine Vie, 2007).

7   Access to mobile phones by the 50+

7.1   In the UK

In the UK, 89 per cent of adults own a mobile phone that they use at least once a month, up from 62 per cent in 2000 (Ofcom, 2009). Moreover, according to statistics from the International Telecommunications Union from 2002, the number of mobile phones per 100 people in France was on average 84.5 (Nation Master, 2011).

However, mobile phone use is not spread evenly across the population. Older adults are less likely to use a mobile phone: 71 per cent of those aged 65–74 and 54 per cent of those aged 75 and over said that they personally used a mobile phone in 2009, compared to 96 per cent of 15–24 year olds, 98 per cent of 25–44 year olds and 91 per cent of 45–64 year olds (Ofcom, 2009). Therefore, the area for greatest potential growth seems to be with the over 65s, with 29–46 per cent of that age group not currently owning a mobile phone.

However, according to research by Continental Research (2008), this group will be harder to convert to long-term users in the future primarily because they are less comfortable with technology generally and less likely to need the mobile phone as a social communications tool. The research quotes this group as having a mobile phone for 'peace of mind' reasons, often in response to encouragement by a close relative, and as a result average revenue per user is relatively low among the over 65s.

7.2 In France

Nearly eight out of ten people in France own a mobile phone (79.6 per cent of people aged 11 and older), according to the results of the Mobile Consumer Insight by Médiamétrie and Nielsen Telecom Practice. Nearly half of the people in the country use their mobile phone for other usage than voice and SMS: they also surf the Internet or use an application (27.8 per cent), send MMS (18.7 per cent), listen to the radio (13.1 per cent) or watch TV (4.6 per cent) (New Media Trend, Watch, 2011).

According to statistics from the International Telecommunications Union from 2002, the number of mobile phones per 100 people in France was on average 64.7 (Nation Master, 2011). This is lower than in the UK where, as we have seen, the equivalent figure is 84.5.

8 How the Internet is used by the 50+

8.1 The case in Britain

We are fortunate in that there is increasing data on the type of Internet activities that the 50+ engage in and the main focus appears to be on social networking and shopping.

Out of the 59 per cent of over 50s who are active on the Internet, 40 per cent belong to at least one social network. Almost all the over 50s know Facebook (93 per cent), with awareness of My space just behind (90 per cent). According to the managing partner at InSites Consulting, Facebook is popular among the over 50s and will be so increasingly in the future (Quigley, 2009). A survey by InSites (Quigley, 2009) revealed that the over 50s online in the UK are far ahead of Belgians and Dutch in their use of social online networks, and a recent survey commissioned by Age UK has shown that 63 per cent of people aged 65 and over who use the Internet feel that since they have been online they have been able to keep in contact with friends and family more than before (TNS Omnibus, 2011).

Moreover, with nearly 1 million older people saying that they are often or always lonely (Agenda for Later Life, 2011), and over half of people aged 65+ (5 million) saying that they consider the television as their main form of company (Age UK, 2009), the Internet can be hugely important in allowing people to keep in contact with loved ones and helping to tackle feelings of isolation and loneliness.

A second activity enjoyed by the 50+ age group is online shopping. According to recent research by Nielsen (2011), the types of websites where people over 50 years old are most likely to be found are a varied mix of health, video, community, travel, fashion, genealogy, cooking and greeting cards. In fact, this research reveals that those aged 50+ account for 31 per cent of people online. In terms of sites that are popular with this age group, health website RealAge has the highest concentration of people this age among its visitors – 89 per cent are aged 50 or over. RealAge is followed by video site Flixxy (80 per cent) and community site Saga – of which 78 per cent of the audience is at least 50 years old. Burmaster, a commentator for Nielsen, has said that 'This age group have a wide appetite when it comes to the types of sites they are using to supplement the interests and needs they have in their lives. Consequently, a number of brands across a range of industries, particularly travel, are showing the rest what a valuable medium online is when it comes to reaching a desired audience who haven't grown up with the Internet' (Nielsen, 2011). Table 3.2 from the Nielsen research illustrates the sectors and sites that are most popular with this age group.

Table 3.2 Most popular UK websites for users aged over 50 by concentration, 2010

Rank	Web brand	% of UK audience 50+ years old	Number of UK visitors 50+ years old (000s)	Site content
1	RealAge	89	101	Health
2	Flixxy	80	108	Videos
3	Saga	78	379	Community
4	WA Shearings	78	123	Travel
5	Fifty Plus	77	122	Clothing
6	FamilySearch	75	128	Genealogy
7	Hand Picked Hotels	75	101	Travel
8	Lurpak	75	163	Food/cooking
9	JacquieLawson	75	239	Greeting cards
10	Cruise.co.uk	74	129	Travel

Source: UKOM/Nielsen. E.g. in May 2010, 89 per cent of UK visitors to RealAge (101,000 people) were at least 50 years old.

8.2 The case in France

Compared to the UK, systematic data about the 50+ generations' use of the Internet exists in France. Tréguer (2002) provided this information, summarised in Table 3.3.

Table 3.3 Usage of the Internet by the 50+ in France

%	Usage	%	Usage
75	E-mail	45	Search for practical information
70	Comparing prices pre-purchase	41	Discovering new ideas
58	Planning and organising travel and going out	40	Administrative tasks
49	Surfing from site to site	39	Reading the press online
48	Managing bank accounts and buying online		

Source: Tréguer (2002)

Clearly, usage of email and searching practical information prevail with 75 per cent and 70 per cent respectively, while managing bank accounts and online purchases is the lowest figure with 39 per cent. Yet, the latter figure seems quite respectable considering the fact that older people might be more concerned about security issues when using the Internet.

9 Marketing opportunities

Academic recognition of the importance of 50+ consumers has been slow to progress. An article in the Harvard Business Review in 1980 (Bartos) was the first publication in the US that redefined this market both in terms of size and buying power. Greco (1986) accepted that grouping all older consumers into one age-based category may result in marketers overlooking crucial segments of this important market. A decade later Moschis (1997) asserted that no other consumer market justifies segmentation more than older consumers, reasoning that as people age they become more dissimilar with respect to lifestyles, needs, and consumption habits. Ten years have elapsed since this paper was written and yet a UK survey of 45,000 over 50s published by specialist marketing agency Millennium (2003) found that 86 per cent of 50+ citizens felt ignored by the marketing industry, and 70 per cent felt patronised by advertising (Demos, 2004, p. 44). These failures make it essential that our understanding of this market is documented in detail.

Moreover, in the field of mobile phones, a survey by Emporia, a mobile firm which specialises in designing phones for the older population, showed that among the over 60s across Europe only 50 per cent own a mobile phone (BBC, 2011). With half of children born today predicted to live to 100, the elderly market is one that manufacturers ignore at their peril, thinks Ian Hosking, an engineering professor at Cambridge University (ibid.). Something similar could be said about the relatively low use of the Internet by older generations. 'Older users are in this world of confusion. They blame themselves for not being able to use devices,' Hosking was quoted as saying. However, without more attention to their needs, according to a spokesperson for Emporia, their market will never take off (ibid.).

According to a report by the Communications Consumer Panel (2011), a great deal could be done to improve mobile phones for older people. The three conclusions that they reached all turn on ways of improving mobile phones for use by older people. The two main recommendations are:

- Increased facility to customise could greatly increase usability for a wide range of users, including older and disabled users.
- Older and disabled people often do not have the information they need to choose a phone that meets their needs, or know where to get that information.

An interview with Arlene Harris (Moss, April 2011), inventor, social technology entrepreneur and co-founder of the company Great Call, provided useful marketing priorities and as we will see, her views corroborate the finding that greater use could be made of customisation. Great Call launched the Jitterbug, a cell phone produced with Samsung with features geared toward seniors (e.g., a large backlit screen, big buttons and a dial tone instead of 'bars'). This mobile phone won the Best Small Business award from the American Society on Ageing. Previous to that, Arlene Harris, a serial entrepreneur, started and ran several wireless ventures. In 1983, she founded Cellular Business Systems, a wireless billing company with Marty Cooper (the inventor of the mobile phone), then selling the company to Cincinnati Bell in 1986. She then started Subscriber Computing, a billing and customer services software company where she conceived several innovative systems to help grow the nascent wireless industry. One such system was the first prepaid cellular management system that opened whole new markets for wireless companies globally, enabling them to securely offer their services to credit challenged customers. The company was sold in 1997.

Harris's success in marketing hi-tech offerings in business and consumer segments and her experience with Jitterbug in particular, a product aimed at seniors, makes her well placed to discuss the elements that need to be in the marketing mix for hi-tech products. She refers to three criteria for building proper solutions, and although her remarks relate to mobile phones they apply equally well to the Internet. The three elements in order of their preference are: (i) invisible elements – these are elements of a user experience or creating an outcome that just works, technology at its best; (ii) familiar elements – with an interface that represents an analogous 'digital' process in the real world that almost any user knows or is already using; and (iii) intuitive elements – these are elements where the process or interaction makes each next step obvious. For many consumers, infrequent 'digital' interaction means that designers should opt for a clear unambiguous process rather than hunt-and-peck menus and unfamiliar icons to produce a desired outcome. Harris takes the view that it is important to understand how older people relate to products at these three levels.

For a familiar example, where mobile phones are concerned, invisible means your mobile phone knows where you are – invisible. Then it provides a one tap 'map' access that assumes you want to know where you are and displays your location – familiar; upon which it gives you a choice of clear and obvious next steps like changing the size of the information display, entering a destination, or getting a different map – intuitive. For clarity, this process started with invisible information development, is displayed with a familiar interface that consumers have used for centuries, and ends with options and an experience only made possible by the use of computer technology. It is these new capabilities and their related 'controls' that make design difficult and adoption by older consumers a real challenge.

Harris also mentions the importance of provoking the right emotional desire to engage with technology. For example, she suggests that if you want people to wear a device for emergencies, then it is a good idea to have that device deliver another service that is fun or interesting to use and keeps them engaged. If there is not a routine use that is meaningful in life, customers will eventually devalue the solution. So, if the same device (in a mobile phone context) counted someone's steps or engaged people in a conversation, then people would be more likely to carry and use this device. The key point, she stresses, is 'to understand the behaviours and needs of the senior'. That said, focusing on seniors is smart for mass-market developers as well. Even though very difficult to achieve, ease of use is a universally desired objective and has been proven to speed adoption of all kinds of new technology by all segments. She cites Apple iPod as the best example – making their personal music devices and service universal primarily because the solution is a complete one and, importantly, easy to adopt and use.

A further point Arlene makes relates to the importance, when designing a product, of being able to customise it. 'It's very hard to build consumer tangible products in large volumes and achieve acceptable costs unless they're customisable – in other words able to behave in different ways for different people' (Moss, April 2011).[7] Extrapolating from this to the Internet, novice seniors should have the applications and especially the benefits of using the Internet explained to them rather than just presented with figure-it-out-for-yourself hardware and 'connected' service features.

9.1 Britain

One of the more dynamic examples targeting 50+ generations is the marketing of the Warner hotel group. After repositioning their brand ten years ago, they succeeded in becoming quite popular among the 50+ age group. The chain's aim was to reach more affluent 'empty nesters' and, according to the marketing director of the group, Ken Johnston, research clearly indicated that this age group enjoyed going to hotels, especially those without children. Lessons from their campaign concerned the importance of not treating the over 50 market as a single, homogeneous one and also not alienating younger customers. Johnston argued for the importance of segmentation and adopting a more targeted approach as well as more extensive use of the Internet.

As a result of a more targeted approach the chain has been very successful, while remaining confident that it can continue to boast the highest occupancy rate of any major hotel chain. Along with Warner Leisure Hotels, Saga, at www.saga.co.uk, also caters towards the 50+ market, offering a range of cruises, insurance and other related products and services.

As for the financial service sector, companies with products aimed at the 50+ market include Legal and General, Rias insurance and Age UK, a leading charity for older people offering a range of financial products and services for the 50+.

9.2 France

The size and economic power of 50+ consumers was recognised by Bergadaà and Hebali (2001) in France when they said that 50+ populations could become an important target for website creators and marketers. Relevant factors include the growth in the purchasing power of the over 60s – increasing seven times over 20 years (Tréguer, 2002) – and the fact that over 55 per cent of new cars and over 70 per cent of camping cars are bought by 50+ citizens.

The power of this group is widely recognised. Jean-Marc Segati of Senioragency International wrote that the 50+ are 'not a share of the market; they are a market share' (Tréguer, 2002, p. 51). In a similar vein, Antoine underlines the importance of the increasing number of 50+ consumers (Antoine, 2003). France has responded with vigour to this challenge. Some retail chains such as the Pinault-Printemps-Redoute group (Fnac, Conforama, Le Printemps) and the hypermarkets Auchan and Cora, have conducted marketing surveys in order to study the needs and demands of the 50+ generation.

In terms of other initiatives, Monoprix has increased its labels for better readability, moved its stores to town centres to offer easier access to older people, and offers home delivery (Tréguer, 2002). Peugeot has promoted the Senior cycle 800 and 805, a bicycle adapted to older people's needs, with shock absorbers, a comfortable saddle, 21 gears and halogen lighting (Tréguer, 2002). In the service sector, the Parisian company Age Design, specialising in generational design, helps businesses which target people over 50 to adapt their design to products and packaging (Tréguer, 2002). The Parisian public transportation system RATP has since 1997 provided free computer training for members of the general public who are in their 50s via the initiative 'les jeudis seniors de la RATP'. These events take place at the Palais de la Découverte, and the RATP also offers gardening, cinema, dancing and genealogy (Tréguer, 2002).

10 Segmentation of 50+ generations

A high proportion of the early studies of the mature market tended to be American and tended to rely exclusively on chronological age groupings, with a study by McCann (1974) segmenting older consumers using housewife age. Later, in response to the realisation that age alone is not sufficient to explain apparent differences in behaviour (Moschis and Mathur, 1993), Leventhal (1991) proposed segmenting older consumers on the basis of chronological age in conjunction with other factors such as buying power, marital status and health. Studies also proposed combining sociological segments with product categories, examples including the development of five segments for over-the-counter drugs (Oates et al., 1996), Morgan and Levy's (1993) segments for health products and food, and four segments for apparel shopping (Mumel and Prodnik, 2005). Two studies also offer ways of segmenting the travel and tourism market for older consumers (Lieux et al.,

1993; Sellick, 2004). Although all may be useful in particular circumstances, the obvious limitation of these models is that they are based on specific product categories and thus cannot be extended beyond those categories.

These limitations make the existence of non-product-specific studies particularly useful. Where American studies are concerned, the gerontographics method proposed by George Moschis and his colleagues (Moschis, 1993; Moschis et al., 1997) is based on a variety of social, psychological and biophysical variables offering four distinctive segments. Subsequent research has found the model to predict responses to consumer behaviour twice as accurately as segments based on chronological age alone (Moschis and Mathur, 1993), providing American marketers the opportunity to target specific segments of older consumers with specific offerings.

Further defining segments are gender and nationality. Where gender is concerned, earlier research (Moss et al., 2009; Moss, 2009) has shown a statistically significant tendency for a person's gender to have a statistically significant impact on the visual and linguistic aspects of the websites produced. This was true of websites produced in the UK and in France as we shall see below. UK research also revealed a tendency in the UK for men and women to show a strong preference for websites produced by people of their own gender, but this research was not segmented by age so information is not currently available on the strength of such a preference among the 50+ age group. Where nationality is concerned, a comparison of websites produced by students in the UK and France revealed a tendency for the websites produced in the UK to have more masculine elements than similar websites produced in France (Gunn and Moss, 2006). Unfortunately, a comparison of websites produced in the UK and France by older people has not yet been made, leaving this as an area for future research.

10.1   Segmenting the 50+ in Britain

In the UK, one piece of commercial research had identified segments of older UK consumers using the target group index to identify five segments differing on attitudes toward money, travel, and media (Silman and Poustie, 1994). Moreover, a recent study (Sudbury and Simcock, 2009) identified five market segments from a sample of 650 respondents. The segments identified were those of 'solitary sceptics', 'bargain hunting belongers', 'self-assured sociables', 'positive pioneers' and 'cautious comfortables'.

For the purposes of this chapter, we will briefly comment on two of these segments: the positive pioneers and the cautious comfortables. Both belong to the 50+ market and have positive attitudes towards advertising and consumerism. The positive pioneers is the youngest segment where chronological and cognitive age is concerned: a 56-year-old person feels ten years younger. They are relatively wealthy, in spite of the fact that their grown-up children might still live with them. They are active travellers and are not particularly price-conscious (Sudbury and Simcock, 2009). The cautious comfortables are particularly interesting as they use the Internet more frequently than any other of the above segments; they are two years older than the positive pioneers and, at the age of 58, they feel ten years younger. They are the most affluent segment and half of them are still working. They are also the healthiest and most energetic segment. Just like the positive pioneers, they enjoy travelling in the UK and abroad.

These are valuable studies which offer snapshots of the consumer at a moment in time. However, Leventhal (1991) has noted that the ageing consumer of tomorrow may be different from that of today and so it cannot be assumed that these categories will continue in the long term. In the short term, gerontographics has been applied to the US health-care market, and longer-term guidance may come from segmenting older consumers using cohort effects (Noble and Schewe, 2003; Littrell et al., 2005). However, the absence of studies addressing differences between cohorts of older consumers on a large number of behavioural variables (Reisenwitz and Iyer, 2007) makes recent calls for further research pertaining to the segmentation of older people of pressing importance (Jayanti et al., 2004; Eastman and Iyer, 2005).

10.2 Segmenting the 50+ in France

With regard to French models of older generations, critics agree that it is useful to differentiate between categories of 50+ consumers in order to avoid being reductionist (Bergadaà and Hebali, 2001; Tréguer, 2002; Guérin, 2008; Antoine, 2003). Tréguer makes the point that a man in his 50s who has a professional life cannot be compared to a woman of 80 (Tréguer, 2002, p. 31), although today's grandmother is no longer a spectacled, knitting lady with a grey knot, sitting in a rocking chair. Instead she might be driving her own car and participating in various cultural, social and sometimes professional activities. In fact, she even has a bank account and might use several credit cards (Antoine, 2003, p. 281).

In his book *Vive les vieux* (2008), Serge Guérin distinguishes between three groups: the *BooBos* or Bohème boomers, the *SeTra* or traditional older people, and the *SeFra* or fragile seniors, the letters '*Se*' standing for the word 'senior'. Guérin states that these three groups are part of the invention of the 50+ age groups, constituting a new social category (Guérin, 2008). According to Guérin, the *BooBos* are the youthful end of the 50+ generations, or *BooBos* are between 50 and 70 and are characterised by their trendy lifestyle. They benefit from the so-called 'golden triangle': available time, purchasing power and health. The *BooBos* are akin to 'young consumers insofar as they have invented eternal youth and want to continue to live, desire and create' (Guérin, 2008, p. 10). There are obvious overlaps between Guérin's categories and those mentioned in the above section focusing on British 50+ generations. For instance, the 'positive pioneers' or the 'cautious comfortables' defined in the Sudbury and Simcock study (2009) with their high levels of energy, who enjoy going out rather than watching TV at home, can be likened to the dynamic French *BooBos*.

In contrast to the *BooBos*, the *SeTra* or traditional seniors are usually over 60 and rather conservative. A more homogeneous group, less inclined to criticise the social structure, the *SeTras*' attitudes toward consumption are more predictable. They expect to be treated like adult citizens and are consumers with high expectations (Guérin, 2008). The *SeFra* or fragile seniors, mostly over 75, are those for whom questions about health as well as physical and mental autonomy are of primordial importance since some of them are physically weak, requiring special help in their daily lives (Guérin, 2008).

Another commentator, Tréguer (2002), proposed four different categories: the Masters (50–59 years), the Liberated (60–74 years), the Peaceful (75–84 years) and the Elderly (85 years+). The Masters generally enjoy a good lifestyle, robust health and they finally have the possibility of fulfilling desires that they could not satisfy previously (ibid.), with the Liberated among them more inclined to spend money on telecommunications, photography, cameras and videos. They are also interested in exploring multimedia and the Internet (ibid.). As for the third category, the Peaceful, they have left their professional lives; their incomes can be compared to those who start their first career (ibid.). Finally, the Elderly are often submerged by solitude and dependency and also more prone to suffer from incontinency or diseases, such as Alzheimer's or Parkinson's (ibid.).

In addition to these lifestyle factors, we can mention factors relating to their design preferences. Research on gender shows a tendency for

French websites to be produced using an aesthetic that is closer to the feminine end of the gender aesthetic continuum than websites in the UK (Gunn and Moss, 2006). In the UK, there was a tendency for younger generations, in blind tests, to ascribe higher evaluations to websites produced by people of their own gender than produced by those of the opposite gender (Moss and Gunn, 2009; Moss, 2009). Similar research to test the effects of gender has not yet been conducted in France, nor has the production or testing of preferences been segmented by age. These are areas for future research.

11 Attitudes towards advertising

Nothing illustrates better the prickly sensibilities of some senior citizens than asking them what they want to be called. When an advertising agency enquired of American senior citizens how they wished to be addressed as a collective group, it rapidly became apparent. The word 'senior' was rejected by 98 per cent of respondents, while 85 per cent disliked the term 'older adult'. Nearly three-quarters prefer to see themselves as 'middle-aged'. Two-thirds did not even like the denomination 'baby boomers'. Even relatively mild euphemisms, such as 'active adult' and '50-plus', are rejected by a clear majority of the over 50s (Demos, 2004, p. 59)

Those aged 50+ are at the youthful end of the 'grey market', and among the younger generation (46–50) Demos (2004) uncovered a large degree of awareness of brands, which are normally considered the preserve of young people. Generally, advertising was regarded with a greater degree of playfulness and reflexivity and as something that could be enjoyed in its own right, unabashed by fears of succumbing to its persuasive powers.

Paramount among the concerns of those aged 50+, however, is a desire not to be patronised, dictated to, or condescended to by those in authority. All of this presents challenges for those in the marketing and communications industry who may be enlisted to nudge idealistic people in this age group into thinking about their 'older' age so that they are prepared and able to deal with it in the best way possible. Rather than being presented with a commercial narrative or image, older people in the 50+ age group also appear to like being presented with useful and objective facts. Indeed, consumers claim that they want straightforward communication that provides them with the facts and allows them to make up their own minds about things (Demos, 2004).

Given the cynicism of those aged 50+ towards established institutions, many of them prefer to have their purchasing guided by their friends and colleagues rather than rely on mass-market advertising, and this attitude presents a challenge for marketers. This will not be easy to address since a 2002 survey of 2,000 people carried out by Millennium, a consultancy specialising in the mature market, showed that 86 per cent of 50+ consumers do not relate to the marketing they see. Similar figures were released in a study by Age Concern entitled 'How Ageist is Britain?' (2004).

12   Conclusion

This article has shown that 50+ consumers constitute a relatively prosperous as well as heterogeneous group and that the importance of cyberspace and digital technologies are steadily increasing for this segment. One clear message arising from the British and French marketing literature is the need for marketers to be clear as to which segment they are targeting. Fifty+ consumers are a heterogeneous group and marketers can fail with their campaigns directed towards the 50+ market, as with any market, because the correct segment has been inappropriately targeted.

Where digital communications are concerned, the challenges for marketers consist in determining how best to use the Internet to target the 50+ age segment. The interactionist approach appears to be particularly suitable as it advocates dovetailing the message to the needs and preferences of the target audience. One complex issue relates to how information concerning different variables (e.g., nationality, generational characteristics and gender) can be prioritised. An additional issue (see below) concerns the extent to which earlier findings regarding differences related to nationality and gender, based as they were on studies of students' websites and preferences, can be generalised to the 50+ groups discussed here. The Internet and mobile telephony offer the potential for a level of flexibility to target segments, which is not so easily available with traditional media, and so more data on this (see below) would be useful.

13   Limitations and future research

The existing literature on the 50+ response to digital communications does not present empirical evidence on how best to use the Internet to target 50+ segments. The three priority areas for future research should be first to examine the preferences of 50+ segments; secondly to examine the role of nationality; and thirdly to examine the impact of gender. This future research would provide new data to marketers, enabling them to follow the interactionist approach and hone their messages more successfully. Including the gender variable could be particularly useful since the extent to which the website productions and preferences of younger males and females differ has been highlighted in recent studies (Moss, 2009; Moss and Gunn, 2009), with evidence not only of male and female students producing quite disparate websites, but male and female students preferring websites created by those of their own gender.

References

Age Concern (2004), 'How Ageist is Britain?', London.

Age UK, *Agenda for Later Life 2011*, March 2011.

Age UK, *ICM Research Survey*, December 2009.

Ahmad, R. (2002), 'The older or ageing consumers in the UK: are they really that different?', *International Journal of Market Research*, 44 (3) 337–360.

All about market research, http://www.allaboutmarketresearch.com/internet.htm, accessed 20 April 2011.

Antoine, J. (2003), 'Un très bon public "cible" pour le marketing', *Fondation Nationale de Gérontologie-Gérontologie et Société 2003*, 106, pp. 279–289.

Bartos, R. (1980), 'Over 49: the invisible consumer market', *Harvard Business Review*, Vol. 58, No. 1, pp. 140–148.

BBC (2010), 'Nearly one in five citizens to survive beyond 100', http://www.bbc.co.uk/news/uk-12091758, December, accessed on 8 April 2011.

BBC (2011), 'Older generation demand smarter mobile phones', http://www.businessofageing.com/www/default/index.cfm/news/older-generation-demand-smarter-mobile-phones/, accessed on 8 April 2011.

Bergadaà, M. and Hebali, M. J. (2001), 'Les seniors utilisateurs d'Internet: typologie induite d'une recherché qualitative en-ligne', Research Seminar on Marketing Communications and Consumer Behaviour, La Londe les Maures, 5–8 June 2001.

Brousseau, E. (2003), 'E-Commerce in France: did early adoption prevent its development?', *The Information Society*, Vol. 19, pp. 45–57.

Carlsson, C., Hyvönen, C., Repo, P., Walden, P. (2005), 'Asynchronous adoption patterns of mobile services', Proceedings of the 38th Hawaii International Conference on System Science.

CIPD (2008), Gen Up – How the Four Generations Work, September.

Claritas Market Research (2003), http://www.claritas.uk.net/internal_market_research.htm.

Clarke, S. and Doherty, N. (2004), 'The importance of a strong business-IT relationship for the realisation of benefits in e-business projects: the example of Egg', *Qualitative Market Research: an International Journal*, Vol. 7, No. 1, p. 58.

Communications Consumer Panel (2011), https://exchange.bcuc.ac.uk/excha
nge/Gloria.Moss@bucks.ac.uk/Inbox/New%20Message-4.eml/Accessibility_
2011_Ofcom_UsabilityRpt_260111.pdf/C58EA28C-18C0-4a97-9AF2-036E93D
DAFB3/Accessibility_2011_Ofcom_UsabilityRpt_260111.pdf?attach=1, accessed on 20 April 2011.
Continental (2008), Mobile Phone Report, Autumn, https://exchange.bcuc.ac.uk/
exchange/Gloria.Moss@bucks.ac.uk/Inbox/New%20Message-4.eml/Accessibi
lity_2008_ContinentalResearch_MP.pdf/C58EA28C-18C0-4a97-9AF2-036E93
DDAFB3/Accessibility_2008_ContinentalResearch_MP.pdf?attach=1, accessed
on 20 April 2011.
Demos (2004), *Eternal Youths* (London: Centrica and Saga Group).
Department of Business Innovation and Skills and Department of Culture, Media
and Sport, 'Digital Britain: final report', TSO (The Stationery Office), June 2009
(available online from www.culture.gov.uk/images/publications/digitalbritain-
finalreport-june09.pdf).
Dutton, W. H., Di Gennaro, C. and Hargrave, A. M. (2005), 'The Internet in
Britain: the Oxford Internet Survey (OxIS)', http://www.oii.ox.ac.uk/research/?
rq=oxis/index.
Eastman, J. K. and Iyer, R. (2005), 'The impact of cognitive age on internet use
of the elderly: an introduction to the public policy implications', *International
Journal of Consumer Studies*, Vol. 29, No. 2, pp. 125–136.
Eurostat (2010), 'Households and individuals', http://ec.europa.eu/eurostat/ict,
accessed on 16 July 2011.
Fiercewireless (2011), Arlene Harris – Top US Wireless Innovators of All Time –
FierceWireless, http://www.fiercewireless.com/special-reports/arlene-harris#
ixzz1I5cMXPXK, http://www.fiercewireless.com/signup?sourceform=Viral-
Tynt-FierceWireless-FierceWireless, accessed on 30 March 2011.
Flatten, K. et al. (2000), 'Internet access for older adults in public libraries', Library
and Information Commission, London.
Gehrt, K. and Yan, R-N. (2004), 'Situational, consumer, and retailer factors affect-
ing Internet, catalog, and store shopping', *International Journal of Retail &
Distribution Management*; Vol. 32, No. 1, pp. 5–18.
George-Hoyau, C. (2008), 'Les boomers déferlent sur Internet', *Pleine Vie*, Sondage
exclusif Pleine Vie/CSA 2007, p. 20.
Gilly, M. and Zeithmal, V. (1987), 'The elerly consumer and adoption of
technologies', *Journal of Consumer Research*, Vol. 12, pp. 353–357.
Gommans, M. et al. (2001), 'From brand loyalty to e-loyalty: a conceptual
framework', *Journal of Economic and Social Research*, Vol. 3, No. 1, pp. 43–58.
Gordon, W. (1999), *Godthinking* (Henley-on-Thames: Admap Publications).
Greco, A. J. (1986), 'The fashion-conscious elderly: a viable, but neglected market
segment', *Journal of Consumer Marketing*, Vol. 3, No. 4, pp. 71–75.
Grover, V. and Saeed, K. (2004), 'Strategic orientation and performance of
Internet-based businesses', *Information Systems Journal*, No. 4, pp. 23–42.
Guérin, S. (2008), *Vive les vieux. Boomers bohème, seniors, retraités, personnes âgées*
(Paris: Michalon).
Guérin, S. (2009), *Société des seniors* (Paris: Michalon).
Gunn, R. and Moss, G. (2006), 'An interactive aesthetic for French and UK
e-commerce', *International Journal of Technology, Knowledge and Society*, http://
ijt.cgpublisher.com/home.html.

Hammer, M. (1995), *Reengineering the Corporation* (London: Nicholas Brearley Corporation).

Ibeh, K. et al. (2005), 'E-branding strategies of internet companies: some preliminary insights from the UK', *Journal of Brand Management*, Vol. 12, No. 5, pp. 355–373.

IITA: Electronic commerce and the NII (1994), Information Infrastructure Technology and Applications. Task Group, National Coordination Office for High Performance Computing and Communications, 13–14 February.

Iwaarden, J. et al. (2004), 'Perceptions about the quality of web sites: a survey amongst students at North-Eastern University and Erasmus University', *Information and Management*, No. 41, pp. 947–959.

Jayanti, R. K. et al. (2004), 'The effects of aging on brand attitude measurement', *Journal of Consumer Marketing*, Vol. 21, No. 4, pp. 264–273.

Jeffery, S. (2003), 'Over 60's reach for the mouse', *The Guardian* (online), 8 July 2003, http://www.guardian.co.uk/uk_news/story/0,3604,994112,00.html.

Joergensen, J. and Blythe, J. (2003), 'A guide to a more effective World Wide Web', *Journal of Marketing Communications*, Vol. 9, No. 1, pp. 45–58.

Johnston, K. (2007), http://www.stoneaston.co.uk/downloads/mature_marketing.pdf.

Kapferer, J. (1992), *Strategic Brand Management* (New York: Free Press).

Karande, K. et al. (1997), 'Brand personality and self concept: a replication and extension', American Marketing Association, Summer Conference, pp. 165–171.

Koo, E. and Cheok, A. (2006), 'Age invaders: inter-generational mixed reality family game', *International Journal of Virtual Reality*, Vol. 5, No. 2, pp. 45–50.

La Tribune (2008), 'Boom de la connexion Internet à domicile des Francais', 22 Janvier 2008.

Lavie, T. and Tractinsky, N. (2004), 'Assessing dimensions of perceived visual aesthetics of WEB Sites', *International Journal of Human-Computer Studies*, Vol. 60, No. 3, pp. 269–298.

Leventhal, R. C. (1991), 'The aging consumer: what's all the fuss about anyway?', *Journal of Consumer Marketing*, Vol. 8, No. 1, pp. 29–34.

Lewin, K. (1936), *Principles of Topological Psychology* (New York: McGraw-Hill).

Lieux, E. M., Weaver, P. A. and McCleary, K. W. (1993), 'Lodging preferences of the senior tourism market', *Annals of Tourism Research*, Vol. 21, No. 4, pp. 712–728.

Lippincott, D. (2004), 'Grey matters: where are the technical communicators in research and design for ageing audiences?', *IEEE Transactions on Professional Communication*, Vol. 47, No. 3, September.

Littrell, M. A. et al. (2005), 'Generation X, baby boomers, and swing: marketing fair trade apparel', *Journal of Fashion Marketing and Management*, Vol. 9, No. 4, pp. 407–419.

Loges, W. E. and Joo-Young, J. (2001), 'Exploring the digital divide: Internet connectedness and age', *Communication Research*, Vol. 28, No. 4, pp. 536–562, http://www.marketinguk.co.uk/Web-Sites/ 'Britains-babyboomers – A MySpace-type website has been launched'. News release, accessed on 25 October 2009.

Melewar, T. C. and Smith, N. (2003), 'The Internet revolution: some global marketing implications', *Marketing Intelligence & Planning*, Vol. 21, No. 6, pp. 363–369.

McCann, J. M. (1974), 'Market segment response to the marketing decision variables', *Journal of Marketing Research*, Vol. XI, November, pp. 399–412.

Millward, P. (2003), 'The "grey digital divide": perception, exclusion and barriers of access to the Internet for older people', *First Monday* (online), Vol. 8, No. 7, http://www.firstmonday.org/issues/issue8_7/millward/index.html.

Mischel, W. (1977), 'The interaction of person and situation', in Magnussen, D., Endler, N. S. (eds), *Personality at the Crossroads: Current Issues in Interactional Psychology* (Hillsdale, NJ: Lawrence Erlbaum Associates) pp. 333–352.

Morgan, C. M. and Levy, D. J. (1993), *Segmenting the Mature Market* (Chicago: Probus).

Morris, A. (2007), 'E-literacy and the grey digital divide: a review with recommendations', *Journal of Information Literacy*, Vol. 2, No. 3, http://jil.lboro.ac.uk/ojs/index.php/JIL/article/view/RA-V1-I3-2007.

Morris, A., Goodman, J. and Brading, H. (2007), 'Internet use and non-use: views of older users', *Universal Access in the Information Society*, Vol. 6, No. 1, pp. 43–57.

Moschis, G. (1993), 'Gerontographics', *Journal of Consumer Marketing*, Vol. 10, No. 3, pp. 43–53.

Moschis, G. and Marthur, A. (1993), 'How they're acting their age', *Marketing Management*, Vol. 2, No. 2, pp. 40–50.

Moschis, G. P., Lee, E. and Mathur, A. (1997), 'Targeting the mature market: opportunities and challenges', *Journal of Consumer Marketing*, Vol. 14, No. 4, pp. 282–293.

Moss, G. (2009), *Gender, Design and Marketing* (Farnham, Surrey: Gower).

Moss, G. and Gunn, R. (2009), 'Gender differences in website production and preference aesthetics: preliminary implications for ICT in education and beyond', *Behaviour and Information Technology*, Vol. 28, No. 5, pp. 1362–3001.

Moss, G., Gunn, R. and Kubacki, K. (2008), 'Gender and web design: the implications of the mirroring principle for the services branding model', *Journal of Marketing Communications*, Vol. 14, No. 1, pp. 37–57.

Mumel, D. and Prodnik, J. (2005), 'Grey consumers are all the same, they even dress the same: myth or reality?', *Journal of Fashion Marketing and Management*, Vol. 9, No. 4, pp. 434–449.

Museums Libraries and Archives Council (2004), The People's Network, http://www.peoplesnetwork.gov.uk/.

Nationmaster, http://www.nationmaster.com/graph/med_mob_pho-media-mobile-phones, accessed on 20 April 2011.

New Media Trend Watch report (2011), http://www.newmediatrendwatch.com/markets-by-country/10-europe/52-france?showall= 1, accessed on 20 April 2011.

Nielsen report into use of internet by people aged 50 and over (2011), http://blog.nielsen.com/nielsenwire/global/users-50-and-older-drive-half-of-latest-uk-web-surge/

Noble, S. M. and Schewe, C. D. (2003), 'Cohort segmentation: an exploration of its validity', *Journal of Business Research*, Vol. 56, pp. 979–987.

Oates, B., Shufeldt, L. and Vaught, B. (1996), 'A psychographic study of the elderly and retail store attributes', *Journal of Consumer Marketing*, Vol. 13, No. 6, pp. 14–27.

Ofcom (2009), Consumer Experience Research Report, http://stakeholders.ofcom. org.uk/market-data-research/market-data/consumer-experience-reports/ce09/, accessed on 20 April 2011.

Office for National Statistics (2008), Demographic Trends, Government Office, London http://www.statistics.gov.uk/default.asp, accessed on 20 April 2011.

Palmer, J. (2002), 'Web site usability, design and performance metrics', *Information, Systems Research*, Vol. 13, No. 2, pp. 151–167.

Pleine Vie/CSA Sondage exclusive (2007), p. 20.

Potter, E. (1994), 'Commercialisation of the World Wide Web', WELL topic in the Internet conference on the WELL, 16 November.

Poustie, R. (1994), 'What they eat, buy, read, and watch', *Admap*, Vol. July/August, pp. 25–28.

Quigley, P. (2009), 'Baby boomers embracing Web 2.0. 4 out of 10 online over-50s in the UK (4,700,000) belong to at least 1 social network, according to recent research by Insites Consulting', http://www.insites.be/02/MyDocuments/PressreleaseInSitesSocialnetworks_22_04_09_UK_EN.pdf, accessed on 19 August 2009.

Reisenwitz, T. and Iyer, R. (2007), 'A comparison of younger and older baby boomers: investigating the viability of cohort segmentation', *Journal of Consumer Marketing*, Vol. 24, No. 4, pp. 202–213.

Samli, A. C. (1995), *International Consumer Behaviour* (Westport: Quantum Books).

Schenkman, N. and Jonsson, F. (2000), 'Aesthetics and preferences of web pages', *Behaviour and Information Technology*, Vol. 19, No. 5, pp. 367–377.

Sellick, M. C. (2004), 'Discovery, connection, nostalgia: key travel motives within the senior market', *Journal of Travel and Tourism Marketing*, Vol. 17, No. 1, pp. 55–71.

Smither, J. and Braun (1994), 'Technology and older adults: factors affecting the adoption of automatic teller machines', *Journal of General Psychology*, Vol. 121, No. 4, pp. 381–389.

Strauss, J. and Frost, R. (1999), *Marketing on the Internet: Principles of Online Marketing* (Upper Saddle River, NJ: Prentice Hall Inc).

Sudbury, L. and Simcock, P. (2009), 'A multivariate segmentation model of senior consumers', *Journal of Consumer Marketing*, Vol. 26, pp. 251–262.

Thayer, S. and Ray, S. (2006), 'Online communication preferences across age, gender, and duration of internet use', *CyberPsychology and Behaviour*, Vol. 9, No. 4, pp. 432–440.

Timms, D. (2003), 'New media: how will the other half live?', *The Guardian*, 3 November, p. 38.

TNS Omnibus 4–13 March 2011 among a weighted sample of 1,117 UK Adults 65+

Tréguer, J. P. (2002), *Marketing 50+. Marketing, Communicating and Selling to the over 50s Generations* (London: Palgrave).

Wedande, G. et al. (2001), 'Consumer interaction in the virtual era: some solutions from qualitative research', *Qualitative Market Research: An International Journal*, Vol. 4, No. 3, pp. 150–159.

Young, G. (2002/3), *The Implications of an Ageing Population for the UK Economy*, www.publications.parliment.uk/ld200203/ldselect/ldeconaf/179/1.

4
Age and Grey Entrepreneurship
Lorraine Watkins-Mathys

1 Introduction

Europe is ageing fast and people are living much longer than previously. The Organisation for Economic Cooperation and Development (OECD) (2005) estimates that by 2050 the 'age dependency ratio' – those dependent on being supported by those in employment within the EU countries – will rise to 55 per cent. This compares to the 20–30 per cent 'age dependency ratio' found in the G7 countries currently. To add to this scenario, some EU economies, notably France, Germany and Italy, are still subsidising early retirements (OECD, 2005), although some like France are making efforts to raise the retirement age from 60 to 62 (BBC, 2010). Hart et al. (2004, p. 3) noted that 'each successive generation of men is less likely to be employed at the age of 50 than the preceding generation'. Medical science for its part is making it possible for people to live and work longer.

Taking into account the demographic and employment trends in developed economies, grey entrepreneurship is becoming something of a 'hot topic'. Despite this, it may seem surprising that grey entrepreneurship remains a relatively under-researched subject (Kautonen, 2008; NESTA, 2009; Singh, 2009).

Against the background outlined above, this chapter aims to provide an overview of entrepreneurial activity across Europe, focusing especially on grey entrepreneurs mainly in the UK. The chapter attempts to answer the following questions:

- How will Grey Entrepreneurs increase in relevance?
- What contribution do Grey Entrepreneurs make and how does this compare with younger entrepreneurs?
- What are the characteristics of Grey Entrepreneurs?
- What drives Grey Entrepreneurs to become entrepreneurs later in life?

- Grey entrepreneurs – what are their characteristics and what drives them to become entrepreneurs later in life?

The chapter is structured in the following way. Section 1 has outlined the purpose and structure of the chapter; Section 2 provides the context for the study of grey entrepreneurship by examining the demographic of ageing and its impact on society. This section concludes by looking at entrepreneurial activity across ages and to some limited extent across OECD countries. The subsequent Section 3 analyses the definitions and terms found in the literature on grey entrepreneurship, then establishes the activities by sector, this is followed by a discussion about the typology and motivation of grey entrepreneurs, then summarises the characteristics of grey entrepreneurs. Section 4 discusses to what extent the future of grey entrepreneurship is important. Section 5 draws together the findings of the chapter by answering the questions posed in Section 1 and highlighting the implications of the findings for entrepreneurship educators, policy-makers and researchers.

2 Ageing across OECD countries

As outlined in the introduction, the evidence from across OECD countries is that our population is ageing (OECD, 2005). This is highlighted in figures 4.1 and 4.2 below, which map out the old-age dependency of our developing economies and also shrinking size of our labour force. The work undertaken by Hart et al. (2004) established that the over 50 age group had risen to over 20 million in the UK and made up 34 per cent of the total population. However, this group of the population tends to have a lower proportion of them in paid work. Furthermore, the report published by PRIME (2004) asserted that those in that category, aged 50–64, who are out of work have only a one in ten chance of becoming employed again. Ageing and ensuring that we maximise the human capital in the 50+ category will become increasingly more important as we head towards 2050.

The data in figures 4.1 and 4.2 below show that the ageing factor in developed economies is leading to a shrinking of available labour. The implications for governments in developing economies are, therefore, that there will be:

- fewer people to pay and support the ageing population;
- fewer people aged 18–64 available to enter and circulate within the labour market;

- greater reliance on older people to remain in jobs;
- greater reliance on older people to use their management and professional experience to start up businesses that contribute to wealth and seek less social security support or pensions;
- a need to keep people healthier and working for longer periods of time;
- a need to review pensions and pension payments.

Added to the scenario above, there are forecasts which suggest more people will live into their third age and live longer. It has been predicted that the proportion of men over the age of 55 will rise from 23 per cent in 2000 to 33 per cent by 2025 and that the average male may extend his life by an additional 19 years by 2051 (NESTA, 2009, p. 23). This is particularly relevant as there are more male than female entrepreneurs (GEM, 2006; NESTA, 2009). The extension of male life expectancy may mean that a larger number of today's young male entrepreneurs may well be able to extend their entrepreneurial activity into their third age.

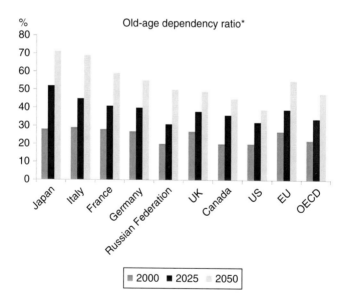

Figure 4.1   Old age ratios will rise dramatically in all G8 countries
* The ratio of the population aged 65 and over to the population aged 20–64.
Source: OECD database on 'The Ageing and Employment Policies', and the UN *World Population Prospectus*, 1950–2050 (The 2002 Revision) for the Russian Federation.

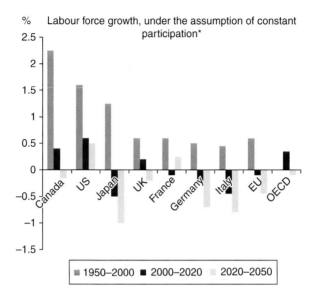

% Labour force growth, under the assumption of constant participation*

■ 1950–2000 ■ 2000–2020 ▨ 2020–2050

Figure 4.2 The size of the labour force will grow little or even fall in some countries
* The projections of labour force growth over the period 2000–2050 assume that age groups and gender remain constant at their 2000 levels.
Source: OECD (2005) Database on Labour Force Statistics and OECD estimates.

2.1 Entrepreneurial activity

The PRIME report (2009) carried out in the UK affirms that one in three of those in the 50–64 age range are without employment, and that interestingly two in every five people in the 50–64 age cohort 'would consider self-employment if they knew there was business support available' (PRIME, 2009, p. 29). On the basis of this survey result in the UK, PRIME (2009) estimates that even if only one of the inactive over 50s were to start up a business it could create 24,000 new jobs and save approximately £175 million in welfare payments.

In Australia in 1998, nearly 50 per cent of those aged 55+ had been unemployed for one year and 35.9 per cent for over two years (Australian Bureau of Statistics 1999 as cited in Weber and Schaper, 2003, p. 4). These statistics highlight that among the over 50s there are people who are potentially available and interested in self-employment, including starting a business. If those people over 50 and not in employment were to start a business it would not only create employment but reduce welfare payments.

Set against this background, the Global Entrepreneurship Monitor (2007) established that 20 per cent of the age 50–64 group are self-employed or owner-managers. However, more than half of them (almost 55 per cent) have businesses that are over ten years old. Only 3.8 per cent of the 50–64 age group were involved in start-up/early entrepreneurial activity in 2006 compared to 7.9 per cent in the 25–34 age range (GEM, 2007 – United Kingdom Report as cited in NESTA, 2009). The entrepreneurial activity, however, of the 50+ age group (see Table 4.1) compares well with that of young entrepreneurs (16–24), which has a total entrepreneurial activity of 3.8 per cent also (GEM, 2007 – United Kingdom Report as cited in NESTA, 2009). In a cross-country comparison between the UK, Ireland, US, Japan and Sweden (Table 4.2) the 55–64 age group accounted for an estimated 11 per cent of all UK

Table 4.1   Total entrepreneurial activity and business formation by age in the UK, 2006

Age Group	Total Entrepreneurial Activity (%)	Proportion of Business Formation (%)
16–24	3.8	9.9
25–34	7.9	25.4
35–44	7.3	31.4
45–54	5.7	20.8
55–64	3.8	12.6

Source: Global Entrepreneurship Monitor (2007) UK 2006 Report as found in NESTA (2009, p. 49).

Table 4.2   Entrepreneurial activity and business formation by age, 2006

Country	Total Entrepreneurial Activity 18–64 Year olds	Total Entrepreneurial Activity 55–64 Year olds	55–64 Year olds: % of all Total Entrepreneurial Activity
UK	5.5	3.2	11
Ireland	8.2	3.4	7
US	9.6	5.8	10
Japan	4.3	3.4	26
Sweden	4.2	2.6	13
EU-average	5.4	2.7	9

Source: Global Entrepreneurship Monitor (2007) Ireland 2006.

new start-ups compared to 13 per cent in Sweden and 26 per cent in Japan (NESTA, 2009).

3 Grey entrepreneurs: who are they and what do they do?

3.1 Defining the terms, the age group and gender

There are many definitions in the literature for entrepreneurship. The focus in this chapter has been on older people starting up an enterprise and, therefore, the definition chosen for the purpose of this chapter is: 'The activities of an individual or a group aimed at initiating economic activities in the formal sector under a legal form of business' (Klapper et al., 2008, p. 3). This fits closely with the definition provided by Weber and Schaper (2003, p. 5) for a grey entrepreneur: '... A rather simplistic definition is to limit the "grey entrepreneur" as someone over a certain age that begins their own small or medium-sized enterprise (SME). Whilst this glosses over the fact that enterprising behaviour is not confined to SMEs, it does allow researchers to make meaningful comparison with published government small business statistics.' Furthermore, Weber and Schaper acknowledge (2003) that this definition excludes those academics who stress innovation, such as Hisrich and Peters (1992).

There are also many alternative terms used in the literature for grey entrepreneurs. In research carried out by Patel and Gray (2006) they identified a number of terms in the literature that could be interchanged with 'grey entrepreneurs'. These included:

- Third age entrepreneurs
- Prime age entrepreneurs
- Senior entrepreneurs (seniorpreneurs)
- Older entrepreneurs (olderpreneurs)
- Elder entrepreneurs (elderpreneurs)
- And second career entrepreneurs (Patel and Gray, 2006, p. 5)

Little distinction, however, if any, was noted between the terms, and Patel and Gray (2006) concluded that they are relatively interchangeable. Nevertheless, authors have differentiated on age when defining grey entrepreneurs. The age applied to grey entrepreneurs ranges, therefore, from 45+ (Blackburn et al., 2000; Hart et al., 2004) to over 60 (Goldberg, 2000). More recent publications (Weber and Schaper, 2003; Patel and Gray, 2006; Kautonen, 2008; NESTA, 2009; PRIME, 2009) define grey entrepreneurs as being over the age of 50. Most of the reports on grey entrepreneurs agree that the greater number of grey entrepreneurs is mainly in the age group 50–54. The percentage of grey entrepreneurs in the higher age ranges starts to decline as the age rises. Entrepreneurial activity and the motivation to become an entrepreneur post 55, and certainly post 65, decline (Hart et al., 2004; PRIME, 2009).

With regard to gender, grey entrepreneurs tend to be predominantly male, and men are three times more likely to start up a business than women (Weber and Schaper, 2003; Hart et al., 2004 Patel and Gray, 2006; NESTA, 2009).

From the literature, four typologies have emerged that help to classify and/or explain the types of grey entrepreneurs. These relate mainly to the older entrepreneur's motivation for becoming an entrepreneur. The four typologies include the:

- Constrained entrepreneur
- Rational entrepreneur
- Reluctant entrepreneur (Singh and De Noble, 2003)
- Lifestyle entrepreneur (Getz and Carlsen, 2000; King, 2002)

The **constrained** entrepreneur is a person who has wanted to start a business for a long time and eventually manages to start a business. Lack of financial or personal/family reasons may have hindered this category of entrepreneurs from starting their business earlier. The **rational** entrepreneur clearly sees running their own business as a way of increasing their personal wealth and that of their family. For this category starting their own business is 'a progression of his or her career' (Weber and Schaper, 2003, p. 4). The **reluctant** entrepreneur is not necessarily somebody with the desire to start their own business. On the contrary, they feel that they are driven into becoming self-employed because there is no employment alternative and/or they have insufficient money to enter retirement. The **lifestyle** entrepreneur, by contrast to the reluctant entrepreneur, is an individual who enjoys the way of life and income generated from owning and running his or her own business (Getz and Carlsen, 2000; King, 2002). Except for the reluctant entrepreneur, who is 'pushed' (Amit and Muller, 1995) into becoming an entrepreneur, the other three typologies are 'pulled' (ibid.) into entrepreneurship.

Table 4.3 highlights that entrepreneurs in the UK are mainly white, male entrepreneurs, with 55 per cent being well educated, having obtained a first degree or equivalent. Less than half (41 per cent) come from a family where one of the parents ran their own business.

Table 4.3 Who are the entrepreneurs in the UK? comparison in percentages of high- and low-growth entrepreneurs

Characteristics	Low growth	Low growth	High growth	High growth	All
	Under 50	Over 50	Under 50	Over 50	
Male	70	90	86	83	75
Female	30	10	14	17	25
White British	92	90	89	100	91
Other ethnicity	8	10	11	–	9
Degree/equivalent	52	63	62	51	55
First time founder	79	45	69	53	71
Parent ran own business	40	45	47	26	41

Source: NESTA Report (2009, p. 19), Telephone Survey.

There are few women entrepreneurs, although three out of ten low-growth entrepreneurs under the age of 50 are women. Non-white ethnic participation in entrepreneurship is very low. At best, one out of ten entrepreneurs are non-white. Comparing high- with low-growth enterprises, there are few significant differences in the characteristics, except where female entrepreneurs are concerned. A greater percentage of under 50s women (30 per cent) participate in low-growth enterprises compared to their counterparts who are over 50 and running high-growth enterprises, where participation rates vary between 10 and 17 per cent.

3.2 What do they do?

Figure 4.3 below identifies the sectors in which older and younger entrepreneurs work. It highlights that there are few differences between older and younger firm founders in terms of the sectors of entrepreneurial activity. It does show, however, that grey entrepreneurs are on balance more active in what is termed 'business services', which include management buy-outs.

With regard to sectoral activity there are relatively few differences between younger and older entrepreneurs. The predominant sector of entrepreneurial activity for both younger and older grey entrepreneurs is focused in business services (up to 40 per cent) that include management buy-outs and consultancy.

The BERR (2008) report established that grey entrepreneurs are less likely to start high-growth start-ups[1] and, therefore, offer fewer

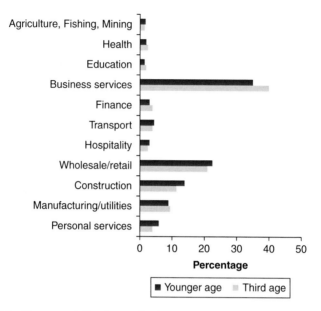

Figure 4.3   The sectoral distribution by founders' age in the UK
Source: NESTA (2009, p. 14).

jobs after five years than businesses run by younger entrepreneurs (Hart et al., 2004).

3.3   Pushed or pulled? Grey entrepreneurs' motivation

Many of the earlier studies on grey entrepreneurship tended to focus on the 'push' factors that lead older people to starting up an enterprise (NESTA, 2009).

However, more recent studies such as the one undertaken by Kautonen (2008) in Finland confirmed that Finnish older entrepreneurs were more likely to be 'constrained' or 'rational' entrepreneurs. 'Push' motives were less evident in his sample (only 10.5 per cent) and concurred with the Global Entrepreneurship Monitor Finland results of 2003 (Kautonen, 2008, p. 9). Furthermore, Kautonen (2008) found that the career history of the grey entrepreneurs in his sample influenced their decision and ability to start up a business.

NESTA (2009) affirmed in their report that while the literature on entrepreneurial motivation is large, few studies exist on the motivation of grey entrepreneurs. Extracting data from the Small Business Service Report (2007) and Barclays Report (2001), however, and comparing grey entrepreneurs and younger entrepreneurs' motivation for starting an enterprise in the UK, NESTA (2009) concluded the following:

- Grey entrepreneurs were less motivated to make money, but instead they prefer to have another source of income to complement their pension;
- Seventeen per cent of grey entrepreneurs compared to 10 per cent of younger entrepreneurs were 'pushed' into starting their own business because they were made redundant;
- More grey entrepreneurs started a business after retiring because they wanted either to work from home after retirement or to have some sort of part-time job.

Except for the above differences, the motivation for starting an enterprise between younger and older entrepreneurs was similar.

NESTA's (2009) report on high-growth grey entrepreneurs in the UK found some interesting contrasts to those cited above. These are highlighted in Figure 4.4.

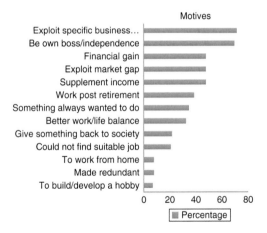

Figure 4.4   Third-age high-growth founder motives: percentage seeing motive as very important
Source: NESTA (2009, p. 21), UK telephone survey.

Grey entrepreneurs in the UK engaged in high-growth enterprises showed that they had different motives driving them. They were much more driven by wanting to pursue a business opportunity or to exploit a business idea. Wanting to work from home came much lower down on the list of motives. However, engaging in entrepreneurial activity for financial gain and supplementing their income was fairly high up on their list of motives.

3.4 Do grey enterprises last?

The literature is divided on the survival rates of grey enterprises. As early as 1994, Storey asserted that enterprises set up by young and older entrepreneurs were most likely to fold owing to a lack of skills and experience among the younger group and lack of motivation and drive by the grey entrepreneurs. This became known as the inverted U-relationship and highlighted the fact that entrepreneurs in the mid-age group 34–40 were most likely to succeed, having gained sufficient experience and skills and being driven to succeed financially. This relationship was more recently confirmed by the work conducted by Green (2008) on new firms in England.

However, the authors of NESTA's report (2009) argued that other factors besides age needed to be included in the statistical analyses. If these other factors were to be included, the NESTA (2009) report argues that age becomes a less important variable. Furthermore, earlier studies found longer survival rates among grey enterprises. Patel and Grey's work (2006) highlights Cressey and Storey's (1995) research, which asserted that survival rates of businesses in the UK run by older entrepreneurs (55+) were more than three times more likely to survive six years in business than any other new businesses.

The divided views in the literature on the survival rates of grey enterprises indicate that further research may be required in this area. More important it would seem, however, is research into establishing what enables enterprises in general, and specifically enterprises run by grey founders, to succeed and survive for longer periods of time.

3.5 Characteristics

Empirical research carried out by various authors (Hart et al., 2004; Weber and Schaper, 2003; Patel and Gray, 2006; NESTA, 2009; PRIME, 2009) identified the following characteristics among grey entrepreneurs. These are summarised in Table 4.4. The literature overview provided in Table 4.4 highlights that while grey entrepreneurship is still relatively under-researched compared to other sub-areas of entrepreneurship, it is quite consistent in its view of the older entrepreneurs.

Three of the typologies for grey entrepreneurs found in the literature can be categorised as opportunity-driven (constrained, rational and

Table 4.4 Characteristics of grey entrepreneurs

Characteristics of Grey Entrepreneurs:	Authors
Predominantly male: men are nearly three times more likely to start up a business than women; in high-growth start-ups men were nearly ten times more likely to do so than older women.	Hart et al. (2004); NESTA (2009); Weber and Schaper (2003); Patel and Gray (2006); NESTA, 2009
They tended to have more management experience; more social, human and financial capital.	Patel and Gray (2006); PRIME (2009)
A large proportion of grey entrepreneurs tended to have a university degree or equivalent.	Kautonen (2008); NESTA (2009)
Failing health (energy levels) result in waning start-up rates post-55.	Curran and Blackburn (2001);
Survival rates of businesses established by older entrepreneurs are higher than those of younger entrepreneurs – this view is somewhat divided.	NESTA (2009); Cressy and Storey (1995); Patel and Gray 2006) support this view.
	Green (2008) argues the inverted U-relationship of age and survival of start-ups.
Approx. 50% in the UK start a business in a related area to their previous job/profession; or, have held a professional job in teaching or management.	Patel and Gray (2006)
Less likely to acquire an existing business than prime-age entrepreneurs.	COM (2003); Patel and Gray (2006)
Their business turnover tends to be lower than that of their younger entrepreneurial counterparts (£70K compared to UK national average of £104K).	Patel and Gray (2006)
More/less risk averse – there is some dispute in the literature about this.	Marsh (1989) – not risk averse; Sorensen and Stuart (2000) – more risk averse. NESTA (2009) found no difference between younger and older entrepreneurs.
Less likely to take over a family business compared to younger founders (only 2% of grey entrepreneurs have taken over a family business compared to 11% of younger age group entrepreneurs).	Barclays Economic Reports (2001)
Marginally less likely to be in high tech but marginally more likely to be working on new or improved product.	Harding (2007)
Less likely to have high-growth new start-ups.	BERR (2008)
Offer fewer jobs after five years than businesses run by younger entrepreneurs.	Hart et al. (2004)

lifestyle entrepreneur), while only the 'reluctant' grey entrepreneur can be seen to be necessity-driven. This tends to concur with the GEM data, 2007, which confirms that across high-earning countries entrepreneurs in general, including grey entrepreneurs, tend to be opportunity- rather than necessity-driven. Grey entrepreneurs tend to work on new or substantially improved products and stay in business longer than the younger entrepreneurs. This, it could be argued, may be due to them making the most of their previous work and professional skills. Having a lower turnover by almost a third compared to younger entrepreneurs tends to explain why grey entrepreneurs might require fewer staff in the business and, therefore, provide fewer jobs. The one issue upon which the literature is not wholly in agreement is the risk propensity of grey entrepreneurs. However, the study by Sorensen and Stuart (2000) suggests that grey entrepreneurs tend to be more risk-averse compared to the study undertaken by Marsh in 1989.

Interestingly, 60 per cent of grey entrepreneurs started enterprises as part of a team rather than on their own. This compares with only 39 per cent of founders under the age of 50.

4   The future of grey enterprise: is it bright?

Across many of the developed economies, the OECD and EU-countries, we can expect a shrinking population of younger people available for the future workforce. The old-age dependency ratios will rise dramatically in all G8 countries (OECD, 2005). Increasingly governments in those developed economies will be pushed into reducing pension payments and other welfare payments such as unemployment benefits and healthcare. With the advancement of medical science the life expectancy among the ageing population will increase. This in turn places greater pressure on supporting people of pensionable age.

Against this background, PRIME's (2009) report found that in the UK one in three of those in the 50–64 age range are without employment and that two in every five people in that age cohort would consider becoming self-employed. The majority of grey entrepreneurs starting a business tend to be in the age group 50–54. The percentage of grey entrepreneurs in the higher age ranges starts to decline as the age rises.

Furthermore, other reports established that in the UK, grey entrepreneurs often started enterprises in order to supplement their pension income (NESTA, 2009). By contrast, grey entrepreneurs of high-growth start-ups are driven by the challenge of starting a business and wanting to pursue a business idea (NESTA, 2009). Grey entrepreneurs are overall well educated and because of their age tend to have more management experience.

Taking into account all of the above demographic changes, it seems that people in the 50–54 age group will provide a dynamic resource for promoting enterprise. If governments were to focus on stimulating high-growth rather than low-growth enterprise this could maximise returns, in particular, as high-growth enterprises generate employment as well as wealth. Furthermore, the survival rate of enterprises run by grey founders is disputed in the literature, and it would seem in governments' interest to find out what would support and enable small businesses to survive longer in general, but specifically grey enterprises, as the latter will grow significantly in importance.

Is the future bright for grey enterprise? In terms of the need to promote grey enterprise in an effort to reduce the dependency on a dwindling younger population and to supplement and/or even replace the income from a pension, then the answer has to be in the affirmative. Do they make a contribution? There are indications from recent reports (NESTA, 2009) that grey entrepreneurs can bring experience and skills into a founding team. However, reports by BERR (2008) and Hart et al. (2004) indicate that currently grey entrepreneurs are more likely to engage in low-growth start-ups and offer fewer employment opportunities through their enterprises. On current performance, grey entrepreneurship contributes less in terms of wealth and employment than start-ups founded by younger entrepreneurs.

Looking into the future it seems that grey entrepreneurship, in general, may grow as a necessity-driven activity among the older population in developed economies. However, by contrast, grey high-growth enterprises seem to be opportunity-driven and hold considerable potential in terms of achieving growth and financial gain as well as offering employment. Encouraging in particular the 50–54 age group may be advantageous for two reasons: first, they may just have left employment (Hart et al., 2004); and secondly, more people in this age group seem willing to start up a business (PRIME, 2009).

Figure 4.5 below conceptualises the main aspects gleaned from the literature and discussions above and conceptualises the key drivers affecting the growth of grey enterprise. These include the characteristics of grey entrepreneurs such as education, career history and experience that build up the social, human and financial capital of the entrepreneur; the institutional, economic and social environment such

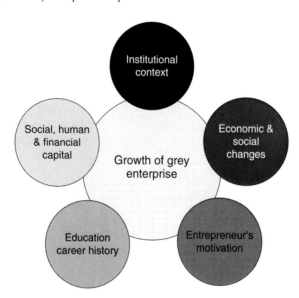

Figure 4.5   Grey entrepreneurship: factors impacting on grey enterprise growth – towards a conceptual model

as the infrastructure, changing demographics, as well as old-age dependency ratio and increasing unemployment of the over 50s; and finally, the grey entrepreneur's own motivation (push or pull factors).

5   Conclusions and recommendations

This section provides answers to the questions posed at the outset of the chapter, general conclusions and recommendations.

5.1   Grey entrepreneurs – what are their characteristics and what drives them to become entrepreneurs later in life?

Grey entrepreneurs, like their younger counterparts, are mainly white and male, well educated to degree level or equivalent. They are not very likely to have had a parent who ran their own business, especially grey entrepreneurs with a high-growth business.

5.2   Grey entrepreneurs – how will they increase in relevance?

The greatest contribution in entrepreneurial activity is currently made by younger entrepreneurs. However, the demographic data predicts a dramatic rise in old-age dependency ratios (Figure 4.1) in G8 countries.

This has many implications, but one important one is the need to retain older people in jobs and to reduce pension payments. Added to this data, Hart et al. (2004) and PRIME (2009) predict that greater numbers of people (men in particular) will be out of employment after the age of 50. Consequently, there is an economic and social need to promote grey enterprise.

5.3 Grey entrepreneurs – do they make a greater contribution than younger entrepreneurs?

No evidence was found in the literature or the research data to suggest that grey entrepreneurs make a greater contribution than younger entrepreneurs. In fact, the opposite may be more likely. Currently, more businesses are started up by younger entrepreneurs – mainly in their late twenties to mid-thirties. In a cross-country comparison between the UK, Ireland, US, Japan and Sweden (Table 4.4) the 55–64 age group accounted for only an estimated 11 per cent of all UK new start-ups compared to 13 per cent in Sweden and 26 per cent in Japan (NESTA, 2009). Younger entrepreneurs make a larger contribution to high-growth enterprises than grey entrepreneurs. In terms, therefore, of economic contribution, younger entrepreneurs make a greater contribution.

The literature was mixed, however, on survival rates: Green. (2008) affirmed that businesses founded by younger entrepreneurs had a better chance of surviving for longer, while NESTA (2009) and Patel and Gray (2006) found contradictory evidence that suggested grey founders were more likely to have businesses that survived beyond six years.

5.4 Conclusions

While there have been some in-depth studies into grey entrepreneurship (GEM, 2007; NESTA, 2009; PRIME, 2009) and interest in the subject by academic researchers, there is general agreement that grey entrepreneurship remains under-researched, especially in certain areas relating to the behaviour and experience of grey entrepreneurs, and the growth and turnover of grey start-up businesses. Moreover, the majority of the literature found offers quantitative data and there appears to be little qualitative data providing case studies and insights into grey entrepreneurs' experiences. Moreover, consistent cross-country comparison on grey enterprise is still patchy, although the most comprehensive work is offered via reports compiled by Global Entrepreneurship Monitor (GEM). Nevertheless, their reports have not to date focused on grey enterprise per se, but included entrepreneurial activity from the ages of 18 to 64.

The literature can be summed up as falling into three categories: descriptive, outlining growing trends among older entrepreneurs (GEM reports); policy implications (Hart et al., 2004; NESTA, 2009); and more recently, studies that have been trying to understand the motivation and behaviour of grey entrepreneurs (Singh and De Noble, 2003; Weber and Schaper, 2003; Patel and Gray, 2006; Kautonen, 2008). There is little comparison at a pan-European level of grey entrepreneurial behaviour and motivation in the European context. Studies on these latter subjects have been mainly country focused (Finland, Australia and UK).

6   Recommendations to policy-makers, researchers and educators

The evidence presented in this chapter, notably on the ageing and longevity of the population and the fiscal implications of this demographic change on governments, makes it imperative for governments in developed economies to examine in greater depth how they might promote grey enterprise in the future. Besides the usefulness of sponsoring more research into grey enterprise, more resources and support for promoting business start-ups among the over 50s group may be needed as the data suggests that 40 per cent of the over 50s, who are not in employment, would consider starting a business.

If more of the over 50s started a business they could help to reduce unemployment among the grey population as well as potentially create more employment, reduce pension or welfare support payments and make tax contributions to the treasury. Enabling grey enterprises to sustain longer survival rates could offer a longer return on investment for organisations supporting grey entrepreneurs. Furthermore, opportunities exist for national governments to share their data and best practice across Europe and other developed countries.

For researchers, the relative paucity of research into grey entrepreneurship provides an opportunity to fill the gap. Obvious gaps include research into older female and older ethnic entrepreneurs and how to stimulate opportunity-driven grey entrepreneurship that leads to high-growth enterprise. Furthermore, much of the literature on grey entrepreneurial activity is quantitative, giving rise for the collection of qualitative data that provide rich and contextualised insights into grey entrepreneurship. Indeed, a qualitative approach may enable us to understand from the grey entrepreneurs themselves the reasons behind their motivation and behaviours.

The literature review has also emphasised the wealth of grey entrepreneurs' human and social capital and how the latter has been especially useful to them in developing and growing their business. While this has been a theme that has received much attention in the general entrepreneurship literature, it has not been studied much in relation to grey entrepreneurs. Table 4.4 highlighted that grey entrepreneurs have lower turnover than their younger counterparts. Furthermore, new start-ups run by grey entrepreneurs tend not to have high growth, offer fewer jobs after five years than businesses run by younger entrepreneurs, and are generally more risk averse than younger entrepreneurs. All of these aspects throw up interesting opportunities for further investigation and research that would be useful for researchers, but also for policy-makers. Furthermore, the dearth of research into these areas across Europe provides an opportunity for European researchers to get together to explore these themes and to learn from respective countries' best practice and experiences. Finally, Figure 4.5 presented above presents a conceptual model that could explore further the growth of grey enterprise.

For entrepreneurship educators the focus has been mainly on promoting entrepreneurship and enterprise among the young, and in building entrepreneurial capability for the future. While this remains an important agenda for educators, it is clear that not enough has been done for the grey generation. There is much that educators could do to assist in researching learning, mentoring and facilitating approaches for supporting grey entrepreneurs, but also in ensuring that any professional training/education contains the development of entrepreneurial skills. The latter is particularly relevant as the empirical studies have shown that older entrepreneurs rely on their previous professional skills and experience when setting up and running their businesses: so, to have had this training experience during their professional career could be useful.

There is also the opportunity to promote grey entrepreneurs in current funded training programmes aimed at other entrepreneurship groups such as creatives, high techs or start-ups in general as well as people who have just lost their jobs, as many of these target groups are likely to have people aged 50+ within these specified groups. Sharing and exchanging best practice at a European level among entrepreneurship educators on skills development and training for grey entrepreneurs could be brought to the fore of entrepreneurship education. This could be done through ERASMUS exchange programmes and EU-funded research programmes.

Note

1. According to the OECD, high-growth enterprises achieve 20 per cent growth annually over a three-year period, as cited in NESTA in the (2009) report.

References

Amit, R. and Muller, E. (1995), 'Push and Pull Entrepreneurship', *Journal of Small Business & Entrepreneurship*, Vol. 16, No. 4, pp. 64–80.

Australian Bureau of Statistics (1999), 'Older People', A Social Report, ABS, Canberra.

Barclays (2001), 'Third Age Entrepreneurs – Profiting from Experience', Barclays Economic Report, Barclays, UK.

BBC (2010), 'French Senate passes Pension Bill', BBC World News, 22 October, http://www.bbc.co.uk/news/world-europe-11610601 (accessed 23.12.2010).

BERR (2008), 'High Growth Firms in the UK: Lessons from an Analysis of Comparative UK Performance', BETT Economics Paper No. 3, London.

Blackburn, R., Hart, M. and O'Reilly, M. (2000), 'Entrepreneurship in the Third Age: New Dawn or Misplaced Expectations?' in 23rd ISBA National Small Firms Policy and Research Conference, Aberdeen University, pp. 1–17.

COM (2003), Entrepreneurship in Europe, Green Paper, 27 final.

Cressy, R. and Storey, D. J. (1995), 'New Firms and Their Banks', Warwick University Business School and NatWest.

Curran, J. and Blackburn, R. (2001), 'Older People and the Enterprise Society: Age and Self-Employment Propensities', *Work, Employment & Society*, Vol. 15, No. 4, pp. 889–902.

GEM (2006), Bosma, N. and R. Harding, R. 'Global Entrepreneurship Monitor: GEM 2006 Summary Results'.

GEM (2007), Bosma, N., Jones, K., Autio, E. and Levie, J., 'Global Entrepreneurship Monitor: 2007 Executive Report'.

Getz, D. and Carlsen, J. (2000), 'Characteristics and Goals of Family and Owner-Operated Businesses in the Rural Tourism and Hospitality Sectors', *Tourism Management*, Vol. 21, pp. 547–560.

Goldberg, S. (2000), 'Senior Startups: Why Older Entrepreneurs are Turning to a Young Person's Game', *Business Week*, online: http://www.businessweek.com/2000/00_33/b3694054.htm (accessed 6.9.09).

Green, F. J. (2008), *Three Decades of Enterprise Culture*, Palgrave Macmillan, Basingstoke, UK.

Harding, R. (2007), 'Technology Entrepreneurship in the UK 2006', NESTA, London.

Hart, M., Anyadike-Danes, M. and Blackburn, R. (2004), 'Spatial Differences in Entrepreneurship: A Comparison of Prime Age and Third Age Cohorts', ISBA 27th Conference Entrepreneurship and SME Development, 'Creating Opportunities: Entrepreneurship and SME Development in Education, Policy and Research', Newcastle Gateshead 2–4 November 2004.

Hisrich, R. D. and Peters, M. P. (1992), *Entrepreneurship: Starting, Developing, and Managing a New Enterprise*, 2nd edition, BPI/Irwin, Homewood, US.

Kautonen, T. (2008), 'Understanding the Older Entrepreneur: Comparing Third Age and Prime Age in Finland', *International Journal of Business Science and Applied Management*, Vol. 3, No. 3, pp. 3–13.

King, S. (2002), 'Entrepreneurs' Measure of Success: Is it More than Profits?' *International Council for Small Business 47th World Conference*, SBANC University of Central Arkansas, 16–19 June, San Juan, Puerto Rico.

Klapper, L., Amit, R., Guillén, M. F. and Quesada, J. (2008), 'Entrepreneurship and Firm Formation Across Countries', *International Differences in Entrepreneurship*, in J. Lerner and A. Schoar (eds), National Bureau of Economic Research, Cambridge.

Marsh, B. (1989), 'Baby Boomers to Continue the Fast Pace of Start-ups in 90s in Entrepreneurial Activity is Forecast', *Wall Street Journal*, 19 June, p. 1.

NESTA (2009), Botham, R. and Graves, A., 'Third Age Entrepreneurs', NESTA Report, London.

OECD (2005), 'Ageing Populations: High Time for Action', Meeting of G8 Employment and Labour Ministers, 10–11 March, London, http://www.oecd.org./dataoecd/61/50/34600619.pdf (accessed 6.9.09).

Office for National Statistics (2003), 'Self-employment in the UK Labour Market', September.

Patel, S. and Gray, C. (2006).

PRIME (2004), 'Towards a 50+ Enterprise Culture: A PRIME Report', PRIME, London.

PRIME (2009), 'Generations Forgotten. Report of a Survey Commissioned by Bank of America on Behalf of PRIME into Attitudes towards Older Entrepreneurship across the UK', PRIME, London.

Singh, G. and De Noble, A. (2003), 'Early Retirees as the Next Generation of Entrepreneurs', *Entrepreneurship Theory & Practice*, Vol. 23, No. 3, pp. 207–226.

Singh, R. P. (2009), 'The Aging Population and Mature Entrepreneurs: Market Trends and Implications for Entrepreneurship', *New England Journal of Entrepreneurship*, Fairfield, Vol. 12, No. 1, pp. 45–54.

Small Business Service (2007), Household Survey of Entrepreneurship 2005, Research Report. Department of Trade and Industry, London.

Sorensen, J. and Stuart, T. (2000), 'Ageing, Obsolescence, and Organizational Innovation', *Administrative Science Quarterly*, Vol. 45, No. 1, pp. 81–112.

Storey, D. J. (1994), *Understanding the Small Business Sector*, Routledge, London.

Weber, P. and Schaper, M. (2003), 'Understanding the Grey Entrepreneur: A Review of the Literature', Conference Paper at 16th Annual Conference of Small Enterprise Association of Australia and New Zealand, 28 September–1 October, 2003, Ballarat, Australia.

Personality

5
Adapting Communications Styles to the Needs of the Market

Holly Buchanan

1 Introduction

Rule number one in copywriting is to write for the audience (Cornelissen, 2000). It is important to know demographics, psychographics, and more specifically what buying process and communication style an audience prefers when shopping for a product or service. The problem is that not all of an audience will have the same preferences. The challenge becomes: how to establish the different preferences, and determine which predominate?

It is important to have a framework with which to segment different audience preferences. The Myers-Briggs Type Indicator (MBTI) test measures psychological preferences in relation to how people perceive the world and make decisions. There are 16 types, and each type has a preferred buying process and communication style. Not all of an audience will have the same type, but one can infer a preferred buying process and communication style by analysing customer communication.

By understanding and mimicking the audience's preferences, copywriters can create more persuasive communication. Research like the 'theory of congruence' and the 'homogeneity principle' show people respond to those they perceive to be like themselves and that persuasiveness can be enhanced by creating similarity between source and receiver. This idea is expanded below.

To be more effective, copywriters need to be aware of not imposing their own personal type, buying process and communication style when they create messaging (unless their preferred type matches that of the target audience). And using MBTI as a framework, analysis can be conducted to determine audience preferences and which preferences are most predominant. Copywriters can generate better results by mimicking these preferences in order to connect with, and persuade, their audience.

2   The homogeneity principle

There is much research that supports the theory that we are attracted to those who are like us, including the homogeneity principle. In her book *Gender, Design and Marketing* (2009) Gloria Moss discusses this principle and she explains there that this principle is one in which a person of one type is attracted to another person of similar type. In a recruitment context, she explains that it is referred to as the 'self-selecting' tendency since it is widely recognised that people tend to prefer other people similar to themselves. People are said to be using 'self-reference criteria' – the use of their own perceptions and choice criteria to determine what is important – and sometimes the process of doing this is unconscious. This means that people are often not aware that they are using self-reference criteria and, in the context of evaluations of communications, may not appreciate that the value of a piece of communications is not absolute but is the product of empathy between object, perceiver and artist. Instead, they make the mistake of assuming that the criteria they employ are applied universally.

Gloria notes that there is some awareness that it may be less than optimum to use universal criteria of excellence. For example, the business guru Michael Hammer, father of the concept of 'business reengineering', spoke of the need for products to be shaped around the 'unique and particular needs' of the customer (Hammer, 1995, p. 21), and for products and services to be 'configured to' the needs of customers (ibid., p. 21). In the field of branding, similarly, an academic, Karande, has expressed the view that there should be congruence between the brand personality and the consumer's self-concept on the basis that purchases are thought to offer a vehicle for self-expression (Karande et al., 1997). This has led to a search for an understanding of the factors that influence congruence.

Moreover, in my own field, that of communications, it has translated into the notion that persuasiveness can be enhanced by similarity between source and receiver (Brock, 1965). In social psychology, it translates into the 'matching hypothesis' or 'similarity-attraction' paradigm, according to which increased similarity leads to increased attention and attraction (Byrne and Nelson, 1965; Berscied and Walster, 1978).

In other words, the person you like is the person who mirrors your own thoughts and views, and may possibly even mirror your looks and behaviour.

Findings continue to emerge about the importance of congruence (or 'rapport' or 'mirroring' as it is sometimes called). At California State University, Sacramento, a study of psychotherapists' successes with their clients showed that those therapists who achieved the best results had the most emotional congruence with their patients at meaningful junctures in the therapy. These mirroring behaviours showed up simultaneously as the therapists comfortably settled into the climate of their clients' worlds by establishing good rapport. When reporting these effects, psychiatrist Dr Louann Brizendine referred to 'mirror neurons' that allow people (mainly women in fact) not only to observe but also to imitate or mirror the hand gestures, body postures, breathing rates, gazes and facial expressions of other people (Brizendine, 2006).

If this emotional mirroring can give psychotherapists the edge, it may do the same for communications specialists. The congruity principle relates to the similarity between source and receiver, and research shows that mirroring the thoughts and views of your audience or interlocutor offers the key to more persuasive communications. The driving force here is to communicate in a style similar to that of the receiver whom you hope to persuade. The important driving force here is to focus on the attributes, benefits and motivations of the person you hope to galvanise into action.

3   Myers-Briggs personality test instrument

The Myers & Briggs Foundation website describes the Myers-Briggs Type Indicator (MBTI) test and the theory behind it.

> The essence of the theory is that much seemingly random variation in the behaviour is actually quite orderly and consistent, being due to basic differences in ways individuals prefer to use their perception and judgment.
>
> Perception involves all the ways of becoming aware of things, people, happenings, or ideas. Judgment involves all the ways of coming to conclusions about what has been perceived. If people differ systematically in what they perceive and in how they reach conclusions, then it is only reasonable for them to differ correspondingly in their interests, reactions, values, motivations, and skills.

MBTI preferences are broken down into four dichotomous personality types, which are described on the Myers & Briggs Foundation website as follows:

Favorite world Do you prefer to focus on the outer world or on your own inner world? This is called Extraversion (E) or Introversion (I).
Information Do you prefer to focus on the basic information you take in or do you prefer to interpret and add meaning? This is called Sensing (S) or Intuition (N).
Decisions When making decisions, do you prefer to first look at logic and consistency or first look at the people and special circumstances? This is called Thinking (T) or Feeling (F).
Structure In dealing with the outside world, do you prefer to get things decided or do you prefer to stay open to new information and options? This is called Judging (J) or Perceiving (P).

Many studies over the years have proven the validity of the MBTI instrument in three categories: (1) the validity of the four separate preference scales; (2) the validity of the four preference pairs as dichotomies; and (3) the validity of whole types or particular combinations of preferences. Many of these studies are discussed in the MBTI Manual (Myers, 1998) and separate studies have demonstrated strong construct validity for the MBTI (Thompson and Borrello, 1986) as well as strong internal consistency and test–retest reliability (Capraro and Capraro, 2002).

By using MBTI preferences as a framework, it is possible to look for patterns in customer communication and behaviour to see which preferences customers display.

4   Methodology

In this research, an online women's clothing company wanted to ensure that the copy on its website was adapted to the preferences of the users of the site. In order to do this, the researcher analysed the language used by those contributing to onsite reviews with a view to identifying the MBTI type of these users and, from that – following the homogeneity or congruity principle – identify the style of language that should be used on the website to match this.

The clothing company was Fit Couture (www.fitcouture.com) an online women's workout clothing company targeting women aged 25–49 who were looking for stylish exercise clothes designed specifically for women. When the researcher first started working with this company, one of the owners was doing most of the copywriting. In interactions with him, the researcher judged him to be an NTJ, the MBTI Intuitive Thinking Judging type, and corroborative evidence was derived from his copywriting style which also appeared to reflect this type. The researcher also read hundreds of customer reviews and, following analysis, judged that the preferred communication style was SFP, the Sensing Feeling Perceiving type. All these traits are in fact opposite in type to those of the owner/copywriter and so, in order to satisfy the preferences of the end-users, the researcher changed the 'voice' of the website and emails from NTJ to SFP.

Pen portraits of these types are presented below so that the reader can appreciate the changes involved in moving from a text appropriate to an NTJ as against an SFP type.

5 NTJ and SFP overview

NTJs are frank and decisive. They quickly see illogical and inefficient procedures and policies, and develop and implement comprehensive systems to solve organisational problems. They are forceful in presenting their ideas. They are sceptical and independent, and have high standards of competence and performance – for themselves and others.

SFPs are friendly, sensitive, and accepting. They enjoy the present moment and focus on what is going on around them. They dislike disagreements and conflicts, and do not force their opinions or values on others. They are exuberant lovers of life, people and material comforts. They are flexible and spontaneous.

In terms of communication styles, the differences between an NTJ and an SFP communication and decision-making style are likely to be as follows:

NTJ:

- Is hierarchical
- Can be sceptical and critical both of themselves and others
- Passes strong pronouncements with words like 'should'
- Uses technical terms
- Focuses on the big picture and generalities
- Uses third person

SFP:

- Focuses on the senses – the look, feel and smell of a product
- Seeks harmony and the positive in people

- Goes with the flow and is generally agreeable
- Is informal and friendly, using slang and contractions
- Focuses on specifics
- Uses first and second person

When reviewing customer communications, the researcher looked for patterns of word use, product benefits discussed, descriptions of motivations and outcomes, and length of review. She looked for frequency of the different patterns to see which were most predominant. Once the preferred type was determined (SFP), copy was revised to mirror this type.

6 Sample copy

Here are samples of the original copy written by the NTJ owner compared with the new copy written in the SFP style.

> **Old copy:** Fit Couture is designed to make you look your absolute best. Choose from comfortable clothes with a flattering fit and moisture wicking fabric.
>
> **New copy:** You're going to love the way you look in Fit Couture. Go ahead, take a second glance in the mirror. Yup, even your butt looks good. And you can sweat in these clothes with material designed to pull away moisture and keep you dry and comfortable.
>
> **Changes:** The use of the third person was changed to the second person and the hierarchical language (*looking the best*) was replaced by language focusing on the senses (*how your butt looks, glancing in the mirror*). Technical-sounding words (*moisture wicking fabric*) were replaced with conversational simple terms (*designed to pull away moisture and keep you dry and comfortable*).
>
> **Old copy**: Real clothes should look great on real bodies, not just on mannequins and models.
>
> **New copy:** Our clothes are designed for women by women. They fit and flatter real women's bodies in all their wonderful variety, shapes and sizes.
>
> **Changes:** The copy, which was judgmental in tone (*should look good, not just on mannequins and models*) was changed to something with a more personal positive feel (*fit and flatter bodies in their wonderful variety of shapes and sizes*).
>
> **Old copy:** No matter how fabulous that outfit looked in the store, if it doesn't make you look great, it doesn't deserve a place in your closet.

New copy: Make room in your closet. Women love Fit Couture pants and clothing so much they often buy three, four, even five pairs. When clothes look and feel this good, why wear anything else?

Changes: Changed critical bias (*if it doesn't make you look great, it doesn't deserve a place in your closet*) to a positive action (*make room in your closet*). Added specific numbers (*three, four, even five pairs.*)

Old copy: Some days it feels like you live in your active wear: from gym to shopping to picking up the kids. Changing clothes for every stop is just not an option. Neither is that threadbare pair of sweats and t-shirt in your drawer.

New copy: Fit Couture's stylish, comfortable clothes have a split-personality – equally at home in the gym as they are outside of the gym. From yoga to grocery shopping to lunch at the neighborhood bistro – just throw on Fit Couture and your favorite lip gloss and you're ready to take on the world.

Changes: The critical bias (*changing clothes … not an option. Neither is*) and judgmental verbiage (*threadbare … sweats*) was amended to having a more positive bias with second person (*you're ready to take on the world*). Also added specifics (*lunch at the neighborhood bistro … lip gloss.*)

Old copy: We're not all the same height, so why should our pants all be the same length? Fit Couture's pants come in lengths ranging from petite to extra long.

New copy: Finally, work out pants that are the right length! Fit Couture's pants come in lengths ranging from petite to extra long. That's right, pick your size, *then* choose the length. No bare ankles, no hemming. How cool is that?

Changes: The word 'should' was changed to a verb with a more positive angle. Moreover, specifics were added (*no bare ankles, no hemming*) and a more informal and conversational tone (*How cool is that?*) was adopted.

7 Results

In an A/B email test, one version was written in the old style (NTJ), one version was written in the new style (SFP), and the new style (SFP) achieved a 27 per cent higher click-through rate. The client was convinced that the new copy was effective and made changes throughout the site.

8 Conclusion

The homogeneity and congruency principle demonstrate the importance of similarity between source and receiver in order for a message to be persuasive. Therefore, it is important to analyse customer communications to discern the customer's preferred buying process, personality type and communication style. Once that pattern has been inferred, it is possible to mirror those qualities back to the customer.

With the Internet this analysis is now a much simpler process. Companies and copywriters can review customer emails, live chats and product reviews, and the MBTI can be used as a framework to look for patterns and preferences.

All messaging should be reviewed and tested to make sure it is persuasive not just to the creator(s) (the copywriter, advertising agency, business owner) but also to the intended audience.

References

Berscied, E. and Walster, E. (1978), *Interpersonal Attraction* (Cambridge, MA: Cambridge University Press).

Brizendine, L. (2006), *The Female Brain* (New York: Morgan Road Books).

Brock, T. C. (1965), 'Communicator-recipient similarity and decision change', *Journal of Personality and Social Psychology*, 1, 650–54.

Byrne, D. and Nelson, D. (1965), 'Attraction as a linear function of positive reinforcement', *Journal of Personality and Social Psychology*, 1, 659–63.

Capraro, R. M. and Capraro, M. M. (2002), 'Myers-Briggs type indicator score reliability across studies: A meta-analytic reliability generalization study', *Educational and Psychological Measurement*, 92, 590–602.

Cornelissen, J. (2000), 'Corporate image: an audience centred model', *Corporate Communications: An International Journal*, 5 (2), 119–25.

Hammer, M. (1995), *Reengineering the Corporation* (London: Nicholas Brearley Corporation).

Karande, K., G. M. Zinkhan and A. B. Lum (1997), 'Brand personality and self concept: A replication and extension', American Marketing Association, Summer Conference, 165–71.

Myers, I. B (1998), MBTI Manual: a guide to the development and use of the Myers-Briggs type indicator, Consulting Psychologists Press, Inc.

Myers & Briggs Foundation website, http://www.myersbriggs.org/my-mbti-personality-type/mbti-basics/, accessed on 22 November 2011.

Thompson. B. and Borrello. G. M. (1986), 'Construct validity of the Myers-Briggs type indicator', *Educational and Psychological Measurement*, 46, 745–52.

Gender

6
Transforming a White, Masculine Organisational Culture

Ian Dodds

1 Introduction

This chapter concerns itself with the impact of unconscious bias in white, masculine organisations. In the West, government, industry and commerce, education, health and so on have historically evolved under the direction of white men. This means that the cultures within them have developed in line with the values and characteristic practices of this group. Hence, they invariably possess white, masculine cultures. These result in individuals who are not white and male experiencing unconscious bias, which can limit both their contribution and their career progression. It not only manifests itself in the workplace, but also at customer, client and service-user interfaces, resulting in lost revenue and business development opportunities. This chapter examines some of the existing research on this topic, particularly in relation to gender. It will then demonstrate its continuing existence from the observations of women and minority ethnic focus group participants' experiences of exclusion and inclusion in their organisations. Finally, it offers methodologies for addressing unconscious bias to gain significant business benefits.

2 Review of the research relating to the nature and causes of unconscious bias

Moss Kanter (1977) was one of the first researchers to recognise and draw attention to the presence of gender in early models of organisations:

> A 'masculine ethic' of rationality and reason can be identified in the early image of managers. This 'masculine ethic' elevates the traits assumed to belong to men with educational advantages to necessities

for effective organisations: a tough minded approach to problems; analytical abilities to abstract and plan; a capacity to set aside personal, emotional considerations in the interests of task accomplishment; a cognitive superiority in problem-solving and decision making.

This remains an issue in many organisations and results in unconscious bias in that male qualities dominate in the selection of talent and in the behaviours characteristically practised both in their workplaces and marketplaces.

Joan Acker (1990) makes the point that 'conversation analysis shows how gender differences in interruptions, turn taking and setting the topic of discussion recreate gender inequality in the flow of ordinary talk'. This was vividly brought home to me in a coaching session I had with a woman who was a member of the UK Executive of an American company. I had feedback on her leadership from her team members and it was extremely positive. Consequently, I had been looking forward to sharing it with her. Imagine my surprise when 20 minutes into the coaching she burst into tears. Initially, she explained her behaviour on the grounds of being stressed as she was so busy. She continued to sob intermittently for 40 minutes as we discussed the feedback. Then, suddenly, she exclaimed that the real problem was that this was such lovely feedback and yet I would not be able to imagine what she had to put up with from her male colleagues. I asked what they did and was told that they interrupted her when she was talking and she never felt that her opinions and ideas were as valued by them as much as theirs. Moreover, they would regularly meet up in a bar after work, supposedly to socialise, but made decisions which they invariably failed to pass on to her. I have undertaken interactive behaviour analyses of discussions in senior manager meetings and have often witnessed women being interrupted and talked over by their male colleagues.

Elisabeth Kelan has pointed out that many researchers on women managers (Gherardi, 1995; Marshall, 1984; Wajcman, 1998) have shown that the fulfilment of the masculine script in managerial work is one way in which gender is portrayed; that is, the ways of leading and managing that are automatically expected in organisations are associated with masculine traits. It is exactly in 'acting gender inappropriately' that women confront multiple problems in masculine work areas. Women are punished for not being 'woman' enough, and so gender accountability, far from being ignored or disrupted, is redoubled. In other words, women experience a double bind in that they are expected to conform to the male norm; but when they do they can find that they face criticism for being unfeminine.

In essence, the 'masculine script' in the West is one which is also white, middle-aged, physically able and heterosexual. Hence, not only are women subject to unconscious bias, but so too are other under-represented groups in senior management. Like the woman executive I referred to earlier they are interrupted more than their white, male colleagues and are likely to feel that their opinions and ideas are less valued. Mary Rowe (1974) describes how this gives rise to under-represented groups experiencing 'microinequities', patterns of negative micro messages; for example, being regularly interrupted, which can result in a lowering of self-esteem and some degree of disengagement.

3 Examples of how unconscious bias plays out in organisations

In the last ten years the author, together with his colleagues, has conducted many focus groups to assess the climate for diversity and inclusion (D&I) in clients' organisations. These are structured on an affinity group basis, for example women's, men's, minority ethnic, and disabled people's groups. They are always facilitated by external consultants of the same affinity identity as the focus group participants, for example women facilitators with women's groups. This is to enable participants to be honest about their experiences of exclusion and inclusion and feel that these will be empathetically understood. These groups have consistently demonstrated that unconscious bias is invariably present and that, as a result, the organisations' workplaces are white, male meritocracies and not inclusive meritocracies for everyone, as is often claimed in their recruitment literature.

The following quotes obtained from focus group participants richly demonstrate the point. First some examples from women:

> 'I feel patronised.... an effort is made to include us because we're women and not because we're good at our work.'
> 'Women don't push themselves and there's nothing in (my company) to help pull us forward.'
> 'Looking in, it looks like a boy's club.'
> 'To get on you have to adopt a more male style – I lead a more masculine life (at work).'
> 'All senior posts come from the sales environment, which is male dominated.'
> 'They take on people like themselves – who fit in with male comfort zones.'

'Old boy network – like this for last 20 years – why fix
what isn't broken?'

'It's a long hours culture and I feel guilty leaving at 5pm to
collect my children.'

'Getting on is all about bringing in the money... you have to be
ruthless and disregard your colleagues.'

'Women are more interactive and want to help people out.'

'In jokes with male-dominated environment – jokes about
who should get tea.'

'Roles are specifically male/female, i.e., males – services/sales, and
females HR/admin and projects.'

'You have to work twice as hard to get your voice heard – male
colleagues will then listen.'

'Many men think that women only work in HR – stereotyping.'

'The attitude is women don't want to get further.'

'Being a woman is a barrier in itself.'

These demonstrate and represent only a sample of many similar quotes
that we have been offered, that women in masculine organisations:

- Often see senior management as 'a boys' club'.
- Have to adopt masculine behaviours in the more masculine culture, e.g. 'lead a more masculine life'; 'be ruthless and disregard your
  colleagues', that is, ambitious, individualistic behaviour; be less interactive than they would naturally be and less supportive of colleagues;
  work long hours.
- Experience structural gender barriers to promotion, such as pro-
  motions to senior management being made from functions which
  tend to be male dominated, for example sales, with organisations
  stereotyping different roles as male or female.
- Encounter attitudes about female levels of ambition; for example,
  'women don't want to get further'.
- Have to work harder to get their voice heard.

Secondly, some quotes illustrating the same point from minority ethnic
employees:

'Conversations take place and you do not feel part of them.'

'We hear about something that affects you later than people
not affected.'

'Managers tend not to include us in decisions.'

'The prejudice can be so subtle sometimes, you can't see it, but you can really feel it.'

'Managers tend to stereotype people; for example, they see Asians as shy and Eastern Europeans as aggressive.'

'Some managers can be patronising and condescending. For instance, one manager described his staff as "these are my Asians and their English isn't very good but they don't mind me asking them to repeat themselves and they won't do anything without me". He thought he was being supportive.'

'We are not expected to want more, the attitude is BAME (black, Asian and minority ethnic) staff are already in the sweet shop, and now they want a ladder to reach the sweets on the top shelf.'

'At our level, advancement is all about networking and communicating well, and this can work against minority ethnic staff if you are not seen as fitting in.'

'Sometimes we are discouraged from advancing within the company with remarks such as "you're fine where you are".'

'Minority ethnics are not given the chance, or get less chance, to advance within the company than other employees.'

Again these represent a sample of many similar quotes that we have been offered from minority ethnic people and these show that they:

- experience exclusion, such as feeling outside of conversations or being overlooked in decision-making.
- feel that they are stereotyped; for example, Asians being 'shy'.
- encounter attitudes about levels of ambition, e.g., 'already in the sweet shop'; 'you're fine where you are'.
- suffer from advancement depending on networking, and minority ethnic staff can have less access to what are often informal networking activities, such as socialising with more senior colleagues in a bar.

4   Case studies of how organisations have addressed unconscious bias

Thus far this chapter has examined research evidence for unconscious bias in white, masculine organisations for individuals not of that identity, particularly women. It has then drawn on experiential evidence from women and minority ethnic focus groups. It is clear that in many Western organisations this is a phenomenon which results in everyday experiences of exclusion for individuals who are not white and male, and it limits their opportunities both for contributing fully and for promotion. This restricts organisations' abilities to obtain the significant benefits available from accessing both 'demographic' diversity and 'cognitive' diversity; that is, diversity encompassing learning styles, communication styles, aspirations and belief/value systems as well as people's attitudes and expectations and the richness, or otherwise, of 'mental models' shared by groups. It is clearly critical that organisations address this issue and this requires a long-term strategic intervention to change white, masculine, organisational cultures into ones which are more inclusive and meritocratic for all.

The author's long experience of working with clients is that before this long-term, strategic culture change effort can begin it is necessary to both convince senior white male managers of the need to act, and engage their will to do so. This involves persuading them of the business benefits: the development and retention of a wider talent pool to promote from; enhanced business problem solving (Harvard professor Scott E. Page has created a theoretical framework, the Diversity Trumps Ability Theorem, to explain why diverse groups often outperform experts); better understanding of diverse markets; and higher levels of performance through staff of whatever diversity feeling more fully engaged in helping the organisation succeed. This is 'the intellectual argument'. However, an 'emotional impact' also has to be made. This is because the senior male managers believe in equality and in putting effort into D&I. However, they are generally unaware that their efforts are undermined by the unconscious biases they demonstrate. This was first driven home to the author when he was presenting the outcome of a global D&I assessment for a leading bank. After seeing the quotes from the women focus group participants, the task force chair stated that he had never realised that the firm was in reality a meritocracy for white males and not for everyone as he had believed. It was the emotional impact of the quotes that resulted in the task force chair driving activity to develop a culture which ensured that its meritocratic principle more fully encompassed women and other under-represented groups. The author was involved in a follow-up D&I assessment five years later for this firm and was amazed at the progress they had made in developing a more inclusive, meritocratic culture, especially for women.

Another means of making an emotional impact is to research stories of how unconscious bias plays out in the organisation for under-represented groups and then depict this by short pieces of drama. We did this for a well-known global company and, again, it was the emotional impact of discovering how women and minority ethnic people's work engagement and promotion opportunities were affected by unconscious bias that persuaded this firm's CEO that action needed to be taken to build a more inclusive, meritocratic culture. This firm has since extended these efforts to its marketplace through introducing activities to increase awareness on the part of sales employees of unconscious bias in their dealings with customers and clients from a different identity group to themselves.

Once the emotional impact has been made and generated the senior management's will to act, it is then possible and productive to develop the long-term culture change strategy which is necessary to transform the white, masculine culture to one which is more inclusive and meritocratic for everyone, whatever their diversity identity. An excellent example is a global organisation the author worked with. It was awarded a World Diversity Leadership Summit Global Diversity Innovation Award for its efforts, an award in which entries were judged by a panel of Fortune 100 companies.

This company's initiative was underpinned by classical transformational change methodology. Upfront the board developed a vision of an inclusive, meritocratic organisation. This offered the workforce a picture of an organisation three years on, which would embrace everyone's contributions and abilities more inclusively. By doing this the vision described how it would improve its ability to solve business problems more effectively and creatively; understand and meet service-users' needs better and improve their satisfaction with the services they received; and promote from a broader talent pool, thereby increasing the proportions of under-represented groups in senior management. The chief executive recorded this vision on a DVD, which was viewed by its global workforce in a one-day behaviourally oriented workshop attended by everyone. Moreover, the workshops were inclusively composed so that they brought together people on a mixed basis across all levels of the hierarchy.

The author's team conducted research to understand how exclusion and inclusion played out in the organisation's culture around the world. This involved interviewing employees from its different levels and from a variety of locations both individually and in small groups. The research informed three short drama scenarios, of 5–10 minutes, scripted by the author's business's theatre producer. A key objective of the scenarios was to enable workshop participants to internalise a picture of inclusive and exclusive behaviour, both in interactions with people of different diversity identities to themselves and in decision-making and problem solving, and to harness the power of difference. The scenarios were also designed to offer interactive learning opportunities for participants to advise and shape the inclusive behaviour portrayed by the actors. Finally, the workshops engaged participants in action planning how they would in future behave differently to be more inclusive. Participants were also required to formulate recommendations for their units' diversity action plans to increase inclusivity in relation to workplace activities and in relating to service-users.

This intervention was positive in its impact in that it resulted in high participant satisfaction scores. However, the author's experience is that one-off training interventions are insufficient to drive sustained, long-term change. The training needs to be reinforced. This was achieved by training regional internal change agents to follow up the training in the units in their regions. Each unit was required to incorporate the recommendations from the workshops into their diversity action plans and these had to be submitted to the group Diversity Strategy Unit (DSU). The regional change agents then worked with their respective units to enable them to implement their diversity action plans. Finally, the DSU monitored progress with the implementation of the units' diversity action plans on a three-monthly basis. This enabled successes to be identified and publicised and shared on the intranet. Progress was measured through developing the organisation's annual employee engagement survey to obtain feedback on respondents' experiences of inclusion. The diversity demographics at the different levels of the organisation were also tracked. The following outcomes were obtained:

- More creative input into problem solving through better cross-team relationships breaking down barriers between staff. This improved the collegiality of the organisation.
- Improved staff development through better cross-organisational learning between teams.
- Individuals bringing new ideas into their own jobs after experiencing other areas of work.
- Better individual understanding of cultural and religious sensitivities.
- Reduced risk of bullying, harassment, victimisation and discrimination.
- Better use of office space through physical barriers to inclusion being broken down.

Another organisation had as its aims to: embrace inclusion and diversity to foster innovation and talent in the workplace and engage more effectively with customers and partners to provide more advanced business solutions in its worldwide marketplace; and shift from a competitive, masculine, task-oriented culture to create a more inclusive, collaborative and truly meritocratic environment. It placed the main intervention emphasis on its majority white male workforce. This group was targeted to ensure that they understood the D&I business case and adopted inclusive attitudes and behaviour, and this part of the intervention involved upfront training sessions for executive team members on unconscious bias.

As in the earlier case discussed, research was conducted to determine how unconscious bias played out in the workplace and in the interface with the market. Scenarios were then scripted to illustrate the findings from the research and portrayed by two actors in workshops delivered to the executives. These again made an emotional impact and generated in the executives the will to act to change the situation. The executives committed to regularly talking to employees on walkabouts and in communications and briefings they led about the importance to the success of the business of D&I. They also challenged everyone to behave inclusively, both in internal and external interactions. A key message was that promotion would be dependent on demonstrating inclusive behaviour. Training on how unconscious bias played out at the customer and client interfaces was delivered to all of the organisation's sales managers. As in the previous example, this training was followed by learning reinforcement activities, for example follow-up discussions with a trainer on the ways in which the sales managers were applying the learning, and setting dilemmas for the sales managers to respond to, publicising successes on the company intranet. The success of the intervention was measured by a comparison of a D&I assessment before and after it had taken place.

The annual employee engagement survey was also restructured to enable an inclusion index score to be generated for each of the diversity strands. Both of these measures demonstrated significant improvements in the extent to which employees experienced inclusion. Finally, examples of new business being won that could be related to the intervention were tracked and some were significant. Also the company found that it was outperforming its competitors in recruiting women graduates.

5 Summary of the steps that need to be taken to address unconscious bias

The examples described in Section 4 demonstrate that the following are key requirements for addressing unconscious bias:

- It is critical that the most senior management reach both an intellectual and emotional understanding of the impact of unconscious bias in order to build their determination to drive the necessary changes.
- It is vital to invest in long-term strategic effort which will transform the prevailing white, masculine culture into one which is more inclusive of all types of diversity.
- The most senior management must regularly offer compelling messages about the business importance of having an inclusive workplace and marketplace. They must identify the behaviour that will drive inclusivity in their organisations and set a consistent example in them.
- The workforce needs not only to understand how the organisation will be more successful if its people think and behave inclusively; but also to be engaged in helping deliver the necessary changes, for example through project teams and task forces.
- Organisations need to invest in training programmes to raise awareness of unconscious bias and the behaviour needed to relate inclusively to colleagues and customers, clients or service-users.
- Training alone is insufficient to drive the necessary cultural shift. It needs to be reinforced by the leadership message and example, and follow-up activities, including the use of internal change agents.
- Progress needs to be measured in terms of both the 'softer' change in inclusion, such as through measuring engagement indices for different diversity strands, and in terms of 'harder' business-related outcomes, for example retention of high potential under-represented employees, new business gains, and customer satisfaction indices by diversity identity group.

References

Acker, J. (1990), *A Theory of Gendered Organizations*, Gender & Society, London: Sage.

Gherardi, S. (1995), *Gender, Symbolism and Organisational Culture*, London: Sage.

Kanter, R. M. (1977), *Men and Women of the Corporation*. R. M. Kanter, New York: Basic Books.

Kelan, E. K. (2010), *Gender, Work & Organization*, Wiley Online Library, Wiley.com.

Marshall, J. (1984), *Women Managers – Travellers in a Male World*, Chichester, UK: Wiley.

Page, S. E. (2007), *The Difference: How the Power of Diversity Creates Better Groups, Firms, Schools and Societies*, Princeton: Princeton University Press.

Rowe, M. (1974), 'Saturn's Rings: a study of the minutiae of sexism which maintain discrimination and inhibit affirmative action results in corporations and non-profit institutions', in *Graduate and Professional Education of Women*, American Association of University Women.

Wajcman, J. (1998), *Managing Like a Man*, Oxford: Blackwell.

7
Maximising the Effectiveness of Advertising for Female Markets

Thomas J. Jordan

Diversity is achieved when organisations are willing to change their status quo and embrace a structure in their companies that accurately represents the population. Today, the word 'diversity' is typically associated with various ethnic groups. However, we should not overlook gender as a major factor as well. In North America and across Europe, most businesses are far from diverse. The top management of the Fortune 500 companies are still mostly older, white men. Women, of all races, have very little representation in these companies. Yet women comprise over 50 per cent of the general population.

And in the field of marketing there is a complete lack of diversity where it matters quite a bit: in the creative departments of the advertising agencies. Over 70 per cent of all advertising is created by men (Farris, 2005). Add the filters of approval, creative directors (over 90 per cent men), and you have advertising created by men and approved by men, that generally appeals mostly to men.

1 Why is this such a big problem?

Because it's been proven, time and time again, that women are responsible for over 80 per cent of all purchases (Barletta, 2006). Not just lipstick and tights: all purchases. And our agency, HY Connect, conducted some proprietary research that suggests that number is actually higher. Published syndicated data shows that a lot of big-ticket items can be a 'dual purchase'. But the question typically asked is, 'Who made this purchase?'

To get a more accurate answer, in the independent research that we conducted online with several hundred men and women, we posed questions a little differently. Such as, 'In the case of a tie, who would be most disappointed if the purchase wasn't their choice?' And, 'Whose opinion carries more weight in deciding the purchase?' Both men and women agreed that over 90 per cent of all 'dual decisions' were really influenced by the woman.

Now, it might be argued that men in the creative departments of advertising agencies could do a satisfactory job of crafting messages that would resonate with women. But recent research proves otherwise. In an online survey (Greenfield, 2002), 91 per cent of the women respondents stated that 'advertisers don't understand them'. Could the answer be as simple as adding more women to the creative departments of advertising agencies?

Unfortunately, quite a few dynamics in this industry would have to change for that 'simple' solution to work. In my book *Re-render the Gender* (2009), I wrote one chapter titled 'That's not a woman baby, that's a MAN', borrowing a quote from the first Austin Powers movie. I point out examples of how women in creative departments usually succeed by acting, writing, talking, presenting and performing much like their male peers. We all laugh at the old-school antics on the popular American television show *Mad Men*. The technology may have changed, the clothing may have changed, but quite a bit of the male-dominated attitudes have not ... especially in the creative departments.

One of the reasons that attitudes have been slow to change can be linked to the emotional rewards given to creative people in advertising agencies via the international creative competitions. If you win a 'Lion', the prestigious award at the Cannes International Advertising Festival, your reputation in the creative community increases, your chance for job advancement increases, and there is a good chance that your salary could increase as well.

The complete disconnect is that the ads are not viewed with an eye as to how effective they may be at reaching their target market but merely on their ability to entertain, influence and impress the judges of these advertising festivals. Historically, over 90 per cent of the judges have been male. And how does one win a Cannes Lion? Is it with advertising that successfully launches a new brand, creates a shift in brand loyalty or increases sales? Unfortunately, the success of advertisements in the real world has nothing to do with winning a creative award.

So, back to the question 'How do you win at Cannes?' The answer is simple: you have to convince the incredibly hip, nearly all-male, nearly all-white judges that your commercial is so hip, so irreverent, so counter to traditional advertising, that you deserve a Lion. In other words, don't do advertising that responsibly tries to sell a product or service and is compelling and works, but instead do advertising that is anything but advertising. That is the dirty little secret. Because most of the work that wins at Cannes is anything but traditional advertising.

So let's recap. The creative departments of advertising agencies are nearly all male. The women, if they hope to succeed, need to act like the men. How do the men act? Like they want to win at Cannes. How do you win at Cannes? Irreverent, hip advertising that impresses the male judges.

That influence follows each creative person every day when they sit down to create advertising. In fact, this 'award-winning' attitude results in advertising that may please an all-male panel of advertising award judges but is often far from female friendly, and this is one of the biggest reasons advertising is not resonating with women. That is why you'll see a commercial trying to sell a snack chip by showing one man hitting another man in the groin with a large glass ball; why a certain cereal maker shows a print ad with a scantily clad woman perched on the counter holding a bowl of cereal (with a half-dressed man behind her) with the headline: 'What satisfies a hungry woman?'; why a certain tyre company demonstrates the desirability of their tyres by showing a married couple confronting a street gang, with the husband shoving his wife out the car door, and leaving her to confront the gang rather than lose his tyres.

This whole approach to advertising has to be corrected before we can do the apparently simple thing of infusing more females into a creative department, thinking that we now have the formula to succeed with the female consumer.

But it gets even worse.

While waiting the whole year to see if anything they've produced is worthy of international recognition, the creative people have to do the work that pays the bills. You know, the real stuff, like banks that want to let people know they have great rates on a loan. Or a hospital that wants recognition for winning the Best Nurses award. And, even though none of this work would even come close to making the shortlist at any advertising award competition, the creative people want to make it look as if it belongs to one of the awards annuals. That's why there's the constant battle to keep the logo small, the copy brief, or non-existent, and the concept 'edgy'.

So, rather than a picture of a group of smiling nurses and a headline for a print ad that says, 'We've always recognized the quality of our nurses and now the entire community has as well,' you'd be looking at a picture of nurse sharks with a headline that says 'We never sleep. And, finally, someone noticed.'

If you think this is an exaggeration, if you think this isn't the prevailing thought in most creative departments, just take a peek in the offices of the creative people in almost every advertising agency. You'll find stacks and stacks of copies of *Archive* and *Communication Arts*, two publications printed quarterly that display the world's most exotic and unusual creative work. However, there is very little mention, if any, as to whether or not these advertisements helped build a brand or sell a product. The functional purpose of the advertisement is of secondary importance to its artistic function, and the very idea that a print ad for a haemorrhoid ointment should be considered 'art' speaks volumes.

Each and every day, most of the creative people are assessing whether the work they are creating would fit in publications like *Archive* and *Communication Arts*. Does the outdoor board they're crafting for the local library have a hip, edgy attitude with type that's hard to read? To be sure, if it doesn't they will be mocked by many of their peers within their own agency. Of course, completely lost and subsidiary in all of this is creating messages that resonate with women.

It's important for me to point out that I'm not merely a disgruntled creative director who is throwing stones at the award shows because my agency isn't capable of winning international recognition. Over the years, we've won at nearly every major advertising competition, so today I speak as a 'converted sinner'. I admit that there was a point in my career that I craved the attention I received in winning at the international advertising competitions, and this craving influenced so much of the work we created. Looking back, I can also say that I have created campaigns that worked very well with women, so maybe I was a good candidate for advocating change in creative departments. The turning point came several years ago when I had an eye-opening experience that changed my point of view and started us on the path of changing how we looked at our industry and communicating correctly with women.

I had entered two television commercials in a local advertising competition that was going to recognise the '99 best advertisements of the year'. One commercial was for the Children's Hospital of Wisconsin and it simply showed a montage of three normal-looking children. Emotional music played in the background and about 20 seconds into the 30-second spot, they revealed, one by one, the scars they had on their chests from open heart surgery.

The other television commercial was to promote literacy. Silently, it started with the titles you usually see at the beginning of a rented film, namely that the screen was adapted to fit their television and that some of the language might have been changed, etc. The final two titles read, 'So forget the movie,' 'Read the book.'

The Children's Hospital spot was, perhaps, the most compelling television commercial of my career. It later went on to win 'Best of Show' at the National Healthcare Advertising Awards, a competition judged by healthcare professionals, not all-male creative directors. However, in a local competition with an all-male judging panel, it did not even make the list of the best 99. There was nothing funny, edgy, hip or irreverent about the ad so maybe this is the explanation. Meanwhile, the other advertisement promoting literacy was the unanimous 'Best of Show'. Maybe its clever allusions to the cinema had appealed to the all-male jury.

At this time I also met Marti Barletta. The combination of the results of the awards show and Marti's insights changed the way I saw the world of advertising. Marti is the author of *Marketing to Women* (2006), a brilliant, breakthrough book that points out the tremendous opportunity marketers could achieve if they focused more accurately on what motivates women. I began to see that nine times out of ten, adverts that focused on what might really motivate women were not scooping up the creative awards. A fog was clearing in front of me and I began to see the error of my ways.

It is a complete contradiction. On the one hand you have Marti with hard facts and figures that indicate the advertising business is wasting a lot of time and money creating ads that don't really resonate with the people doing most of the buying. On the other hand, you have advertising agencies largely ignoring many of the techniques that would help their clients' businesses.

In 2009, Gloria Moss wrote a book entitled *Gender, Design and Marketing*. This invaluable reference was the result of over 15 years of research on colours, shapes, shades and styles that each gender finds the most engaging. It describes experiments she conducted into men and women's preferences, finding on repeated occasions that women tended to like designs produced by women, while men tended to like designs produced by men, even though neither group knew the gender of the designer. Over the years, Moss had done work for big companies that had seen the benefits of using designers who were in tune with the preferences of the target market. However, many had chosen to ignore her proven, insightful findings. Why? Because it didn't agree with their preconceived beliefs and would have meant changing the male-dominant demographic of design.

A recent book published by two social psychologists (Tavris and Aronson, 2007) explains why all of us can find ways to justify what we believe, even in the face of facts that clearly prove us wrong. This book should be required reading for everyone. It explains why the chief marketing officer of a company won't acknowledge research that proves his, or her, current advertising campaign is not effective – why marketers can hear the brilliance of a Marti Barletta, proving the merits of targeting women and be told, 'We get it completely. We have women in our ads.'

Of course, it is not enough to just 'have women' in your ads. What are they saying, what are they doing and does it all ring true with the women in the audience? And, did a nearly all-male team create this work?

A quick recap: women do the buying of the majority of products and services. Men create and approve the advertising for those products and services. The motivating factor for the advertising creatives is to become famous by doing advertising that is *not* advertising. That advertising is judged primarily by men at the award shows. To succeed, women have to create award-winning advertising that appeals to men. Even the work that has no chance to make a creative person famous is influenced by the ads they will study in *Communication Arts* and *Archive*, nearly all of which ignores all the valuable findings that Gloria Moss discovered in her years of research on design. The marketing to women experts, including the world-renowned Marti Barletta, experience standing ovations at their speeches, and yet witness little change in the advertising that companies run. No surprises then if the chief marketing officers continue to justify millions of dollars of expenditure on work that doesn't resonate with most women.

But still, it gets worse.

Today, there are schools that teach writers and art directors how to do award-winning work. These 'portfolio centers' take smart, talented, impressive people and pound into their heads what it takes to create the work that will win at Cannes. They are called portfolio centres because the students leave school with a portfolio of ads that, hopefully, get them hired at an advertising agency, and their graduates are now employed at nearly every medium to large advertising agency.

On occasion, these portfolio schools will bring in guest speakers to help impress upon these young folks what life will be like in an advertising agency. One of the speakers is a creative director who has bathtubs full of advertising awards. He speaks to a number of these classes. At one he was addressing the need to be simple in your communication. But the tone and manner in which he delivers this message sends other signals altogether. What he tells this class is this:

> The clients love their products. They believe they're faster, cheaper. You are going to spend your whole job, your whole career 'stiff-arming' them to keep some of the facts they tell you out of your ads. So get ready for a long, horrible career of all these schmucks in suits who come in with charts proving to you that all the facts and figures they're showing you are correct. All you're going to have is your gut ... and what I'm telling you.

So, he's telling these students that the advertising belongs to them and that they don't need to listen to the client because they're just 'schmucks in suits' who should be ignored, despite the fact that they have facts and figures proving their point of view.

And now, it really gets worse.

What about cultural, racial and ethnic differences? Your massive female population includes African-American, Hispanic, Asian. The 'too hip for the room' white guys at the advertising agencies don't have a clue how to reach even Anglo women. Women of colour are not even part of the conversation for the majority of mass media even though they generate nearly one trillion dollars in consumer spending. It is a fact that for marketers willing to embrace gender and cultural differences, the potential opportunities are enormous.

Fortunately, some people are offering in-depth insight into this area. For example, in her book, Muley (2009) demonstrates how women of colour are often completely left out of the equation when clients are creating their marketing plans, and agencies are creating the ad campaigns. This book points out many of the reasons why marketers should avoid grouping all women together. For instance, she discusses the evidence that women of colour place a higher regard on motherhood than other groups, quoting a study by Yankelovich (2005) showing that Latina and African-American women are more likely to state that 'having a child is an experience every woman should have'. Seventy-four per cent of Hispanic women agree with this statement, compared with 57 per cent of African-American women and 49 per cent of non-Hispanic white women.

Another book (Miller and Kemp, 2005) examines the cultural complexities of the black market, offering concrete examples of the importance of having a product adopted by black trendsetters. It also discusses how to break through stereotypes to better understand the African-American consumer. They also offer insight confirmed by our own independent research that a white audience can relate very well to African-Americans in TV commercials. In fact, one spot for Tide detergent showing an African-American man asleep with his child scored so well that it had the highest performance score among other Tide commercials.

As for reaching the Hispanic market, the fastest-growing ethnic segment in the United States, a recent book (Soto, 2006) offers a 'thorough understanding of the environment in which you will compete for it, identifying which of those consumers will allow you to generate profit, and defining how well an organization and its environment and target consumer are aligned'. The author points out that marketers sometimes look for a 'cultural solution' when the secret is really understanding the behavioural context and drivers of the target market. She also points out that businesses should not expect to be able to imitate another company's strategy and achieve the same results. According to the author, there are no 'cookie cutter' solutions, and the entire organisation needs to be in tune with the Hispanic market.

One of the most misunderstood and overlooked markets is that of Asians. It is true that Japanese, Koreans, Chinese and others have their distinct cultures, but there are overlapping characteristics shared by Asians that must be understood to communicate to them successfully. A useful book (Hyun, 2005) provides invaluable insight into why Asian men and women are hired out of college at a proportion much higher than other ethnic groups but often fail to advance to management positions. This is not a marketing book, per se, but one that offers insight into what obstacles, real and self-imposed, Asians face today.

Ironically, perhaps, the characteristics of Asians, both men and women, parallel many of the characteristics of women in general. Hyun demonstrates the cultural characteristics of 'not tooting your own horn...not bragging...expecting to be recognized for your hard work...wanting to please others' are found among Asians and are some of the same reasons men, and women, do not get promoted at the same rate as white mainstream men.

Some clients are smart enough to hire agencies that specialise in ethnic advertising, and enlightened women are helping to craft their messages. However, traditional agencies are bottom-line oriented and don't want to see money go out of the door. They are seldom willing to share any of the client's money for anything, be it media buying and planning or any 'ethnic' effort. So they will hire a 'specialist' or two to help convince the client that they are the 'one-stop shop' for all their communication needs. Can the reader guess the gender of most of these specialists?

So I've painted a rather bleak picture of how things are. Is there light at the end of the tunnel? Yes. Since Marti Barletta and others have published on the topic of women, marketing and design, the snowball has just started to roll down the snowy mountain. Today she speaks to large audiences all over the world, and slowly, but steadily, more men are attending and hearing.

A decade ago, Marti and researchers like Gloria Moss were practically alone. Ironically, when Tom Peters, the well-known (male) marketing guru co-wrote a book with Marti, her messages started to get traction. On the heels of Marti's efforts, others, like Amanda Stevens (2007) and Holly Buchanan (2007) have taken up the battle cry. Today, there are dozens of other authors and speakers on the subject of marketing to women, and the enlightened companies that are embracing the opportunity are winning. Moreover, as we saw earlier, there are now great books that hold the keys to reaching the various ethnic groups. The secret is to blend understanding, research and an open mind to find the path to reach the female target with the right insight, the right message, the right media.

The research we have conducted has led us to discover techniques that we now use when crafting our messages. I'd like to share a few of them now to help other advertisers succeed in reaching women. These Six Guidelines are paths and suggestions that we have found successful.

1. Don't insult women

This may seem obvious. But a lot of the advertising created by men can often be oblivious to the subtle insults and put-downs that women perceive. In an effort to be 'funny' women may be the butt of a joke or insulted in some manner. A famous comedian once said, 'Seventy-five per cent of all humour, of all jokes, succeed because someone is a victim.'

Women don't like to see innocent people hurt or ridiculed, especially other women. A recent Volkswagen television commercial shows a young man and a young woman riding along with the windows down. The young lady keeps explaining to the man, 'The wind is ruining my hair.' His response: 'I can't hear the engine with all your yakking.' When we tested this commercial with a variety of women, there was a close on 100 per cent negative reaction to that comment. One wrong word, one false note, and you're spending a lot of time, effort and money turning off the very people you're trying to reach.

2. Look for 'we' not 'me'

As the protectors of family and friends, women can be selfless and seek what is best, right or good for others. It's why mom takes the smallest piece of cake, is willing to go toe-to-toe with anyone bullying her children and is primarily concerned about the safety of her family.

Knowing this, you can win her by showing a picture of a world that she would like to live in . . . even when she's not in the picture: a shot of a young boy or girl looking up at the mom who is off camera; a tender moment of children with dad; a grandmother teaching a granddaughter how to bake cookies. So, creating situations involving a mother who cares about her family, and she will care about you.

3. Be sincere

Women have a 'BS' meter that can sense a lie a mile away. How often have you heard a woman say about a certain other man or woman, 'I don't know . . . there's just something there I'm not sure of.' They read eyes, smiles, posture, body language. Those same antennae are always out when you're preaching your message.

How can you expect any woman to feel deeply about your product or service if you're stretching credibility? Are your claims believable? I don't mean true . . . I mean believable. Maybe your detergent does remove all grease stains, works in cold or hot water, and actually makes the colours more vibrant than before you washed them, and even eliminates the wrinkles. If it sounds too good to be true (even if it is true) stay within the lines of believability. You may want all the glory for being the creator of a flashy advertisement but why not settle for a sale?

You need to check whether the people creating your advertising have a deep, honest passion for your brand, or whether some of your advertising is conveying the fact that you are the sparky copywriter at the ad agency and these clever words are your way of showing that you don't really understand the product or the consumer and you're proud of that. Rather than that, you want to craft your message so that the consumer hears the voice and soul of your brand.

4. Real, not ideal

Gorgeous, flawless, air-brushed models. Children with perfect smiles and no hair out of place. Dad on the beach with six pack abs and a smile so white you need sunglasses. The sister at the door with the Coco Chanel coat.

That's not her world.

We tested two ads for a cabinet company to see which kitchen women preferred. One ad showed the old white painted cabinets in a kitchen setting. The other showed the really cool, new cherry wood cabinets in a modern kitchen setting. We did not understand the women's feedback showing that the ad with the old cabinets was much preferred over the new ones until we read the women's comments showing that the older kitchen was preferred because it gave the impression that someone really lived there. We examined the ads and, lo and behold, there was an old gym bag on the chair in the one ad versus the perfect, pristine kitchen. Lesson learned.

Another lesson: never, just use testing for a score. Use it to learn. We pour over the verbatim feedback that we receive in order to glean the real nuggets such as the 'gym bag' example.

5. Tell a story

Women love stories. In the past it was all about performance – how well people performed with the product. However, Barletta drew our attention to the fact that interest in product performance is something that can be conveyed in different ways to audiences of men and women. If you take a ski product, *he* may be interested in who goes down the hill the fastest while *she* may want to know about the participants. Did 'Anna' suffer from polio when she was growing up in that small Swiss village and did she train endlessly for the chance of representing her country? They will watch, cheer and cry even if Anna comes in last. Why? Because they feel they know her because you told them a story.

In fact, we tested reactions to the Google TV spot that told the story about the man who woos the French girl, moves there, marries her and then poses a final question to Google: 'How to build a crib?' When we tested this spot, we found that women, and many men, were actually moved to tears and said how much they loved the brand.

6. Incorporate humanity

Studies have been conducted comparing the reactions of infant boys and girls to people as against things. A study by Professor Simon Baron-Cohen and his colleagues at Cambridge University exposed one-day-old newborn babies to two stimuli – the face of a woman and a rounded mobile. The results showed that the girls looked for longer at the face and the boys at the mobile (Connellan et al., 2001).

As Gloria Moss shows (2009, p. 89), the female bias towards the personal shows up in other experiments too. In one, a group of boys and girls were invited to look through a pair of binoculars which showed in the left and right eyes two different images at the same time, one of an object and the other of a person. The children were shown exactly the same images but when asked what they had seen, the boys reported seeing significantly more things than people, and the girls more people than things (Moir and Jessel, 1989). One possible explanation is that women are more focused on people than men are, and if you compare magazines aimed at men and women, the covers of those targeting men are dominated by gadgets and 'things' while those aimed at women are dominated by people and headlines advertising stories about relationships.

We created some print ads to test this. One was for a car company, one for a manufacturer of ice cream and one for a snack biscuit, with a common denominator being that people were absent from all of them – there were not even hands, or shadows, or even distant shots of people. So, we changed the advertisements in just one way: we added humanity and then we ran the tests a second time with women. The new set of ads were preferred by around three to one. We also tested these ads with male art directors and found that they preferred the ads with no people.

So, if you're a chief marketing officer, what do you do with this information?

You may want to start with a frank discussion with the heads of your advertising agency. You need to make sure the creative directors, art directors, Internet creatives, as well as social and rich media mavens, know that you want new thinking in crafting your messages. You may want to provide a list of the many books (quite a few of them I've mentioned in this chapter) that can help them understand how to modify their thinking when targeting women.

A final thought:

There is one memorable scene in the animated movie, *Finding Nemo*. Nemo is confronting the huge shark who confesses that it has taken a lot of effort not to just bully his way through the ocean and eat the fish, because 'Fish are our friends.'

Is it possible for the male-dominated world of creative departments to craft advertising that will succeed in connecting with a female audience? I believe it is but that it takes an open mind, an honest effort and a lot of support throughout the agency.

Just like that shark, I'm asking the other males in the creative community to change their bullying ways in the halls of advertising agencies.

This world is for men and women, and advertising is there to increase a firm's profitability. Let's change it. Let's embrace true diversity and all profit from it.

References

Barletta, M. (2006), *Marketing to Women: How to Increase Your Share of the World's Largest Market*, Dearborn Publishing.

Buchanan, H. (2007), *The Soccer Mom Myth*, Wizard Academy Press.

Connellan, J., Baron-Cohen, S., Wheelwright, S., Batki, A. and Ahluwalia, J. (2001), 'Sex differences in human neonatal social perception', *Infant Behavior and Development*, 23, 113–118.

Farris, K. (2005), *Motivated Reasoning and Social Basis*, University of Texas at Austin.

Greenfield Online for Arnold's Women's Insight Team (2002), *Adweek*, 27 May, 2002, p. 2.

Hyun, J. (2005), *Breaking the Bamboo Ceiling: Career Strategies for Asians*, Collins.

Jordan, T. (2009), *Re-render the Gender*, Booksurge.

Miller, P. and Kemp, H. (2005), *What's Black About It? Insights to Increase Your Share of a Changing African-American Market*, Paramount Market Publishing, Inc.

Moir, A. and Jessel, D. (1989), *Brainsex*, Great Britain: Mandarin.

Moss, G. (2009), *Gender, Design and Marketing*, Farnham: Gower.

Muley, M. (2009), *The 85% Niche: The Power of Women of All Colors – Latina, Black and Asian*, Paramount: Market Publishing Inc.

Soto, T. (2006), *Marketing to Hispanics: A Strategic Approach to Assessing and Planning Your Initiative*, Kaplan Publishing.

Stevens, A. (2007), *SheSelling: the Psychology of Selling to Women*, Splash Publishing.

Tavris, C. and Aronson, E. (2007), *Mistakes were Made. But not by Me*, Harcourt, Inc.

Yankelovich Monitor Multicultural Marketing Study (2005), accessed on 20 November 2011: http://buzzologysurveys.blogspot.com/2007/09/yankelovichs-20072008-monitor.html.

8
Professional Services Firms and Gender Diversity

Gloria Moss

Research into diversity in organisations has focused on exploring how workforce diversity influences organisational life (Jehn et al., 1999) and the barriers diverse individuals can face within organisations (Kanter, 1977; O'Neill et al., 1999; Thomas and Gabarro, 1999; Moss, 2007, 2009). This emphasis has left a gap in organisational scholarship, with little information available about the processes and practices that foster greater diversity (Akinola and Thomas, 2008), and a gap too in terms of the hoped-for benefits. This is true of the legal, IT, accountancy, management consultancy, and design and marketing areas, and this chapter makes a start in filling these gaps by reporting on indicative interviews with a sample of senior managers in the legal, IT, design, accountancy and professional recruitment. These views can be balanced against the academic and practitioner literatures on the general benefits of and obstacles to diversity in this sector.

1 Professional services firms

Professional services firms are knowledge intensive firms (KIFs) and the long-term success of KIFs is contingent on two objectives serving the goal of achieving financial success, these being to 'deliver outstanding client service' and 'to provide fulfilling careers and professional satisfaction [to employees]' (Maister, 1997, p. 3). These two objectives imply the need to 'satisfy the demands of the client marketplace' and 'the people marketplace for staff' (ibid., p. 3), and satisfying these two primary objectives, according to Maister (1997), turns on making appropriate strategic choices. As he says, 'professional service firms compete in two marketplaces: they compete for clients and they compete for staff' (p. 189). In his view, these elements are integral to competitive strategy and their strategic importance warrants a more detailed focus in the next two sections:

1.1 The client market

Maister, the author of a classic text on managing the professional services firm written in 1997, wrote that '... a primary means of achieving a competitive advantage is to have a better understanding of the wants and needs of clients than does the competition' (p. 61). He then expresses the view that according to the supply chain management literature, achieving prominence involves the simultaneous production and consumption of services (Sampson, 2000) and that the professional services provider is as much in the business of managing the client's experience with respect to professional services as in the business of executing technical tasks (ibid., p. 71). Moreover, pointing out that the way a professional deals with a client 'is an essential determinant of the client's judgement of the value received' (ibid., p. 81), he concludes that not only is 'power in all professions moving from the professional to the client' but that the professional firm must increasingly demonstrate a willingness to be 'cooperative, responsive and adaptable in order to win the confidence of today's client' (ibid., p. 74).

1.2 The people market for staff

The strategic view of the client resource matches the strategic view of the employee resource, with Maister predicting that 'in the next decade and beyond, the ability to attract, develop, retain and deploy staff will be the single biggest determinant of a professional services firm's competitive success' (1997, p. 189). He makes the point that 'if you have paid a lot for a resource, and invested a lot in its training, the last thing you want is for that resource to disappear. Retention will become a major strategic issue' (ibid., p. 198). According to Maister, the achievement of partner status is the goal to which employees aspire: 'To be accepted into the partnership represents an anointing and admission into the ranks of the full professional. To be denied partnership is to be condemned to second-class status' (ibid., p. 186).

Since the ultimate goal of those in professional services firms will be the attainment of equity partner status we can see that, in terms of positioning in relation to the concept of 'Total Rewards' (one that recognises that there are financial as well as non-financial motivators as shown in Figure 8.1), the emphasis within professional services firms is

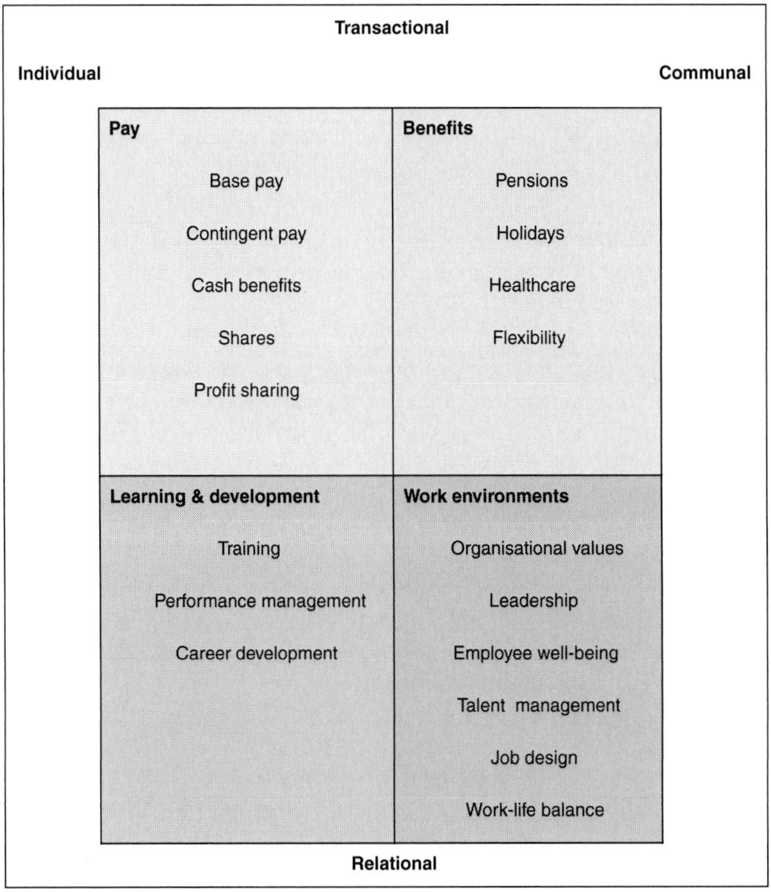

Figure 8.1 Total rewards model

still largely on payment-based rewards, with rewards focused on pay and ultimately profit-sharing goals (top left-hand quadrant of Figure 8.1).

So, how easy is it for employees to achieve partner status? In terms of career structures, the majority of professional services firms utilise flat/hierarchical structures with a high ratio of junior to senior professionals. The skill development and career progression for junior professionals revolves in large part around the degree to which they are invested in by senior professionals who serve as mentors and coaches, creating the conditions that can guide high rates of skill development, motivation, and commitment from junior professionals (Akinola and Thomas, 2008).

The impediments consist of time constraints on senior profession-als for whom the need to balance revenue-generating, client-building activities with these mentoring and coaching activities for junior pro-fessionals, can create a disincentive to invest in junior professionals (Wilkins and Gulati, 1996; Akinola and Thomas, 2008). The conflict-ing priorities facing senior professionals can lead them to selectively offer coaching and mentoring, confining their attention to those 'stars' thought to have the highest future value to the firm (Lorsch and Tierney, 2002). How easy in fact is it for them to identify staff with potential?

A fascinating study (Kumra and Vinnicombe, 2008) investigated the perception of the promotion process within a management consultancy, concluding that there was sex bias in the promotion to partner decision-making process. Two areas of potential disadvantage for females were identified as the self-managed nature of the career advancement pro-cess and a prevailing success model within the firm that is moulded on predominantly male behaviours. As the authors write:

> Characteristics of this 'type' were individuals with 'gravitas', good technical expertise and skills, those who were overtly ambitious, good team players and who worked well with clients. Physical presence was also seen as being important (p. S70).

It is apparent from this study that professional services firms are not as gender-neutral as they might imagine themselves to be and uncon-scious bias can pose a hidden barrier to the promotion of women in the firm. As a result, a firm's ability to achieve its objectives in terms of resourcing and retaining staff for competitive advantage can be severely compromised.

Given the importance of the client and employee base for competitive advantage in professional services firms, we will now look at what we know of obstacles to the achievement of a diverse workforce.

2   Obstacles

According to Akinola and Thomas (2008), research on workforce diver-sity has highlighted the obstacles faced by minorities in organisations as including a lack of mentors and role models (Ragins and Cotton, 1996; Thomas and Gabarro, 1999), exclusion from informal networks of communication (Kanter, 1977; Ibarra, 1993; Giscombe and Mattis, 2002), stereotyping and preconceptions of roles and abilities (Waters,

1992; Bertrand and Mullainathan, 2004), and lack of significant line experience, visible and/or challenging assignments (Hurley et al., 1997). These barriers can hinder career progression and prevent organisations from moving forward in their efforts to maintain a diverse workforce. We can add to these barriers those posed by criteria or processes that favour one group over another (Moss and Daunton, 2006; Kumra and Vinnicombe, 2008; Moss, 2009), leading to the development of unconscious bias against groups who do not exemplify these characteristics and in favour of groups who do. This finding makes the concept of 'merit' a more complex one than commonly assumed, since the concept of 'best' is not absolute but relative to the criteria of appointment selected. We can also add to the obstacles cultures, structural arrangements and embedded organisational routines that can blunt diversity-oriented transformations (David, 2010).

3 Achieving diversity within professional services firms

It has been said that single-threaded diversity solutions, such as reliance on recruitment or single-approach management techniques, for example those requiring every employee to take diversity training, do not create lasting change or sustainable advantage (David, 2010, p. 24). By contrast, Wheeler's model of change (1998), focuses on four levels at which change can be achieved, from the process of creating and developing diversity through to leveraging diversity for competitive advantage. The ultimate goal is to reach a stage in the organisational diversity process where leveraging diversity for competitive advantage is achieved (David, 2010, p. 36). The first level in Wheeler's model is that of 'creating' (includes creating a diverse workforce and structure); the second level is that of 'managing' (includes attraction/retention of staff; open closed/governance models); the third level is that of 'valuing' (includes a move from compliance to internalisation and integration); and the fourth level is 'leveraging' (drawing on the strategic resources and capabilities of the organisation).

According to Akinola and Thomas (2008), the barriers to achieving a fully diverse workforce can only be overcome with structural, cultural and behavioural changes, with structural change focused on change within the formal systems that guide and control the work of the organisation (Holvino et al., 2004). A focus on organisational culture would also be needed, with special attention given to the values, beliefs and ideologies of the organisation, particularly as they relate to informal norms or mental models (Senge et al., 1999; Trefry, 2006). Behavioural change refers to the behaviours, attitudes and perceptions within and between individuals and workgroups that support or hinder the goals of diversity, and Ely and Meyerson (2000) focus on challenges to existing power relations and the dismantling of practices that have long been institutionalised.

The areas within which attitude and behavioural change might be needed could relate to a spectrum of factors, from management paradigms to organisational models. The former point could include attitudes to optimal styles of leadership with evidence pointing, overall, to a male and female preference for transactional as against transformational leadership respectively (Moss and Daunton, 2006). Attitudes to flexible working may also be segmented by gender since evidence shows that 80 per cent of women compared with 17 per cent of men are responsible for looking after the children or arranging childcare facilities (Barclays, 2000) and that childcare can be both difficult to find – there is a severe shortage of registered childcare places with only enough childcare places for 25 per cent of children aged under eight (Daycare Trust, January 2005) – and expensive, since a full-time nursery place for a child under two typically costs over £7000 per year (ibid.). With the pressures of childcare acting primarily on women, the need for flexible working is likely to be felt more sharply by women than by men.

Against this backdrop, we can now examine the position of men and women within the legal, accountancy, design, management consultancy and software sectors.

4 Legal sector

Research carried out by the Law Society and the InterLaw Forum (*The Lawyer*, 2010) reported on the presence of women and ethnic minorities in UK law firms. This research highlights the proportion of partners and equity partners in the top 30 UK firms, and this is important since equity partnership brings significant rewards – more then £1 million a year at a UK 'magic circle' firm (it should be said that in return, the demands are onerous with an 80-hour week not uncommon as well as frequent travel and constant demands from clients). The report in *The Lawyer* also reports on initiatives to widen opportunities and this information, taken with other information currently available, is summarised using Wheeler's change model (Table 8.2), with the name of the firm(s) operating a particular initiative shown in brackets.

According to the senior partner at Allen and Overy (one of the top ten firms of UK solicitors) this data does not necessarily provide insight into the depth or impact of these initiatives and this point is corroborated by a corporate partner at Simmons and Simmons, Daniel Winterfeldt, who states that 'Our studies show that there's a lot of window dressing in the legal profession, but little cultural change' (*The Lawyer*, 2010). The problems posed in the culture are emphasised in research by Spurr, both singly and in conjunction with Sueyoshi (1990 and 1993 respectively), examining men and women's promotion experiences in legal firms. In a detailed study of the promotion process within large law firms Spurr (1990) found substantial differences between the employment and promotion experiences of male and female lawyers with women half as likely as men to be promoted to partner positions. This is despite the fact that he found no significant differences in quality between male and female lawyers as measured by quality of school attended or achievement of academic distinction in law school. Spurr concluded that his findings were strongly suggestive of discrimination (Kumra and Vinnicombe, 2008).

Interestingly, Spurr raised the possibility that while male and female lawyers may be equal in ability, female lawyers may exert less effort in competition for partnership; 'indeed, the incentive of women might be weakened by the lower likelihood of promotion' (Spurr, 1990, p. 409). In a later study, Spurr and Sueyoshi (1993) found that there was still a sex difference in likely promotion to partner in law firms (though diminished) but that a factor in this might be discrimination in the promotion to partner decision-making process.

In 2010, the percentage of women who were partners and equity partners of top ten firms in the UK (ranked by turnover) were as follows (*The Lawyer*, 2010):

Table 8.1 Percentage of female partners and equity partners, in 2010

Top ten firms by turnover	Ranked by female percentage of all partners	Female percentage of equity partners
Eversheds	22	15
Slaughter and May	19	19
Lovells (legacy)	18	17
Ashurst	17	15
Norton Rose	17	15
Allen and Overy (A&O)	15	13
Herbert Smith	15	10
Clifford Chance	14	11
Linklaters	14	13
Freshfields	11	11

Source: *The Lawyer* (2010).

Table 8.2 Initiatives pursued in the top 30 law firms in the UK to widen partnership opportunities for women (initiatives that appear not to be currently undertaken are indicated in the boxes within quadrants 3 and 4)

2. MANAGING (attraction /retention of staff; open/closed/governance models)	3. VALUING (move from compliance to internalisation and integration)
Pre-employment *Bursary scheme* (Bird and Bird) *Work placements for BME students* (A&O; Freshfields) **Management of diversity** *Diversity committee* (many e.g., Ashhurst, DLA Piper, Norton Rose and Withers) *Monitoring diversity* (e.g., A&O; Nabarro; Norton Rose; Addleshaws + 57 per cent of signatories to the Diversity Inclusion Charter) **Management systems** *Mentoring* (Freshfields and passim) *Performance reviews – diversity targets for partners or counsel* (Bristows) **Reward systems** *Reward systems,* e.g., not exclusive reliance on billable hours targets (Bristows; Haynes and Boon in the US) which includes *rewards for leadership and business development activities*	*Affinity networks* (Herbert Smith; Ashhurst) *No presenteeism* (Bristows) Pilot project on flexible working (Freshfields); p/t working (A&O; Beachcroft; Herbert Smith; Norton Rose; Withers) *Facilities for religious observance* *Training in Diversity (SJ) or unconscious bias for partners* (Simmons and Simmons; Norton Rose; Freshfields) **Initiatives not apparently currently undertaken:** (a) Research on cognitive and behavioural diversity in promotion criteria, work and communication styles, values, attitudes and expectations; (b) Examination of the culture of organisation; (c) The potential for better work-life balance; (d) The potential for greater use of Total Rewards (see Figure 8.1)
1. CREATING (creating a diverse workforce and structure)	**4. LEVERAGING** (drawing on the strategic resources and capabilities of the organisation)
Recruitment *Casting the net wide at recruitment* (Trowers and Hamlin) *Objective interview process* (Trowers and Hamlin) *Balanced representation on the recruitment panel* **Targets** *Targets for numbers of women and target dates* (Addleshaw Goddard) **Working structures** *Part-time working* (A &O) *Home working* (Addleshaw Goddard; Trowers and Hamlin; Pinsent Masons Leeds); *job sharing* (Trowers and Hamlin)	**Measurement of the following not currently undertaken:** (a) Workplace climate (b) Financial impact (e.g. reduced recruitment, turnover and training costs) (c) Diversity mindset within the senior management team (d) Learning and growth Extent of NPD; improved understanding of customer needs and improved customer loyalty

Source: Wheeler (1998); The Lawyer (2010)

On average, women achieve partnership one year earlier than men at 38.9 years old but they also tend to resign from their respective partnerships 2.3 years before the males, meaning that they spend on average 5.9 years at the same firm compared with 8.2 years for men. They also leave at a younger age on average, with most women leaving their original firm by the time they are 44 and men at 48. This has an impact on the fee-earning capability of the departing partners when they arrive at their new firms, as it takes some time for them to build up to peak performance (McLeod-Thomas, 2010a).

In terms of some of the initiatives listed in Table 8.2, the act of setting targets and target dates for the proportion of female partners was initiated for the first time in a major firm in the UK in November 2010 (McLeod-Thomas, 2010b). Moreover, a woman's network was established for the first time in London firm Clifford Chance in 2008 (Smith, 2008). A journalist commenting on this wrote:

Law firms to date are some way behind other professions at encouraging diversity. The accounting firms, for one, have had women's networks for years. Aurora (2008)

In the US, 25 per cent of the partnership at solicitors Haynes and Boone is female and one initiative that is thought to have had a positive impact on women's integration has been a compensation system that rewards people for teamwork, not individual accomplishments, 'staving off the dog-eat-dog competition for clients and assignments that pervades many firms' (O'Brien, 2006). Compensation is also said to be based on a number of other factors, including leadership and business development activities, among which billable hours are just one component (ibid.).

A view from the inside: Allen and Overy

In-depth interviews held separately with the senior partner and global HR director of Allen and Overy revealed the strength of the case for increasing the proportion of women at partner level, but also the obstacles. This firm, with a £1bn revenue and 60 per cent of revenues deriving from outside the UK (from 76 offices in 26 countries) and only 40 per cent of its partner base in its London office, has an international profile which puts it in the top three or four global law firms. Its partners' average salary is £1m plus.

The business case. The firm perceives three main sources of competitive advantage for increasing women's representation at partner level. The first relates to the fear of losing its talent. In the words of the senior partner: 'We are a people business and so the future success of the firm stands or falls on the quality of the partnership and you've got to search high and low to find the people who can grow the business and attract clients. It is statistically obvious that the bigger the pool, the higher the quality of the people you are going to get. Today, 62 per cent of law school graduates are women and if women leave the firm, you are losing a lot of your future partners.'

Another argument relates to the better performance perceived to derive from a better balance of men and women in the workforce. As the senior partner at Allen and Overy says, 'Research shows that this brings with it a better performance and I've seen it myself. It is good for productivity, imagination, ideas, innovation and progress.' This view is echoed by the global head of HR there when she says that 'difference can make for strength' and speaks of 'technicolour thinking'. She describes the importance of a mix as 'the most compelling business case' and draws an analogy with the structure of a building. 'You don't create strength by everything running parallel – you need intersections – points at which things cross over one another.'

Another business advantage for increasing women's presence at partner level, according to the senior partner, is that women's choice of firm will be based on where they are 'likely to do best'. So, a healthy proportion of women at partner level will attract more applicants to the firm.

Obstacles. In terms of the difficulties of achieving change, the senior partner described the political job needed to persuade partners of the necessity for change. 'You can't have fundamental change without the agreement of the partners and nothing changes unless the partners want it to change.' He goes on to explain that, as a constituency, this is not a unified group:

'A lot of the men in this group are not engaging in the debate because they fear they might be accused of being chauvinist – the debate tends to be dominated by extremists on both sides and many men are reluctant to engage in the debate. In fact, our audience tends to divide into three groups: about 40 per cent simply ask what the problem is since recruitment and promotion procedures are completely gender neutral and there are no obvious biases against women. They assume that women must not be committed enough even though they won't say this publicly. On the other hand there is another perhaps 30 per cent of the male partners who have personal experience of the difficulties women have in progressing their career and so are more sympathetic to the hidden issues affecting how women progress and the fact that the world of business is configured to suit men and doesn't always suit women. Then there is a group in the middle, representing perhaps 30 per cent of the partners, who have not spent a great deal of time thinking about the issue, its causes or the impact and they could go either way.'

Moreover, he confirms that opinion varies on a country by country basis: 'At one end of the spectrum, in China, it is perfectly accepted that women will occupy senior roles in business and politics. In Germany and Switzerland, however, a more conservative position is found, and the UK and the US occupy a place somewhere in the middle. In a global law firm like our own, you have to accommodate differences in culture around the world, and in the end, you're playing three-dimensional chess to get anything changed.'

The global HR director at Allen and Overy speaks of other difficulties. 'One of the challenges is that this subject risks being perceived as "political correctness" when it is actually about competitive strength. The other difficulty is actually facilitating a healthy debate. If you focus solely on women, men can feel excluded and concerned that they might not get equal treatment.' She recalls the time that she organised a women-only reception at a global partner event in 2008. 'We had nearly 100 per cent attendance and the room was buzzing. We had identified the retention of female talent as a key strategic priority and knew that we were losing too many of our best female associates so wanted to try to understand why. To kick start the debate I thought it was a good idea to start with the group most likely to have experienced some of the issues firsthand – namely our female partners.'

However, not everyone saw it that way. On rejoining the event, one male partner expressed his anger at being excluded and another spoke of 'how inappropriate it was to organise a woman's only function'. The global HR director commented that it struck her that this was possibly the first time the male partners had felt excluded or treated less favourably on the grounds of gender. They were experiencing what it felt like not to be invited to join a group, which is something many woman have experienced during their careers.

The other big challenge was trying to effect a shift against a backdrop of a partnership comprised of over 80 per cent men. As she said, it is very natural for people to feel more comfortable with that which is familiar to them – whether that be gender, background or beliefs. So, when you're trying to effect change in terms of number of female partners for example, you have to raise consciousness and make sure everyone is alert to the possibility of bias and take steps to ensure it doesn't impact decisions. As you can see, it's a very complex issue which plays out on a number of different levels.

The complexity of the issue is one reason why the firm is undertaking studies to better understand the obstacles. From her own experience, she expects that many of the issues will revolve around the problems of juggling work and parenthood. 'My working life has been made much more complicated by the fact that I am a mother... the logistics of combining motherhood and work are a constant challenge.' She also recollects times when she has been outside 'the majority group'. As she goes on to say:

'I have often found myself as the only woman, or one of a minority of women, in a meeting. You become aware, as certain conversations develop, that you see things from a different perspective, one that might not be immediately apparent or understood by others. However, it could be that it is critically important to the debate. You therefore have to think about how to get your view across such that it can be understood and given sufficient consideration. She goes on to say: 'With so much organisational history being dominated by men in leadership roles, the unwritten rules of the game are often inherently masculine in character. I have seen men confused by certain female behaviours, finding them difficult to understand, so important points of view can get lost or misunderstood. With a greater mix round the table I think the debate is much richer which ultimately can only lead to a better outcome.

Solutions The solutions? According to the senior partner, a lot of firms delegate down to diversity committees and 'nothing happens'. For this reason, he says that 'we don't have a diversity committee and we don't want one…I don't want talking shops and lip service.' The firm did, however, introduce a scheme to allow partners to apply to work a four-day week for a maximum period of eight years. 'The average age at which women are made partner is 35 and five years before and after are typical times when women are thinking about having a family – so without an offer of flexible working, a lot of women will look at a firm and say "I'm not going to enter that race". So, we introduced our system of part-time working for partners in January 2010. No other law firm has got as far as Allen and Overy has. We are the first major law firm to do something as structurally significant as this and we've made it available for men and women so that women are not stigmatised by it."

A view from the inside: another top ten law firm

An in-depth interview with the recently appointed head of diversity of another top ten UK firm of solicitors revealed twin factors prompting the call for greater diversity. Firstly, there was an internal drive, fuelled by private sector clients, for greater diversity within the firms they did business with. In fact, supplier diversity was a key driver of diversity initiatives for many organisations. Secondly, there was an internal drive from the law firm itself to hire the best talent and to explore a range of different profiles and backgrounds to match and mirror the backgrounds of clients.

How does the firm factor in diversity? The head of diversity said: 'We don't want a homogeneous workforce and we pride ourselves on having a relaxed culture. You see, it has become increasingly important to open up access to the industry. Firstly, we don't want identikits – largely because we are after the best talent and also because of the nature of our global business. Secondly, our clients are from different social backgrounds and it helps our business if we can mirror the client base. For example, in-house legal counsel often tend to be female so there's a business case for employing lawyers in our firm who can mirror this demographic. Some practice areas are more diverse than others. Property and employment law are areas with a relatively high proportion of women while corporate law has a lower proportion. This is transactional law with longer hours and the combination makes it less attractive to women who want to start a family and don't want to work ridiculous hours.' The cultures within the different practice areas are different. In property, there are more female role models and the flexible working culture is better, both of which will attract more women into the area. Corporate law makes bigger personal demands on lawyers' time. The nature of the role impacts the culture and how attractive the area is to women.

Many male partners with children and a wife working full or part time, will want to leave work at sensible times at least a few times a week in order to see them. Often the partners who struggle with requests for flexible working are those with wives or partners who are not working, showing how influential personal lifestyle is on how others are viewed in similar circumstances.

5   Discussion

It can be seen that law firms are taking steps to improve the proportion of women partners although, as Table 8.1 shows, the percentage of women equity partners among the top ten UK firms by turnover is still under 20 per cent, ranging between 11 and 19 per cent. In terms of types of reward, high reliance is placed on financial rewards (the 'pay' category in the Total Rewards model in Figure 8.1) and less on factors in the 'work environment' such as organisational values, the quality of leadership in the firm, employee well-being, talent management, job design and work–life balance. It is conceivable that if more were done on these elements, the masculine cultures found in many law firms would start to change.

Just as rewards are focused on one part of the Total Rewards model, so too are efforts to increase diversity concentrated in the first two quadrants of Wheeler's model of change ('creating' and 'managing') with relatively few initiatives relating to the more culturally intrusive approaches to change found in the 'valuing' and 'leveraging' quadrants. The views offered by the senior partner and global HR director at Allen and Unwin highlight the political difficulties in achieving change where a large partnership body needs to be convinced, and the head of diversity's view, at the second law firm, that a major determinant of a partner's attitude is whether a partner's spouse is working or not may explain why it is difficult to move efforts up a notch by progressing to 'leveraging' and 'valuing' initiatives. Were it possible to provide a greater focus on these areas, it would be easier to achieve attitude and culture change, creating an environment which is better adapted to the needs of women with families.

Those initiatives that might fall into the 'valuing' category include:

- Research examining the cognitive and behavioural criteria underpinning promotion to partner level. This research could seek the views of associates as to the promotion criteria operating in a firm (the methodology used in Kumara and Vinnicombe's 2008 work on partnership promotion criteria in management consultancy) with a study of the leadership constructs used by recruiters in the selection process (the methodology used in Moss and Daunton's 2006 study). Doing this would make it possible to compare the success criteria assumed by associates with those actually used by recruiters.
- Examination of the organisational culture of the law firm.
- A study of the potential for better work–life balance.
- Consideration as to the potential for greater use of 'total rewards' attention moves away from a single focus' on pay, one of four motivational categories in the Total reward model (see Figure 8.1).

In a further step, attention could focus on moves to assist law firms to leverage the benefits of a diverse workforce. These initiatives could include regular measurement of the following elements:

- Workplace climate.
- Financial impact (e.g., reduced recruitment, turnover and training costs).
- Diversity mindset within the senior management team.
- Improved understanding of customer needs and improved customer loyalty.

Once initiatives in quadrants three and four have taken root, one might expect to see an advancement in the proportion of women at partner level.

6 The design profession

In the UK, figures from *The Business of Design: Design Industry Research*, a UK Design Council Report in 2005, puts male designers at 61 per cent of the profession and female at 39 per cent. A more detailed picture of the gender demographics of the industry emerges from membership statistics of the Chartered Society of Designers (CSD), the professional body for designers in the UK. The proportion of male and female members for 2006, by design discipline, is shown in Table 8.3. A quick glance

Table 8.3   The proportion of men and women members (and by grade of membership, and whether as 'Member' or a 'Fellow') of the Chartered Society of Designers, 2006 (Moss, 2009)

Discipline	Males (%)	Females (%)
Design management		
Member	86	14
Fellow	84	16
Design education		
Member	86	14
Fellow	70	30
Product design		
Graduate members		34
Member	92	8
Fellow	92	8
Graphic design		
Graduate members	44	56
Member	79	21
Fellow	88	12
Fashion and textile		
Graduate members	25	75
Member	30	70
Fellow	53	47
Interiors		
Graduate members	30	70
Member	30	25
Fellow	75	12

shows men outnumbering women in all the design disciplines with the exception of fashion and textiles, with the proportion of female members decreasing with seniority. Overall, 9 per cent of fellows are women, 18 per cent of members and 40 per cent of graduates. The absence of women is particularly acute in product design (a discipline classed as covering furniture, ceramics, jewellery, automotive, glass and industrial products) where women constitute a meagre 8 per cent of members at all levels (Moss, 2009).

The CSD does not keep data on the relationship of membership grade to job seniority, but one might reasonably expect membership seniority to correlate with professional status. So, following this logic, one might assume from the CSD's figures that the vast majority of middle and senior ranks of design managers, design educators and product designers in the UK are male. It is only in the case of fashion and textile design (and then only at member and graduate level) that female members outnumber males. At the highest level of fellow, even in this otherwise female-dominated field, men outnumber women. A tentative conclusion, therefore, might be that the design profession is one in which small proportions of women move up the ranks (ibid.).

We should note that the declining position of female designers in institutional life contrasts with the position of boys and girls at school leaving stage. In 1996, an analysis of art and design examinations showed that the majority of candidates at both GCSE and particularly 'A' level were girls (Moss, 1996), and also showed that the majority of those achieving 'A' grades were also girls. Ten years on, the situation at this stage remains largely unchanged, since the 2006 report (Women and Work Commission, 2006) refers to 'A' level Art and Design as a subject favoured by female candidates. Not surprisingly, the majority of design students at tertiary level are then female (60 per cent), but the question poses itself as to why the surplus of women over men at this level – equivalent to the demographics we saw in the legal sector – falls away in the senior reaches of professional life.

One contributory factor may be the shortage of part-time opportunities available for women, who see part-time work as a way of combining childcare with work. As we saw earlier, women have the primary responsibility for childcare in the UK (Barclays, 2000), and the shortage and cost of full-time childcare, together with the lack of part-time working opportunities for women in the design sector (Moss, 2009), may force women into self-employment and freelance work. The Design Council Report, *The Business of Design: Design Industry Research* (2005), showed that as many as 40 per cent of designers are self-employed and since, according to Christina Martinez-Tsyrklevich of the Chartered Society of Design and Design Association, the lack of full-time or part-time opportunities are the major prompts for women working on a freelance basis (Moss, 2009), and since the evidence is that women build smaller businesses than men (Global Entrepreneurship Monitor, 2004, p. 28), women's relative inability to climb the career ladder may be related to the difficulties design firms have in delivering options for part-time working.

A further contributory factor may be the impact (albeit unconscious) of gender on production and preference aesthetics, since it has been shown gender can leave its mark both on what is created (the 'production' element) and also on how people respond to that (the 'preference' element). Extensive research has revealed the strong tendency (again unconscious) for men and women to greatly prefer designs produced by people of their own gender and this applies to graphic, product and web design. Presumably, the men and women are picking up on the significant differences that have emerged in terms of the type of designs produced, with the elements distinguishing the male and female work principally those of colour, shape, detailing, dimensionality and type of thematic material used (Moss, 2009; Moss and Gunn, 2009).

The tendency for men to unconsciously prefer designs produced by other men could lead male recruiters to judge women's work to be of lesser value compared to equivalent men's work. So, if the senior people in design responsible for recruitment decisions are, for the most part, men, then one could expect them to rate the male candidates' work more highly than the females'. In fact, there are no surprises here. Peter Souter, creative director of advertising and brand agency AMV, and former president of the British Design and Art Direction Association (D&AD), has said that the male domination of these creative industries rests on the fact that 'people are slightly guilty of hiring themselves' (Moss, 2007). This is tantamount to acknowledging the all-pervasive impact of what is known as the 'homogeneity principle' – the tendency for people to like to associate with others like themselves.

Souter's own reaction is to impute negative consequences to this in the advertising and design industries, describing this as a 'lamentable state of affairs'. He points to statistics showing that '75 per cent of all purchase decisions are made by women' and concludes from this that the demographics do not make sense 'if you believe that the person *writing* the ad should know as much as possible about the person receiving it'. He is referring here to the economic and marketing arguments for design reflecting the preferences of the end-user who, as we know, will tend to be female. We can understand, however, the tendencies at work in a male-dominated workplace that will sanction the preference of designers with work exemplifying the male production aesthetic. Unless steps are taken to stop this happening, this will continue to occur and the forces of congruity within the organisation will impede the achievement of congruity with customers outside it. Clearly, the process by which managers are selected is of enormous importance, and a way of overcoming the effect of the homogeneity principle inside an organisation needs to be found if customers are to be provided with designs that are maximally effective.

Souter is not a lone voice espousing the recruitment of people who mirror the demographics of the target market. Debbie Klein, chief executive of advertising agency WCRS, and the author of the 2000 Institute of Practitioners in Advertising report on women in advertising, supported the notion of employing more women in the creative industries on the basis that 'it would bring different ways of looking at things' (Doward, 2000).

However, while there are attractions to involving people in organisations who offer a different perspective, academics have long been aware, at a theoretical level, of the extent to which design paradigms are concentrated around the male production and preference aesthetic, and the way this can create barriers for those whose thinking may be different. Buckley (1987), for example, speaks of the fact that male designers promote a particular approach to design and that the dominance of the profession by men makes it difficult for a female approach to gain acceptance. We can see this in the fact that design is defined in terms of mass production design, the design favoured by the male sex; and craft design, the design traditionally favoured by women, is accorded secondary status. In this way, the interests of the dominant group are presented as 'universal' rather than just a reflection of the interests of the dominant group, and this leads Attfield and Kirkham (1989) to a hierarchy of design values in which industrial design and the 'machine aesthetic', areas which she describes as 'more obviously masculine', are accorded pride of place. Meanwhile, areas which are more obviously 'feminine' are ascribed lesser importance. This notion that there is a specifically male set of values has been further developed by Professor Penny Sparke, pro vice-chancellor for the arts at Kingston University and a prolific writer on design. As she writes in *As Long As It's Pink* (1995), her book on gender and design, that 'women's tastes stand outside the "true" canon of aesthetic values of the dominant culture', noting that:

> Architectural and design modernism imposed on goods and their design a stereotypically masculine aesthetic, not only because it was undertaken by men but because it was now embedded within masculine culture. (p. 10)

So, while injecting staff with a new way of thinking into an organisation may appear on the face of it to be a useful strategy, in practice it can be problematic. Aside from the demographic difficulties in finding the necessary staff (as a result, for example, of the shortages in female product and web designers), actually succeeding in hiring a new style of recruit whose demographics and values may differ from that of the majority in the organisation may be difficult. One solution, where the market is predominantly female, is of course to ensure that the majority of staff are female or at least very diverse. These are the singular cases of the two organisations showcased below, Appetite and Cherry London, successful companies with women at their helm.

A view from the inside: Appetite and Cherry London

Interviews took place with Laura Haynes, chairman of Appetite and the Design Business Association (DBA), and Tamara Gillan, managing director of Cherry London.

Appetite is a strategic communications and design agency which effects change on an internal organisational level. In order to do this, they need staff who are open-minded and can intimately understand different perspectives. So, they need staff with a high level of empathy and understanding and people who can work hard at continually learning about other people's perspectives. Cherry London is a marketing and design agency specialising in brand partnerships and has a female-dominated audience with brands such as Marie Clair and Anna Sui.

Appetite has found that the empathic skills they need can best be found in a diverse workforce, and in autumn 2010 when the interview took place, the agency employed people from their twenties to their sixties, of diverse national origins (from the US, New Zealand, France, Brazil, India, Ireland and Britain), and a mixture of men and women, with men primarily in a design role (industrial, graphic and digital design) and women in a strategic client-facing role.

In Haynes's words, 'there are natural cultural and gender characteristics that feed into the way that we interpret the world, and because our work is about understanding different perspectives it is important that we have an effective mix'. She goes on to speak of the importance of 'questioning and learning and being ever curious since this makes us do our job better', and the importance of diversity where a visual medium is involved in communications, since 'people respond to visual stimuli on a number of levels – rationally and emotionally – and there's a reaction that comes from cultural and gender programming. If you look at the creative outputs, you will see the rational and non-rational influences that create visual solutions although designers are often not remotely aware of what influences their work. Often they won't be able to articulate why they've done something and their backgrounds will create a different understanding of the use of space, line and colour. So it is important that we have an effective mix.'

Haynes also speaks of the benefits of having mixed teams: 'the results can be very effective where we have a very analytical person working with a high empathy person with a facilitator'.

She contrasts this diversity approach with that of organisations staffed by 'professionals who have received similar education and training and who share similar prejudices'. She adds that 'there are lots of professions like this'.

At Cherry London, Gillan describes how important diversity is in marketing. 'Understanding differences in consumer groups, since our starting point is the consumer and brand values, and employing people from that demographic can provide vital insights. For example, we have hired one girl straight out of school and she has an absolute understanding of the youth segment. She has brought us a fresh perspective on youth brands, how to target the youth market and how youths engage and use new channels. This experience has changed our perception about who we should be recruiting and the necessity of employing graduates. 'In the same way, we've had mums working for mums' campaigns since they have a natural affinity with the audience. If you are the target market as much as a marketer you have a headstart, and so we do assign people to jobs on this basis. This way, when you talk about something, you're talking from experience.'

Cherry London is unique also in bringing brands together for a campaign. So, the skills of building relationships between brands is a vital one and, according to Gillan, 'building, engaging and listening to the client is a much more female trait'. How is this diverse mix of staff achieved? At Appetite, the answer lies in careful recruitment, spending a lot of time with people. As Haynes says, we 'look for people with different ways of thinking'. At Cherry London, task-related interviews were introduced and this made a dramatic difference to the success of recruitment.

7   IT and software

If we turn to the information technology (IT) and computing fields, we find sectors on which there is a sizeable literature discussing the participation rates of men and women. Average participation rates for women in IT and computing fluctuated during the 1990s between 19 per cent and 22 per cent (Robertson et al., 2001) but there was an overall dominance of men at all levels and across the three fields of information systems, information technology and computer science (ibid.). The situation varied only in different parts of the world and different IT specialisms. For example, in the US, the proportion of women among computer professionals fell in the 1990s from 35.4 per cent to 29.1 per cent. While in the UK in 1994, women made up 30 per cent of computer scientists, 32 per cent of systems analysts, 35 per cent of computer programmers, 10 per cent of ISS directors, 18 per cent of project leaders and 14 per cent of applications for development managers (Baroudi and Igbaria, 1994/5).

If we are looking for trends, then clearly the proportion of women in IT is on the decline. So, while the 1980s saw an influx of women into IT, with a fourfold increase between 1980 and 1986 in the number of women awarded bachelor's degrees in computer science and a three-fold increase in the number of women with master's degrees (Igbaria and Parasuraman, 1997), recent years have seen a sharp decline in the number of women pursuing undergraduate and postgraduate degrees in computer-related fields (ibid.). Figures for the IT profession in 2002 (see Table 8.4) show the consequences of this, namely a male-dominated industry (Robertson et al., 2001).

The consequences, according to a paper by Black et al. (2005), are that in the UK:

> The number of women entering into the field of computing is very low and the percentage of women in senior management positions is behind that of other neighbouring countries such as the United States, Canada and Ireland. In the fields of software engineering, women only account for just 8% of the workforce and a report by the UK Government on women in ITEC (Information Technology, Electronics and Communication) showed that the barriers women encounter in IT-related fields is mainly responsible for the decline.

Table 8.4 Percentage of men and women in the IT profession (Equal Opportunities Commission, 2002)

Occupation	Males (%)	Females (%)
Software professionals	84	16
ICT managers	83	17
IT operations/technicians	71	29

What are these barriers? According to one paper, the skewed distribution of men and women in IT has produced a 'masculine computer culture' with a 'masculine discourse' and a prioritisation of technical issues (Robertson et al., 2001). These are thought to deter women from entering or remaining in the field (ibid.) and the authors suggest that it is only by including a 'broader set of skills and discursive practices' that a more diverse group of people can be attracted into the profession, and that the masculine nature of the culture can be altered.

Further light on the obstacles comes from an interesting Swedish study (Petersen, 2007) which examined the extent to which the IT consultant work ideal (that is, the abstract idea about the necessary competence for an IT consultant to possess and display) reflect masculine or feminine values. The study involved 31 interviews with IT consultants and managers in three Swedish IT consultant companies. At the time, many consultants were being shed from IT consultancy and the respondents were asked to differentiate between the characteristics of those who remained from the consultants and those who were laid off, in relation to having or lacking specific qualities, skills, behaviour, knowledge, experiences and education. From this, it would be possible to discern the work ideal that constituted the basis for the interviewees' distinction between valuable workers and those understood as without (or with less) value.

The comments of male and female respondents indicated that work associated with men and masculinity was interpreted not only as different from, but also better than, and with a higher status than, work associated with women and femininity. The men's work was described as being technical and the women's (as design, interface profiling and application architects) was described as 'soft'. The soft work was implied by many of the male respondents as having a lower value and status (because perceived as requiring less important competence and less technical skill) than the work typically assumed by men of developers, systems analysts and systems architects. In fact, consultants working in soft fields were laid off as a matter of course, since they were the ones understood as not valuable and not ideal workers.

Moreover, in terms of social competences, those retained were referred to as having skills involving the ability to sell, self-promote and exhibit a go-ahead attitude, with a lesser emphasis on listening and relating skills, thereby prioritising skills associated with masculinity as against femininity (Rees and Garnsey, 2003).

Some would say that it is only when an organisation perceives the strategic benefits of diversity that the strangle-hold of culture can be broken, and the next 'view from the inside', from a large, global software provider, suggests the kind of strategic thinking that can bring about change. As can be seen, the company draws great strength from its diverse salesforce since this allows the organisation to match sales staff with client demographics, something thought to increase synergystic thinking.

A view from the inside: a global software provider

The following are the views of a sales manager in the software industry working for a global software company with its headquarters in the US.

The importance of diversity in sales teams

Good selling is about getting to know your customer and understanding their business so that you can position products and services according to their business goals while helping them achieve their objectives. While many of the products I sell such as infrastructure software are standard across vertical markets (meaning that the products are not tailored towards any given industry), the method involved to sell them, and more importantly the objectives underpinning purchases, will differ from company to company and vertical to vertical.

Experienced sales executives or account managers quite often specialise in a certain enterprise space such as finance, telecommunications, utilities, public sector, manufacturing or pharmaceuticals. In the commercial space specialisation could be at a more niche level such as restaurants, garages, tradesmen or even a localised territory. So while all of the above companies have similar infrastructure software requirements (for example, backup software), that is the only similarity.

For a sales executive to get to know their customer, quite often they may have worked for that customer or indeed made a career out of managing that customer with different suppliers.

Quite often you will find that the sales executive and the customer are of a similar background and that a professional relationship has been built up over many years. Results often prove that sales executives who specialise in a specific vertical segment or customer over their career quite often enjoy the most success.

So while the role of selling is similar across different verticals and customers, the sales individuals will be very different even though they are doing the same role. Quite often sales management will look for specific individuals that have either a proven track record of working with specific customers or would match a profile of the 'type' of people within that organisation. Why is this? Ultimately, people buy from people and therefore the sales process is about building a relationship with your customer. You have to know the customer and the best way is to be on a similar level to them. In some cases the more similar the customer-facing organisation is to the customer in terms of backgrounds, age, gender and religion, the greater the chance that the rapport between the client and the organisation will succeed. In the same way, the more events such as corporate hospitality that can be tailored to the customers' needs, the greater the chances that the event will be enjoyed. The vast majority of customers want to feel that you understand them and their business objectives, so you can appreciate the importance of careful targeting of employees and events.

Examples? If you wanted someone to focus purely on selling to Indian restaurants, then someone from a similar background, for example, of Indian descent, may well be most suited especially if any language barriers exist. In the case of a different type of environment, for example an investment bank in the City of London, if I was managing a team interfacing with them, I would expect the best salesperson to have previously worked in the City in some capacity, to have a very polished appearance (smart suit), perhaps be privately educated, to have a fast 'clock speed' (i.e. be very dynamic) and to have a similar background as well as likes and dislikes to the client.

Achieving this would help build a relationship with the customer.

Again, if you wanted to sell to someone in the public sector, you would need a sales person with an understanding of their budgetary constraints and pain points. So, if I wanted someone to manage the Department of Work and Pensions for example, I would look for someone who may be ex-Department of Work and Pensions (or at the very least who had experience in managing them as a supplier) and who understood the pain of the organisation and its 'hot buttons'. The profile of the successful sales person here would be very different from that in the investment bank.

From a legal perspective, there's no discrimination because anybody could apply for any of the roles. Ultimately, you need someone capable of doing the job and most likely to build a relationship with the customer. In our business, we sell to all the FTSE 1000 companies as well as to the public sector. So the client-facing organisation – the sales team – will be very diverse in order to be able to cater for different parts of the customer base. While the software offered is standard to different clients, what is not standard is the way that it is sold to them. In fact, you will find increasing national diversity in IT teams in the UK today, with much personnel from the BRICK countries (Brazil, Russia, India, China and Korea). If we take the case of India, there are many Indian professional services firms operating globally and with a base in the UK. They employ some very knowledgeable graduates who come to the UK and elsewhere and who may come and work for us subsequently.

Where does gender fit into this diversity? Just as with nationality and educational background, it is helpful to have a gender match between the customer and salesperson. This is one way of avoiding the obvious embarrassment should one person get the wrong idea and think that this is more a personal than a business relationship.

How to organise diverse sales teams

You do a lot of profile matching in an informal sense. While companies would not proactively look for specific traits or certain diversities, in match profiling a customer to a sales person, the best candidates are quite typically ones from a similar background to that of the prospective clients so typically you will end up with a diverse sales team within an organisation. Many sales organisations end up with a group of people from diverse backgrounds in order to satisfy their clients' requirement; typically it can happen this way unconsciously as opposed to being the result of a strategic decision to employ diversity to increase sales effectiveness.

First, of course, people are recruited into the organisation and the methods used here are 'standard'. Then, the sales team produce group client companies into 'sales patches' that would be deemed similar, for example mobile telephone operators or investment banks or local authorities. Sometimes territories are also geographical, for example Scotland. Then when seeking the most experienced person for that given vertical or territory, you'd expect to see CVs of people with similar experience to that which is required and a proven track record.

I would expect to see a different 'type' of person for each of the four territories listed above. For example, the best person to sell to Scottish companies would probably be someone living in Scotland (in order to reduce travelling time to clients and maximise productivity) and/or of Scottish descent since they're more likely to have the level of contacts required and local market knowledge. As for the planning, typically it is done from a ROI perspective looking at where you can get the best return. So, for example, if there are three possible vacancies to manage clients, you might ask which clients are spending more at present and which will deliver the best return?

Once you have identified the most profitable target, you would plan your search for staff with a similar background and demographics to those working in that organisation.

Ultimately, no sales manager wants to see people fail, so by profile matching skills, traits and characteristics as closely as possible to the client or territory you are maximising your chances of success.

8 Management consultancy, accountancy and other professional services

8.1 Accountancy profession

8.1.1 Pay

Research in 2003 by Accountancy Age and Robert Half Finance and Accounting revealed that women were twice as likely to be in the lowest income bracket of the profession, earning less than £25,000 a year. By contrast, men were almost twice as likely as women to earn more than £50,000 a year and five times more likely to earn more than £70,000 a year (Hester, 2003). This survey also revealed that male finance directors (FDs) earn an average of 20 per cent more than female FDs (ibid.).

Six years on from this, a report by the Equality and Human Rights Commission in 2009 (Metcalf and Rolfe, 2009) showed that women working full time in the finance sector earned 55 per cent less annual gross salary than men. This compared with a pay gap of 28 per cent for the economy generally (Dunbar, 2009). The report also shows that this gap has increased in the case of the highest paid positions.

Partners. Research conducted in 2003 showed that women made up just 10 per cent of partners, while some big firms admitted to having no female partners at all (Hester, 2003). Although in 2010 women make up an increasing proportion of new entrants to the accountancy profession, with almost 50 per cent of the accountancy trainee intake being female and over half of the members and students of the Association of Chartered Certified Accountants (ACCA) being women (Hudson, 2010), a recent report by the Equality and Human Rights Commission (2011, p. 9) noted that women are 'significantly under-represented' in managerial jobs, including those at the most senior level. An exception in the UK is KPMG where the percentage of partners in 2007 rose from 14 per cent in October 2000 to 19 per cent in March 2007 (Davidson, 2007).

Coaching and mentoring. Global research from ACCA in their 2008 publication on mentoring, suggests coaching and mentoring is being poorly practised across the finance professions, revealing a lack of understanding of good practice and ultimately leading to poor returns on training investment. This is an area where better systems are needed.

8.1.2　Discussion

It would appear that the accountancy sector suffers many of the problems found in the legal sector and has, if anything, further to go in making workplaces female-friendly places. In terms of the four quadrants in Table 8.2, it would appear that effort needs to be focused on quadrants two, three and four.

8.2　Management consultancy and professional services

In management consultancy and professional services firms women typically represent between 30 per cent and 40 per cent of the intake (Kumra and Vinnicombe, 2008) with 7–14 per cent reaching partner level at the big four consultancies of Accenture, Andersen, BearingPoint, CapGemini, Deloitte & Touche, Ernst & Young, KPMG and PricewaterhouseCoopers.

In terms of flexible working, a survey in 2007 of Scottish 'Big Four firms' revealed that financial services firms continue to adopt a macho culture, particularly in relation to the working week, and this culture makes it difficult to achieve an acceptable work–life balance within the environment of a professional accountancy firm. So, although the survey shows that flexibility is available, working less than a full week is generally viewed in a negative manner. Consequently, unless a cultural change is made to the working environment that could be of benefit to all employees, it is difficult to envisage a situation where women accountants will progress to partnership in the same proportion as male colleagues (ICAS, 2007). Moving outside Scotland, an exception again is KPMG, which has increased flexible working options – open to all but taken up mainly by women. In recognition of its progress in this area the firm was recently given Opportunity Now's City award, for an institution that develops 'a culture which encourages flexible working' (ibid.).

In terms of promotion criteria, a study of the promotion criteria at a UK management consultancy through interviews with 34 male and female non-partners (Kumra and Vinnicombe, 2008), revealed that to advance within the firm it is necessary to understand and emulate the prevailing model of success; in essence the people who were made partners were those who fitted a more masculine than feminine model of success, with typical criteria being 'physical presence', 'being one of us' (both p. S70) and 'being a good bloke' (p. S71). The sought-after physical characteristics included looking like existing partners, a predominantly male group, and the authors of this important study concluded that 'the expectation that men and women must both adopt a particular masculine standard of partnership, whilst constraining to men, is particularly problematic for women'.

A view from the inside: an interview with the director of diversity and inclusiveness – EMEIA at Ernst and Young, one of the big four professional services firms

Of our graduate entrants 48 per cent are female, and 18 per cent of our partners are female. This is not about fixing the women but about changing the way we go about our business. One key focus to develop a level playing field has been to teach our line managers about the impact of unconscious bias on their decisions. This virtual training has recommended ways of counteracting unconscious bias in the evaluation of talent, and tips included: pausing before you take a view; looking at specific outputs rather than style only; talking more around a topic objectively.

So, for example, if in an appraisal someone is described as 'lacking in *gravitas*', you could ask the question 'what do we mean by gravitas?' Another tip is to avoid comparing one person with another but instead comparing people with their objectives. 'You can't cure unconscious bias but you can give people the benefit of the doubt.'

The training also included case studies to show up unconscious bias at a basic level. For example, one involves introductions to two people, a man and a woman, with the first approaches being made to the man on the assumption (which may be wrong) that he is the more senior of the two.

In some locations, 'Career Watch' programmes have been rolled out which focus on sponsorship. To support this work, sessions are organised on topics such as micro-inequities. One micro-inequity that has been identified is the way men may not pick up on an idea when voiced by a woman but when voiced subsequently by a man, the idea is discussed.

It is very important to get this right since the key competitive advantage of the organisation is the 'differentiated people culture'. All the big four management consultants attract good graduates and 'it is very hard to differentiate across the big four. It is literally our people that make the difference.'

For example, discussions may have reached an impasse but one person may say something that changes things completely.

8.3   Recruitment

Lord Davies' review (2011) into women in the boardroom recommended that UK listed companies in the FTSE 100 should be aiming for a minimum of 25 per cent female board member representation (up from the level in 2011 of 12.5 per cent of non-executive directors). He also recommended that headhunters and executive search firms produce a voluntary code of conduct, British headhunters have now produced a code of conduct to ensure that at least 30% of candidates presented to clients on every long list are women.

An interview with the CEO and co-founder of recruitment agency Green Park, according to its website, the fastest growing recruitment agency in the UK, highlighted some of the obstacles in the way of greater diversity. This agency, named the UK's 19th fastest growing private company in the Sunday Times Fast Track 100, is a minority owned business and Stonewall Diversity Champions. Its strong focus on diversity recruitment means that the agency has experience of encouraging and achieving diversity within the UK context. The views of the co-founder and CEO are shown in the following views relating to the achievement of diversity in professional services firms.

A view from the inside: CEO of Green Park recruitment consultants

The headhunting industry and the process whereby people are assessed in this country has a significant level of institutional bias. So, you can never really increase representation in your board-room until you increase representation in your supply chain; in other words, the talent coming into the organisation and how you develop the talent that you have got.

From what we see, it is much easier to foster diversity in small organisations than it is in large blue chips. In my view, this is because the responsibility for recruitment needs to move out of HR into a discipline with a financial responsibility. There is also a massive difference between organisations that portray a good picture and organisations that actually deliver diversity. For example, there are many large FTSE 100 organisations that have good reputations on diversity, but if you look at the shape of their boards you will find a very different picture.

My view is that if you judge people on capabilities rather than on their demographic, and you have a diverse talent pool, you will end up with more diverse management teams. In professional services firms, we need to get a discussion going on the talent pool.

Solutions?

There's no silver bullet. There's no one thing but rather a range of strategies. There has been a view that nothing ever happens unless you have a critical mass of role models or hold the diverse people you have up as role models so that they serve as talent magnets. How do you get to that point? There has been a view that nothing ever happens unless you link behaviour change to compensation, so focusing on compensatory mechanisms is one way of affecting change. Other strategies include:

- direct recruitment strategy
- internal mobility
- giving people promotion opportunities
- including diverse groups in succession planning decision-making
- understanding how your organisation is seen
- proactive market mapping

- creating a really understood business case, sometimes linked to a more efficient delivery of service. For example, research shows that in a straight line culture, a mono culture will outperform a diverse team; but in the world we live in, we no longer live in a straight line culture and innovation is the way forward and diversity is key to achieving this. Unless there is a clear business case, the whole idea of diversity is in the air.

Professional services firms like to be seen to be active in the area of diversity but if you asked them why it is important for their firm, they would probably offer completely different answers. Until a true understanding is developed and is made accountable through bonus schemes, the whole thing is mere rhetoric.

9 Conclusions

There is growing recognition from the representatives interviewed of the sectors discussed here – legal, design, IT, accountancy, management consultancy, and recruitment – of the business benefits of achieving diversity. These benefits are perceived as:

- retaining the talent base (legal sector);
- mirroring the client base and creating better and longer-lasting relationships (legal and software sectors);
- more innovative solutions (legal sector; design agencies; management consultancy and recruitment consultancy);
- the perception that a firm that offers good opportunities for women will attract talented women (legal sector).

A key point from the recruitment consultancy that specialises in diversity recruitment relates to the importance of maximising the impact of role models and using the compensation system to steer desired behaviours.

References

ACCA (2008), 'The coaching and mentoring revolution – is it working?', http://www.acca.org.uk/pubs/mhc/research/previous/coachingandmentoring.pdf
ACCA (2009), 'Equality: women in financial services', September, http://www.accaglobal.com/pubs/about/public_affairs/unit/global_briefings/equality.pdf

Akinola, M. and Thomas, A. (2008), 'Defining the attributes and processes that enhance the effectiveness of workforce diversity initiatives in knowledge intensive firms', working paper of Harvard Business School, accessed on 24 December 2010 at http://www.hbs.edu/research/pdf/07-019.pdf.

Attfield, J. and Kirkham, P. (1989), *A View from the Interior: Feminism, Women and Design* (London: Woman's Press).

Aurora (2008), 'Tough Lady Lawyer', http://www.auroravoice.com/pressarticle.asp?articleid=698, accessed on 19 November 2011.

Barclays (2000), 'The barriers start to fall', references in the 'Women's enterprise taskforce', accessed on 1 January 2011 at http://www.womensenterprise.co.uk/about_wetf.asp

Baroudi, J. J. and Igbaria, M. (1994/5), 'An examination of gender effects on career success of information system employees', *Journal of Management Information Systems*, 11(3) 181–202.

Bertrand, M. and Mullainathan, S. (2004), 'Are Emily and Greg more employable than Lakisha and Jamal? A field experiment on labor market discrimination', *American Economic Review*, 94 (4): 991–1013.

Black, S., Jameson, J., Komoss, R., Meehan, A. and Numerico, T. (2005), 'Women in computing: a European and international perspective', Conference: 3rd European Symposium on Gender & ICT: Working for Change, Weston Conference Centre, UMIST Manchester UK.

Buckley, C. (1987), 'Made in patriarchy: towards a feminist analysis of women and design', *Design Issues*, 3 (2): 3–14.

David, A. (2010), 'Diversity, innovation and corporate strategy', in G. Moss (ed.), *Profiting from Diversity*. Basingstoke: Palgrave Macmillan.

Davidson, C. (2007), 'Feminine women can succeed too', BBC, 27 June, http://news.bbc.co.uk/1/hi/business/6568649.stm

Davies, Lord (2011), Women on Boards.

Design Council (2005), *The Business of Design: Design Industry Research*, London: Design Council.

Doward, J. (2000), 'Why adland is still lad land', *Observer*, 19 November, http://www.guardian.co.uk/business/2000/nov/19/pressandpublishing.media1> or http://www.guardian.co.uk/Archive/Article/0,4273,4093039,00.

Dunbar, J. (2009), 'Equality commission claims financial services undervalue women', FT Magazine: Financial Adviser, 10 September 2009.

Ely, R. and Myerson, D. (2000), 'Advancing gender equity in organizations: The challenge and importance of maintaining a gender narrative', *Organization*, 7 (4): 589–608.

Equality and Human Rights Commission (2011), Sex and Power.

Giscombe, K. and Mattis, M. (2002), 'Leveling the playing field for women of color in corporate management', *Journal of Business Ethics*, 37 (1): 103.

Global Entrepreneurship Monitor (GEM) (2004), Report on Women and Entrepreneurship, The Center for Women's Leadership at Babson College, http://www.gemconsortium.org/download/1293898598172/GEM_Womens_Report.pdf

Hester, J. (2003), 'How does the gender situation for UK FDs compare to Europe?', *Accountancy Age*, 30 October, http://www.accountancyage.com/aa/analysis/1759468/how-gender-situation-uk-fds-compare-europe#ixzz194o C8pyv

Holvino, E., Ferdman, B. M. and Merrill-Sands, D. (2004), 'Creating and sustaining diversity and inclusion in organizations: strategies and approaches', in M. S. Stockdale and F. J. Crosby (eds), *The Psychology and Management of Workplace Diversity* (pp. 245–276). Malden, MA: Blackwell.

Hudson, V. (2010), 'Women and accountancy: still a way to go', 8 March, http://blogs.accaglobal.com/pamrblog/2010/03/women-and-accountancy-still-a-way-to-go.html

Hurley, A., Fagenson-Eland, E. and Sonnenfeld, J. (1997), 'Does cream always rise to the top? An investigation of career determinants', *Organizational Dynamics*, 26 (2): 65–71.

Ibarra, H. (1993), 'Personal networks of women and minorities in management: a conceptual framework', *Academy of Management Review*, 18: 56–87, http://www.icas.org.uk/site/cms/contentviewarticle.asp?article=5091

ICAS (2007), Gammie, E., Gammie, B., Matson, M., Duncan, F., 'Women of ICAS reaching the top: the demise of the glass ceiling', Institute of Chartered Accountants, Scotland, http://www.icas.org.uk/site/cms/contentviewarticle.asp?article=5091

Igbaria, M. and Parasuraman, S. (1997), 'Status report on women and men in the IT workplace', *Information Systems Management* 14 (3): 44–54.

Jehn, K. A., Northcraft, G. B. and Neale, M. A. (1999), 'Why differences make a difference: a field study of diversity, conflict, and performance in workgroups', *Administrative Science Quarterly*, 44 (4): 741.

Kanter, R. M. (1977), *Men and Women of the Corporation*, New York, NY: Basic Books.

Kumra, S. and Vinnicombe, S. (2008), 'A study of the promotion to partner process in a professional services firm: how women are disadvantaged', *British Journal of Management*, 19: S65–S74.

Lorsch, J. W. and Tierney, T. J. (2002), *Aligning the Stars: How to Succeed When Professionals Drive Results*, Boston: Harvard Business School Press.

Maister, D. (1997), *Managing the Professional Service Firm*, New York: Free Press.

McLeod-Thomas, L. (2010a), 'Revealed: Top UK firms make poor showing in female partner stakes', *The Lawyer*, http://www.thelawyer.com/revealed-top-uk-firms-make-poor-showing-in-female-partner-stakes/1005590.article

McLeod-Thomas, L. (2010b), 'Addleshaws sets out goals to boost diversity', 1 November 2010, http://www.thelawyer.com/addleshaws-sets-out-goals-to-boost-diversity/1005942.article

Metcalf, H. and Rolfe, H. (2009), Employment and earnings in the Finance Sector: a gender analysis, National Institute of Economic and Social Research, Equality and Human Rights Commission.

Moss, G. (1996), 'Do males and females make judgements in a self-selecting fashion?', *Journal of Art and Design*, 15 (2): 161–169.

Moss, G. (2007), 'Psychology of performance and preference: advantages, disadvantages, drivers and obstacles to the achievement of congruence', *Journal of Brand Management*, 14 (4): 343–358.

Moss, G. (2009), *Gender, Design and Marketing*. Farnham: Gower.

Moss, G. and Daunton, L. (2006), 'The discriminatory impact of deviations from selection criteria in Higher Education selection', *Career Development International*, 11 (6), 504–521.

Moss, G. and Gunn, R. (2009), 'Gender differences in website production and preference aesthetics: preliminary implications for ICT in education and beyond', *Behaviour and Information Technology*, 28 (5): 1362–3001.

O'Brien, T. (2006), 'Why do so few women reach the top of big law firms?', 19 March, http://www.nytimes.com/2006/03/19/business/yourmoney/19law.html?pagewanted=4

O'Neill, R. M., Horton, S. and Crosby, F. J. (1999). 'Gender issues in developmental relationships', in A. J. Murrell, F. J. Crosby and R. J. Ely (eds), *Mentoring Dilemmas: Developmental Relationships within Multicultural Organizations* (pp. 63–80). Mahwah, NJ: Lawrence Erlbaum Associates.

Petersen, H. (2007), 'Gendered work ideals in Swedish IT firms: valued and not valued workers', *Gender, Work and Organization*, 14 (4): 333–348.

Ragins, B. R. and Cotton, J. (1996), 'Jumping the hurdles: barriers to mentoring for women in organizations', *Leadership and Organizational Development Journal*, 17 (3): 37–41.

Rees, B. and Garnsey, E. (2003), 'Analysing competence: gender and identity at work', *Gender, Work & Organization*, 10 (5): 551–578.

Robertson, M. et al. (2001), 'The issue of gender within computing: reflections from the UK and Scandinavia', *Information Systems Journal*, 11: 111–126.

Sampson, S. (2000), 'Customer-supplier duality and bidirectional supply chains in service organizations', *International Journal of Service Industry Management*, 11 (4): 348–364.

Senge, P., Kleiner, A., Roberts, C., Ross, R., Roth, G. and Smith, B. (1999), *The Dance of Change: The Challenges to Sustaining Momentum in Learning Organizations*. New York: Doubleday.

Smith, C. (2008), 'Kathy Honeywood: "Being the only woman is quite tough"', 9 April, http://business.timesonline.co.uk/tol/business/law/article3707079.ece

Sparke, P. (1995), *As Long As It's Pink*, London: Pandora Press.

Spurr, S. J. (1990), 'Sex discrimination in the legal profession: a study of promotion', *Industrial and Labor Relations Review*, 43 (4): 406–417.

Spurr, S. J. and Sueyoshi, P. (1993), 'Turnover and promotion of lawyers', *Journal of Human Resources*, 29 (3): 813–842.

The Lawyer, Diversity Report (2010), www.thelawyer.com

Thomas, D. A. and Gabarro, J. (1999), *Breaking Through: How People of Color and the Companies They Work for Can Overcome Barriers*, Boston, MA: Harvard Business School Press.

Trefry, M. (2006), 'A double-edged sword: organizational culture in multicultural organizations', *International Journal of Management*, 1 September, http://www.allbusiness.com/company-activities-management/management-corporate-culture/13477475-1.html

Waters, H. (1992), 'Minority leadership problems', *Journal of Education for Business*, 68 (1): 15–21.

Wheeler, M. (1998), 'Measuring diversity: a strategy for organisational effectiveness', *Employment Relations Today*, Spring, John Wiley and Sons Inc.

Wilkins, D. and Gulati, M. (1996), 'Why are there so few black lawyers in corporate law firms?: An institutional analysis', *California Law Review*, 84 (3): 493–625.

Women and Work Commission (2006) 'Shaping a fairer future', http://www.ukces.org.uk/assets/bispartners/ukces/docs/publications/women-and-work-shaping-a-fairer-future.pdf, accessed on 19 November 2011.

9
Profiting from Diversity in the Banking Sector

Isabelle Maque, Audrey Becuwe, Isabelle Prim-Allaz
and Alice Garnier

1 Introduction

The participation of women in entrepreneurship has increased tremendously over the last decades and is now significant in most developed countries and in many developing countries (Brush, 1992; Minnitti et al., 2005). In France, small and medium businesses and very small firms of Industry, Trade and Services (ICS) numbered 2,613 million (INSEE, 2005). Women represent only 28 per cent of all entrepreneurs in small and medium businesses and they constitute 46 per cent of the workforce. In the United States, they represent 48 per cent of all entrepreneurs (APCE, 2007). The increase of female entrepreneurs has attracted academic interest, and female entrepreneurship has developed as a separate research field (Verheul, 2005). However, little attention has been devoted to a feminine perspective of business ownership (Bird and Brush, 2002). Entrepreneurship is often depicted as a form of masculinity (Mirchandani, 1999; Bird and Brush, 2002; Bruni et al., 2004), with entrepreneurs described in terms that are associated more with men than women, for example, 'the conqueror of unexplored territories, the lonely hero, the patriarch' (Bruni et al., 2004, p. 407).

Prior studies on women entrepreneurship have often concentrated on objective measures of success based on business size (e.g., number of employees, sales) or financial performance (e.g., profits, return on investment) rather than more subjective 'lifestyle' measures and business manager perceptions (Walker and Brown, 2004). Many studies have also focused on investigating gender-based differences. More precisely, studies on gender-based differences in debt financing have focused on two related themes (Carter et al., 2007): the complex relationship between gender of entrepreneur and bank finance; and whether gender-based differences are a consequence of supply-side discrimination by bank lenders, demand-side aversion to debt or risk by women entrepreneurs, or simply the result of structural dissimilarities. If structural dissimilarities (e.g., size, turnover, sector) explain most differences between male-owned and female-owned businesses, the explanations of residual differences remain controversial. Thus, this present study is designed to contribute to the entrepreneurship literature in many ways. It responds to the call for research on entrepreneurship as a gendered process (Mirchandani, 1999; Bird and Brush, 2002; Marlow and Patton, 2005). Based on feminist theory (liberal and social), we examine how a business owner's gender influences his or her education, his or her sensitivity towards the management mode of his or her firm, and bank finance. This chapter takes a social constructionist or poststructuralist feminist position and uses the term gender in the original sense of the word, that is, as socially constructed.

Therefore, after a review of the literature on female entrepreneurship and banking relationships (see Section 2.1 below), we introduce the concept of gender and feminist theories (Section 2.2). In the next section we clarify the research method (3.2). Our study is based on 382 respondents, top managers of French small and medium-sized enterprises (SMEs). We define entrepreneurship broadly, that is to say both women creating their own business and women managing firms that they did not create themselves.

It should be noted that existing research on female entrepreneurship largely considers data from Anglo-Saxon countries such as the US and UK (Ahl, 2002) and the investigation of gender differences in self-employment in other countries is seen as a promising direction for new research (McManus, 2001).

Our study is based on data collected in a French context, which broadens the existing knowledge on this subject. In terms of findings for feminism, our results appear to invalidate the liberal feminist theory while validating the social feminist one (Section 3.2). Then, in a discussion of gender identity (Section 4), we note that some researchers call for studies on the influence of gender socialisation (Ruble and Martin, 1998) – a phenomenon which encourages individuals to exhibit traits associated with gender stereotypes – on business owners' attitudes and behaviours (Mirchandani, 1999; Bird and Brush, 2002; Marlow and Patton, 2005). In response to this call, we examine the role of gender identity, a psychological construct that has been theoretically and empirically linked to gender socialisation (Bem, 1993; Ruble and Martin, 1998; Eagly et al., 2000), in predicting business owners' sources of behaviours and bank relations. We end this chapter by formalising two research proposals.

2 Section 1: Review of the literature

2.1 Gender-based differences and bank finance: further investigation and explanations are needed

Carter et al. (2007) state that studies investigating gender-based differences in debt financing have focused on two related themes:

> First, researchers have sought to unravel the complex relationship between gender of entrepreneur and bank finance with regard to the volume of finance lent, the terms of credit negotiated, and the perceived attitudes of bank lending officers to female entrepreneurs.
>
> Second, researchers have attempted to demonstrate whether gender-based differences are a consequence of supply-side discrimination by bank lenders, demand-side aversion to debt or risk by women entrepreneurs, or simply the result of the structural dissimilarities of male-owned and female-owned businesses.

It is the case that many research studies highlight clear differences between male-owned and female-owned businesses but if such structural dissimilarities explain most, the explanations of residual differences remain controversial.

2.1.1 The characteristics of women-owned businesses and their female owners

Only a few studies on an entrepreneur's gender and financial constraints are firm-level based and most of them are based on US data (Muravyev et al., 2009). Thus, the recent study by Cole and Mehran (2009) relies upon the very much used database on privately held businesses drawn from the Federal Reserve's Surveys of Small Business Finances (Coleman, 2000; Robb and Wolken, 2002; Coleman, 2007). This study seeks to establish a 'baseline of "stylized facts" concerning the role of gender and entrepreneurship in the United States' using a set of four surveys covering a 16-year period. The study finds that female-owned firms compared to their equivalent male-owned firms are significantly smaller (measured by sales, assets and employment), younger (measured by age of the firm), more likely to be organised as proprietorships and less as corporations, more likely to be in retail trade and business services and less likely to be in construction, secondary manufacturing, and wholesale trade, and inclined to have fewer and shorter banking relationships (but this disparity with male-owned businesses has narrowed over time). Moreover, the univariate analyses show no significant differences in profitability by gender. Compared to male owners, female owners are also significantly younger (but one to two years in magnitude and the difference declines in each survey), less experienced (4.5 to 5.2 fewer years) and not as well educated. Moreover, in a multivariate analysis, older firms are significantly more likely to be female owned (after controlling for owner experience and firm size).

The study by Muravyev et al. (2009) is based on the data from the 2005 Business Environment and Enterprise Performance Survey conducted by the European Bank for Reconstruction and Development and the World Bank, and covers 34 countries. In terms of contributor countries, 23.9 per cent of the firms are made up of the oldest member states of the EU (although French data is not included) as well as 26 post-socialist economies of Eastern Europe and Central Asia like Korea, Turkey and Vietnam, 26 per cent of the businesses of which are women-owned. On average, female-owned firms tend to be smaller, younger (1.5 years), less likely to export and in a less competitive business environment; female-owned businesses are also relatively rare in construction and manufacturing but more common in the service sector.

2.1.2 *Gender and bank finance management: persistent differences*

Carter et al. (2007) declares that previous researches provide unequivocal evidence that women-owned businesses start with both lower levels of overall capitalisation and lower ratios of debt finance. If structural dissimilarities between male-owned and female-owned businesses account for many of the differences by gender, the underlying factors behind these residual differences remain controversial. Supply-side practices might be one explanation – thus Fay and Williams (1993) found discrimination against women when the applicant for a loan had high-school education but not when the applicant was university educated – but there is also evidence of demand-side risk and debt aversion, with a lower preference for risk among women as a recurrent finding (Watson and Robinson, 2003). Risk aversion to assume business debt but also to engage in fast-paced business growth (Cliff, 1998; Bird and Brush, 2002) was another feature characterising women's small business behaviour. Notwithstanding these differences, it has been found that gender differences in risk preferences are smaller and often non-existent among certain groups of the population, most notably managers and professionals (Croson and Gneezy, 2009).

Thus, Cole and Mehran (2009), on US data, find strong univariate evidence of differences in the availability of credit. Female-owned firms are more likely to report not seeking credit during the three years prior to the survey and are disproportionately likely to report that while they needed credit, fear of rejection kept them from applying. Female-owned firms are also significantly more likely to be credit-constrained because they are more likely to be denied credit when they apply. Having said this, in a multivariate analysis, these latest differences are rendered insignificant when other firm and owner characteristics are controlled (firm's size and industry, owner's age, experience and educational attainment).

Treichel and Scott (2006) also find, on a different US survey, that women-owned businesses are significantly less likely to apply for a loan and that this outcome persists over time after controlling for business characteristics. Again, if women-owned businesses more frequently report being turned down for a loan, it appears that it is because of size, legal form, firm age, growth, industry or size of current bank finance but not on account of gender. They also find that, even after controlling for firm risk (size and years in business) and loan terms variables and size effect (women-owned businesses are smaller), women-owned businesses persistently report a smaller loan size. This smaller loan size is linked, according to the authors, to the limited need for bank loans in the sectors in which women-owned businesses are frequently found, namely retail and services. Differences might also be due to concerns women business owners have concerning control of their lives: women start or buy businesses to have greater control of their lives, and to seek external funding might imply a loss of control over the business. *Thus, rather than discrimination, these outcomes may be the result of self-selection by women-owners.* However, having selected firms in the service and retail industries only, Coleman (2007) found a significantly lower percentage of women business owners having any type of loans and lines of credit. Moreover, this study (ibid.), studying the impact of human capital (education, prior business experience, age and maturity, family history of firm ownership) and financial capital (the firm's ability to secure external debt capital and its willingness to apply for it) on the firm's profitability, also highlights the fact that measures of human capital had a more important role in determining profitability in women-owned businesses, whereas measures of financial capital assumed more prominence for men. For women also, firm growth appeared to be largely unaffected by measures of human or financial capital, suggesting that growth in women-owned firms was determined by variables not included in this analysis.

Muravyev et al. (2009), on international data, find that on average, female-owned firms have a smaller fraction of bank financing than male-owned firms. Again, the authors find results corroborating the US data insofar as they find that the share of non–borrowers among women is much higher than among men, and women are more discouraged from borrowing than men (having said that, the rejection rates by gender are very close in the full sample). Using a multivariate analysis, controlling for firm characteristics, female-owned businesses were found to have a lower likelihood of obtaining bank credit and were found to pay, on average, higher interest rates (0.45 per cent more on average). The study also found that differences between men and women reduced with the level of development of the country, with women-owned firms in more financially developed countries more likely to receive loans, pay lower interest rates and face lower collateral requirements than in less developed countries. This shows that discrimination is somewhat linked with the level of development of the country, although the authors suggest that competition among providers of capital reduces the scope for discriminatory behaviour (consistent with Becker's view (1957)).

2.2 For reading gendered: the contribution of feminist theories to work on entrepreneurship

Several authors maintain that research on women entrepreneurs suffers from a number of shortcomings, which include the absence of a power perspective, and the lack of an explicit feminist analysis (Reed, 1996; Mirchandani, 1999; Ogbor, 2000). As a result, the 1990s brought a more explicit call for a feminist theory of entrepreneurship (Stevenson, 1990; Hurley, 1991).

In this section, we initially discuss the concept of gender and then present the relevant feminist theories. While liberal feminist theory accounts for the differences between the achievements of men and women by emphasising discrimination and/or systemic factors that deprive women of essential opportunities such as education and experience, social feminist theory explains these differences by referring to the ongoing socialisation process that leads men and women to believe that they differ inherently.

2.2.1 What is meant by gender?

Most studies on female entrepreneurship address the gender aspect in terms of identifying the differences between women and men entrepreneurs. These search features associate with one sex or the other and identify obstacles and problems specific to women in business creation (access to networks, access to financing, etc.). There is a logic of differentiation that is of interest but this school of thought has a very narrow vision of what can make a reading of gender-related phenomena.

Consequently, feminist scholars introduced the term gender to distinguish between biological sex (human bodies with male or female reproductive organs) and socially constructed sex, i.e., social practices and representations associated with femininity or masculinity (Acker, 1992; Ahl, 2006). This chapter takes a social constructionist or poststructuralist feminist position and uses the term gender in the original sense of the word, that is, as socially constructed. The term 'gender' refers to what is regarded as masculine or feminine and is used as being independent of a person's biological sex, with gender understood as being the result of upbringing and social interaction and therefore varying in time and place. When gender – not sex – is in focus, this means that the study object goes beyond men and women so that we can speak of professions, for example, being gendered, and likewise with entrepreneurship (Ahl, 2006; Constantinidis et al., 2006).

2.2.2 Two feminist theories: liberal feminist theory and social feminist theory

According to Fischer et al. (1993) there are two perspectives that help organise and interpret past research, and highlight avenues for future researches. These perspectives are liberal feminism and social feminism.

The first group is liberal feminist theory, which is a theory of inequality in which liberal feminist theory sees men and women as essentially similar. It is inspired by liberal political theory, that is, this perspective assumes that both sexes possess equal capacities for rationality. However, the view is taken that women are disadvantaged relative to men due to discrimination and systemic factors that deprive them of vital resources such as business education (Fischer et al., 1993) and experience. This inequality is seen to arise from the structural organisation (or macro influences) of society and not from any biological or personality differences between men and women. Liberal feminism assumes that women will evolve and become like men when all forms of discrimination in a society are eliminated, believing that it is possible to change this gender inequality through the equalisation of opportunities (Trebilcot, 1973).

The second stream is the social feminist theory. This theory suggests that men and women differ inherently due to differences in early and ongoing socialisation. It posits that men and women exhibit fundamentally different views of the world because of differences in their socialisation. For Chodorow, 'An important dynamic of gender division of labour is the process of socialization [Chodorow, 1971] which, in the broadest terms prepares males and females for the fulfillment of different roles; a process which influences the shaping of personality differences' (Chodorow, 1978 in Mills, 1989). The theory holds that different socialisation of men and women results in the emergence of feminine and masculine modes of knowing and, extrapolating from this, that male and female entrepreneurs might differ in their traits, behaviours and experiences, while their ventures may differ in their characteristics and outcomes. In summary, social feminism holds that there are differences between male and female experiences through different socialisation methods from the earliest moments of life, resulting in fundamentally different ways of viewing the world (Fischer et al., 1993).

A liberal feminist perspective would expect to find that men and women may differ in their level of formal education, possession of management skills, and choice of sector, while a social feminist perspective would more likely expect a gender difference in terms of bank finance, financial communication and the sensitivity vis-à-vis the management mode of his or her firm. In the second section, we look at the results of empirical work to see which of these two approaches (if either) are validated.

3   Section 2: Research method and results

3.1   Research method

3.1.1   *Sample definition*

The empirical section of this chapter is based on a database of 382 French SMEs. Interviews were conducted from January to June 2010. The primary objective of this data collection was to identify the levers used by businesses to pass different stages of growth. The study was limited to firms in Rhône-Alpes, a French economically dynamic region, and in order to get enough data on a longitudinal basis, only firms older than four years old were selected. Small companies with a turnover below 500,000 euros were excluded from the study and companies belonging to foreign groups were not taken into account. Companies that met all these requirements formed the study population (around 17,000 SMEs in the Rhône-Alpes area). In total, 432 questionnaires were completed by top managers and, after discarding incomplete questionnaires, our database included 382 complete and usable questionnaires representative of the wider population. The questionnaire consists of four parts: (1) general information on the company, its environment and its markets; (2) the company and its strategy; (3) organisation, resources and tools; and (4) Governance Officer.

In terms of the questionnaire returns, 83 per cent of respondents are males and 17 per cent females. The observed distribution in the sample is identical to that of the French population in 2008 (INSEE, DADS 2008) and the observed imbalance of our two subsamples (83 per cent men and 17 per cent women), and the fact that this imbalance is reflected in the general entrepreneur population in France, enhances the statistical significance of the results obtained. Thus, the huge difference in the size of our two subsamples (men and women) has a strong statistical impact: the significance is all the more significant when results are significant.

Incidentally, in terms of the origin of the businesses in question, 47.7 per cent of the female entrepreneurs and 50 per cent of the male ones in our sample are the initial founders of the firm (no statistical significant difference). For 81 per cent of men, the business which is the current focus of attention is one that they have created, while for 19 per cent of them it is a takeover of a business. By contrast, for 75 per cent of the women, the business in question is one that they have created, while for 35 per cent of them, it is a business that has been taken over (no statistical significant difference between men and women on these points).

3.1.2   *Measures and procedure*

The measurement tools come from different sources and the items in the questionnaire are the results of a wide literature review on entrepreneurship and growth and of a strong qualitative exploratory phase (about 30 in-depth interviews within ten different companies). The data collected through the questionnaires were completed by financial and longitudinal data proposed by the Diane database and the questionnaire had been pre-tested on representatives of professional trade unions and on about ten SME CEOs. The questionnaire used a variety of measures and the questions were phrased in the form of statements scored on a five-point Likert-type scale, most of them being: $1 =$ 'strongly disagree'; $3 =$ 'neither disagree nor agree'; and $5 =$ 'strongly agree'. Statistical tests were performed on SPSS 18 using chi-square tests, the t-tests and analyses of variance (ANOVA).

3.2 Results – descriptive statistics

As discussed earlier, our sample consisted of 83 per cent men (N = 317) and 17 per cent women (N = 65) for a total sample of 382 respondents.

3.2.1 *Entrepreneurs' characteristics*

Age. Men are slightly older than women (p = 0.099) by an average of two years. Thus, the average age for men in this sample is 51 years and 49 years for women. This runs counter to trends in the population as a whole since in France the APCE (2001) finds that women entrepreneurs are more likely than men entrepreneurs to belong to the category of less than 25 years old. In North America (Canada and US), women entrepreneurs are also younger than their male counterparts (Légare and Saint-Cyr, 1999) with Cole and Mehran (2009) highlighting in a recent study the fact that in the very much used Federal Reserve's Surveys of Small Business Finances data, the same difference in age of two years is identified.

Education and experience. Entrepreneurs in our study, that is to say men and women, have a high overall level of education. Indeed, 30 per cent of them have completed five years of study following their first degree.

Highlighting this result could be very important when analysing our findings since very often there are no significant gender differences between men and women. Thus, according to Croson and Gneezy (2009), gender differences in risk preferences are smaller and often non-existent among certain groups of the population, most notably managers and professionals; the same decisive argument, that is to say the high level of education of our female managing directors, could explain our numerous 'no significant gender differences'. Moreover, there is a correlation between age and training (p = 0.008) with a high proportion of older people about three to five years on average more than other groups. So, our findings do not corroborate those of Cole and Mehran (2009) who, using US data, find that female entrepreneurs are not as well educated as male entrepreneurs. Nor do they corroborate the findings of Saint-Cyr et al. (2003) who find that American women entrepreneurs have a higher educational level than equivalent men and often no previous experience in their industry. Thus, 36.4 per cent of men and 21.5 per cent of women have created other companies (p = 0.02). Among them, 36.4 per cent of men and 42.9 per cent of women are within the same sector (but in this case, the difference is not significant: p = 0.421).

Skills. To the question 'What are your specific skills?', several items were offered to respondents, such as production, research and development, IT, management/strategy, accounting/finance, marketing, sales and human resources. Statistical tests show that there are differences on specific competences with 15.5 per cent of women having accounting and finance as their prime skill with this being the case for only 7.59 per cent of men ($p = 0.006$). Moreover, 35.5 per cent of men and 36.9 per cent of women benefited from long training periods, with these positive factors yielding no significant difference between the facts reported for men and those reported for women ($p = 0.349$).

Shareholding. There is a significant difference relative to being a shareholder, with only 68.75 per cent of women being shareholders of their firm as compared with the higher figure for men of 86.39 per cent, ($p = 0.001$).

Serial entrepreneurship. Men are significantly more often simultaneously managing other firms (33.5 per cent) than women (9.23 per cent), $p = 0.000$.

3.2.2   Business characteristics and performance

Size of the firm measured by firm employment. On average, the number of people managed by men is 33.8 and 32 for women, a result that produces no significant differences between the genders ($p = 0.814$). Moreover, firms are on average 28 years old, whether managed by men or by women ($p = 0.895$). These results do not corroborate the literature in which firms managed by women are found to be both smaller and younger (Coleman, 2000; Cole and Mehran, 2009; Bellucci et al., 2009). Could it be because of the high-levelled female managing directors' explanation mentioned above? Indeed, North American and European statistics show that most businesses managed by a woman were created to offer self-employment, to reconcile professional and personal lives, mainly in the services sector, or to create work after a period of unemployment (see 'pull' versus 'push' motivations). Consequently, their primary objective is not to develop the size of the firm. In the case of the firms in our French sample, however, the women directors are managing firms the same size as men, are as educated as men, and there is no real difference in the economic sector. We explain this lack of difference by the fact that the selection of firms in our sample was based on being a growing firm.

Sector. Our study shows no clear sector differences for firms managed by men or women. This may be because of the very large and detailed number of French official sectors and the groupings we were forced to use. Thus, among the service sectors in which there are no significant differences in the sectors in which male and female entrepreneurs are active, 32.41 per cent of men and 24.07 per cent of women have their business related to a broadly defined sector of industrial services, which includes car mechanics as well as transport/storage. In prior research, female entrepreneurs were found to be more likely to head retail and service firms and less likely to head manufacturing and wholesale firms (Brush, 1992; Cliff, 1998). According to the study in late 2007 coordinated by the French National Agency for Business Creation, women entrepreneurs emerged as very active in the area of personal services (38 per cent of female entrepreneurs).

Firm situation relative to export and competitive environment. Our data show no significant differences, unlike Muravyev et al.'s findings (2009) that show, on average, that female-owned firms are less likely to export and are more likely to work in a less competitive business environment.

Performance measured by the turnover or return. The turnover of the firms managed by women in our study, over the eight years of data, is always significantly lower compared to the turnover of firm managed by men: for example, the turnover in 2009 is 4,798,000 euros for men compared with 4,438,000 euros for women but the difference, while significant, is not of high significance ($0.05 < p < 0.10$). Moreover, on all measures of return – whether return on assets or return on equity – there are no significant differences between the female- and male-owned companies. We should not perhaps be surprised since our results corroborate results on US data that show no differences on return.

Growth. We asked the managing directors for the decisive events in the history of the firm: in terms of the 'number one' event, stability in the growth of the firm's activities is significantly more highly prioritised by women than it is by men. Our results show a stronger tendency for men than women to prioritise growth but with no significant difference in their response. This result is consistent with the recurring finding of a lower preference on the part of women for risk or risk aversion to engage in fast-paced business growth.

3.2.3 Bank finance: access and perceptions

Funding strategies. Our results show no differences relative to funding (self-financing, external equity or bank finance), in contrast to the literature, which highlights the fact that women use more self-financing and less bank funding and if they resort to external sources, tend to use smaller amounts. From our survey, the only significant difference relates to short-term financing (overdraft, factoring and credit notes) with 58 per cent of female managing directors using it as compared with 44 per cent of men (p = 0.048). This is a significant difference that we do not know how to explain, especially given that there is no difference where working capital is concerned in male- or female-managed firms.

Managing directors were also asked to provide their funding priorities and the only significant difference that emerged related to short-term financing with this seen as a higher priority by men than by women (p = 0.033). On a five-point Likert scale, the average score for men is 3.04 and only 2.43 for women. This result is consistent with our previous result.

Difficulties of funding. Managing directors were asked both about the funding difficulties they faced during the last ten years (insufficient self-financing, weakness of the initial funding of the firm, difficulties to obtain banking funding – excessive financial conditions, denials of bank fundings – difficulties of obtaining more commitment from present shareholders, and difficulties of convincing new equity investors), and about the intensity of these difficulties. In general, the women's answers present a higher score than the men's although the differences between the scores of the two genders is never significant. There is only one slight significant difference (p = 0.067), which relates to excessive financial conditions (3.76 for men versus 4.50 for women on average on a scale of 5). Summing up, women do not perceive that they are being treated worse than men.

Number of banks. On average, woman have 2.10 banks and men 2.28 banks but the difference between these figures is not significant. By contrast, according to Cole and Mehran's study (2009), women use significantly fewer banks than men.

3.2.4   Behaviours, relation with their bank and external financial communication

Relationships with external investors. Managing directors were asked to describe their relationship with investors where the use of external equity funding was concerned. A five-point Likert scale was offered to respondents ('strongly disagree' to 'strongly agree') with the options being as follows: support for assessing the value of new ideas; contacts offered to develop markets; help in recruiting new employees; advice on the management of the organisation; and the development of policy/strategic ideas.

Statistical tests show that women seem to rely less on investors than men, with the female average lower on all items and significantly lower for two of them, namely (i) help with recruiting new employees (p = 0.083) and (ii) contributions to policy/strategic ideas (p = 0.02).

Relationship with the main bank. Respondents were asked to characterise their relationship with their main bank on a five-point Likert scale. Six items were available to respondents: you provide crucial information on the evolution of the company to your bank; you are heavily involved in those relationships; your bank heavily invests in your business life; your banker has visited your business or might conceivably do this; your main bank supports you more than other banks. The average is consistently higher on all items for women and is significantly different on two items, namely (i) your main bank supports you more than other banks (p = 0.084) and (ii) you are satisfied with your relationship with your main bank (p = 0.07). On these two items, the female respondents were more satisfied than the male respondents.

External financial communications. Respondents were asked if they had an external financial communications strategy, with 'yes' or 'no' answers available. It appears from a chi-square test that women communicate more than men, with 17.2 per cent of them communicating as against 8.6 per cent of men (p = 0.038). This result is significant.

Sensitivity of the managing director to growth. To the question 'for you, a strong period of growth is...', nine items were offered to managers: a motivating challenge; a source of danger and disruption; a source of personal satisfaction and gratification; an opportunity to improve the well-being of employees; a source of financial enrichment; an increased ability to control and monitor operations; a means to increase the independence of the company from its customers, suppliers and financial improvement; an opportunity to increase the sustainability of the company; a situation that the company can easily manage. Five-point Likert scales were proposed to the entrepreneurs (with options ranging from 'not at all agree' to 'strongly agree') and a significant difference in response emerged in relation to the 'possibility of improving the well-being of employees', with women more concerned about this than men (p = 0.044).

Growth seen by the entourage of the leader. This question asks respondents to indicate how others close to the entrepreneurs see their company growth. Those identified as close to the entrepreneurs are family, friends, shareholders, customers, employees, managers, leadership team, financial partners and counsellors. The five-point Likert scale ranges from 1, 'not necessary at all', to 5, 'absolutely necessary', and the results highlight the fact that most men consider growth to be a necessity for their shareholders (p = 0.017) while more women consider growth to be a necessity for their close advisers (p = 0.032).

Main objectives of the owners of the company. In response to the question, 'What are the main objectives of the owner of the company?', respondents were asked to indicate on a Likert scale ('not at all agree' to 'strongly agree') the relative importance of six items: (1) independence; (2) heritage interests; (3) growth; (4) profitability; (5) sustainability of the company; (6) selling the company. The results show that women have significantly less intention to sell their business than men (p = 0.043). This result corroborates the result on US data (Cole and Mehran, 2009), where older firms are mostly managed by women.

Ease of providing funding to the firm. Men feel equally at ease compared to women in providing funding for the activity of the firm, with the average score for men at 3.50 for men and 3.47 for women as measured by a five-point Likert scale. This result is consistent with the earlier finding that accounting and finance is the prime skill of 15.5 per cent of women and only 7.59 per cent of men.

3.2.5   *Summary of the statistical results obtained from the survey*

As can be seen, our study highlighted a total of 19 significant differences (see Tables 9.1, 9.2, 9.3, 9.4) in the responses of the men and women. These differences relate to entrepreneurs' characteristics, with women being slightly younger, having less experience in terms of creating other

Table 9.1   Entrepreneurs' characteristics

Variable	Women value	Men value	Significant differences
Age	49 years old	51 years old	P = 0.09*
Education			No difference
e.g., Master degree (b)	29.75%	32.81%	
Experience			
Creation of other companies (b)	21.50%	36.40%	P = 0.02*
Creation of other companies within the same sector (b)	42.9%	36.4%	No difference
Skills			
Accounting and finance as a prime skill (b)	15.50%	7.59%	P = 0.006**
Long training periods (b)	36.9%	35.5%	No difference
Shareholding	68.75%	86.3%	P = 0.001**
Serial entrepreneurship	9.23%	33.5%	P = 0.000**

(b) % of 'yes' answers; (*) slightly significant; (**) very significant

Table 9.2 Business characteristics and performance

Variable	Women value	Men value	Significant differences
Firm employment (number of people managed)	32	33.8	No difference
Firm age	28	28	No difference
Sector			No difference
Industry	31.48%	29.64%	
Industrial services	24.07%	32.41%	
Services	44.44%	37.94%	
Turnover	4438 K€	4798 K€	P = 0.066*
Return[1]			No difference
Stability in the growth as a choice	70.00%	26.19%	P = 0.014**

(*) slightly significant; (**) very significant

Table 9.3 Bank finance: access and perception

Variable	Women value	Men value	Significant differences
Funding strategies			
Use of short-term financing	58.00%	44.00%	P = 0.048**
Short-term financing as a priority (a)	2.43	3.04	P = 0.033**
Use of bank finance	42.00%	46.00%	No difference
Bank finance as a priority (a)	3.56	3.13	No difference
Difficulties of funding			
Insufficient self-financing (b)	27.42%	34.95%	No difference
Intensity of insufficient self-financing (a)	4.00	3.47	No difference
Insufficient initial funding (b)	19.67%	18.89%	No difference
Intensity of insufficient initial funding (a)	4.13	3.65	No difference
Denials of bank funding (b)	11.11%	11.04%	No difference
Intensity of denials of bank funding (a)	4.50	4.09	No difference
More commitment from present shareholders (b)	3.28%	6.98%	No difference
Intensity of more commitment from present shareholders (a)	4.50	4.05	No difference
Difficulties of convincing new equity investors (b)	6.45%	3.67%	No difference
Intensity of difficulties of convincing new equity investors (a)	4.25	4.40	No difference
Excessive financial conditions (b)	14.29%	13.92%	No difference
Intensity of excessive financial conditions (a)	4.50	3.76	P = 0.067*
Number of banks	2.10	2.28	No difference

(a) on a five-point Likert scale; (b) % of 'yes' answers; (*) slightly significant; (**) very significant

Table 9.4 Behaviours, relation with their bank and external financial communication

Variable	Women value	Men value	Significant differences
Having a main bank	75.81%	77.85%	No difference
Relationship with external investors			
Recruiting new employees (a)	1.16	1.50	P = 0.083*
Contribution to policy/strategic ideas (a)	1.72	2.44	P = 0.02**
Relationship with the main bank			
Provide crucial information on the evolution of the firm to the bank (a)	3.77	3.58	No difference
Firm manager heavily involved in the relationship (a)	3.51	3.36	No difference
The bank heavily invests in the firm business life (a)	3.02	2.78	No difference
The banker has visited the business or could do so (a)	4.26	3.96	No difference
Main bank support (a)	3.76	3.35	P = 0.084*
Satisfaction (a)	4.09	3.58	P = 0.07**
External financial communication	17.2%	8.6%	P = 0.038**
Sensitivity of the managing director to growth			
Possibility of improving the well-being of employees (a)	3.67	3.97	P = 0.044**
Motivating challenge (a)	4.13	4.22	No difference
A source of danger and disruption (a)	2.40	2.50	No difference
A source of personal satisfaction (a)	3.69	3.89	No difference
A source of personal satisfaction and gratification (a)	3.97	3.67	No difference
A source of financial enrichment (a)	3.55	3.55	No difference
An increased ability to control and monitor operations (a)	2.31	2.55	No difference
A means to increase the independence of the firm (a)	3.50	3.58	No difference
An opportunity to increase the sustainability of the firm (a)	4.08	4.17	No difference
A situation that the firm can easily manage (a)	3.16	3.20	No difference
Growth seen by the entourage of the leader			

A necessity for their shareholders (a)	2.64	3.19	P = 0.017**
A necessity for their close advisers (a)	3.40	2.99	P = 0.032**
Main objectives of the owners of the company			
Intention to sell the business (a)	2.07	2.49	P = 0.043**
Independence (a)	4.46	4.33	No difference
Heritage interests (a)	3.53	3.50	No difference
Growth (a)	3.97	3.96	No difference
Profitability (a)	4.55	4.40	No difference
Sustainability (a)	4.68	4.61	No difference
Ease of providing funding to the firm			No difference

(a) on a five-point Likert scale; (b) % of 'yes' answers; (*) slightly significant; (**) very significant

companies, being more likely to have accounting and finance as a prime skill and being less likely to be a serial entrepreneur. Differences also emerged in terms of business characteristics and objectives, with women's turnover being lower than men's and stability in growth having a higher priority for women than men. Consistent with this last point is a lesser intention on the part of the women to sell the business than is expressed by the men. Other differences relate to the fact that women place less reliance on external investors and higher levels of satisfaction with the support received from a bank. In terms of the management of the business, the women were shown to be more concerned about improving the well-being of employees compared to the men in the sample. These results illustrate, we believe, the need to take gender into account in future research and also in the way that financiers and banks deal with women. Awareness of these differences can lead financiers and banks to profit from diversity by honing their products to the preferences of male and female entrepreneurs.

In contrast to these differences, the results do not highlight any significant differences between men and women in their level of formal education and choice of sector.

There are several possible explanations for these findings and the authors of this chapter believe that these results are related not to internalised gender differences but to masculine versus female values (gender identity), and the conceptual background to this way of thinking is explored in the next section. This is in line with a social femininist approach.

4   Section 3: Discussion and conclusion

Gender stereotypes are sets of attributes ascribed to the groups of men and women by the virtue of their sex (Deaux and LaFrance, 1998; Eagly et al., 2000), and one way of explaining some of the results is with reference to stereotypes. A stereotype is a cognitive mechanism to simplify and organise the complex world around us, and the male stereotype is characterised by high amounts of 'masculine' traits that are task-oriented or agentic (e.g., dominance, autonomy and achievement), while the female stereotype is characterised by high amounts of 'feminine' traits that are interpersonally oriented or communal (e.g., deference, nurturance and affiliation). Gender stereotypes are both prescriptive and descriptive; that is, beliefs about the traits that males and females actually possess translate into beliefs about the traits that males and females should possess (Eagly et al., 2000). Gender socialisation during childhood and adolescence, which is facilitated by parents, schools, peers and the mass media, encourages adherence to gender stereotypes (Deaux and LaFrance, 1998; Ruble and Martin, 1998; Eagly et al., 2000).

Some might explain these differences, moreover, with reference to gender identity, which describes the extent to which an individual believes that he or she possesses traits associated with traditional gender stereotypes (Bem, 1974, 1993), with gender identity framed by two independent dimensions: *masculinity*, or beliefs about the extent to which one possesses traits associated with males (such as aggressiveness, ambition, dominance and independence); and *femininity*, or beliefs about the extent to which one possesses traits associated with females (such as compassion, sensitivity to the needs of others, understanding and warmth) (Bem, 1974, 1993; Eagly et al., 2000). Business owners of both sexes may vary from high to low in masculinity and from high to low in femininity. Individuals develop a sense of themselves through the social categorisation and identification process (Tajfel and Turner, 1986; Ashforth and Mael, 1989) and not just through biological sex which refers to a physiological property of individuals (e.g., Bem, 1993; Fischer et al., 1993) and does not necessarily determine what he or she values as a business owner.

According to this way of thinking, since sex is a highly visible basis for self-categorisation, individuals identify with personal traits attributed to members of the same sex, and being categorised as male or female motivates individuals to adopt the corresponding gender identity. Thus, we might expect business owners' sex to be associated with their gender identity such that male business owners are higher in masculinity and lower in femininity than female business owners (Bem, 1974, 1993; Deaux and LaFrance, 1998).

Although gender identity is thought to be influenced by socialisation experiences during childhood (Deaux and LaFrance, 1998; Eagly et al., 2000; Ruble and Martin, 1998), it is also said to be somewhat malleable in adulthood as people age (Markus and Wurf, 1987) and is influenced by life experiences (Kirchmeyer, 2002; Kasen et al., 2006).

The literature review has highlighted studies focusing mainly on comparisons between men and women and differences in managing the relationship between banks and entrepreneurs. The results of our study and discussion on the concept of gender advocates an inclusion of a more detailed assessment of these differences, not only based on comparisons in terms of biological sex but also in terms of degrees of masculinity and femininity as conceptualised in the literature. According to one academic (Bem, 1981), gender is a psychological orientation determined by an individual's personal attitudes, values and self-concept and is not determined by biological sex. Bem developed the Bem Sex Role Inventory (BSRI; Bem, 1974, 1981), a widely used instrument to measure gender role perceptions and androgynous attitudes, i.e., attitudes that display both stereotypical masculine and feminine traits (Bem, 1974). Bem (1981) has developed a short 30-item version of the scale and the authors of this chapter think that this Bem scale could be used in future research.

In terms of the directions that future research could take, we would argue in favour of the integration of the gender concept (degree of masculinity versus femininity, regardless of the biological sex of the respondent), leading us to formulate the following two propositions.

Proposition 1: Satisfaction of his/her principal bank will be positively related to the femininity dimension of gender identity. It would now be interesting in further research to cross gender and the relational mode of managing bank relationships. For instance, an analysis based on the respondent sex shows that females tend to communicate more and have a greater sense than males that their bankers are more benevolent than males so, looking at these results through the lens of the social contract theory (Macneil, 1980), the proposition that gender may have an impact on the way managers manage their relationships could be relevant. Indeed, Macneil (1980) defines transactional and relational exchanges on process characteristics such as the level of social interaction and communication, the level of contractual solidarity, the ability to transfer rights, obligations and satisfactions to other parties and the level of cooperation (Dwyer et al., 1987). It seems that differences between male and female exist on these dimensions. So to cross gender and relational mode of managing bank relationships could help understand both still unexplained gender differences and the relational mode of managing bank relationships.

Proposition 2: The mode of managing bank relationships will be positively related to the femininity dimension of gender identity, while the mode of relationship management in banking of a transactional nature will be linked to the dimension of masculinity of gender identity.

In order for banks better to profit from diversity, we invite banks to put to one side any stereotypes that they may have of male and female entrepreneurial behaviour in order to make the most of the relations they have with firms. A typology that makes space for entrepreneurs' gender identity will permit a more relevant understanding of expectations of entrepreneurs than one based solely on biological gender.

Note

1. Return has been studied with data available on Diane database (2002–2008): return on assets; return on equity.

References

Acker, J. (1992), 'Gendering organizational theory', in Mills, A. and Tancred, P. (eds), *Gendering Organizational Analysis* (pp. 248–260). London: Sage.

Ahl, H. (2002), 'The making of the female entrepreneur. A discourse analysis of research texts on women's entrepreneurship', *JIBS Dissertation Series 015*, Jonkoping University.

Ahl, H. (2006), 'Why research on women entrepreneurs needs new directions', *Entrepreneurship Theory and Practice*, 30 (5), 595–621.

APCE (2001), Annual report from the APCE (French Agency for Firm Creation), http://www.apce.com/pid266/etudes-et-publications

APCE (2007), Annual report from the APCE (French Agency for Firm Creation), http://www.apce.com/pid266/etudes-et-publications

Ashforth, B. E. and Mael, F. (1989), 'Social identity theory and the organization', *Academy of Management Review*, 14, 20–39.

Becker, G. S. (1957), *The Economics of Discrimination*. Chicago: University of Chicago Press.

Bellucci, A., Borisov, A. and Zazzaro, A. (2009), 'Does gender matter in bank–firm relationships?' Evidence from small business lending, MOFIR, Working Paper No. 31, October.

Bem, S. L. (1974), 'The measurement of psychological androgyny', *Journal of Consulting and Clinical Psychology*, 42, 155–162.

Bem, S. L. (1981), *Bem Sex Role Inventory Professional Manual*, Palo Alto, CA: Consulting Psychologists Press.

Bem, S. L. (1993), *The Lenses of Gender: Transforming the Debate on Sexual Inequality*, New Haven: Yale University Press.

Bird, B. and Brush, C. (2002), 'A gendered perspective on organizational creation', *Entrepreneurship Theory and Practice*, 26 (3), 41–65.

Bruni, A., Gherardi, S. and Poggio, B. (2004), 'Doing gender, doing entrepreneurship: an ethnographic account of intertwined practices', *Gender, Work and Organization*, 11, 406–429.

Brush, C. G. (1992), 'Research on women business owners: past trends, a new perspective and future directions', *Entrepreneurship Theory and Practice*, 16 (4), 5–30.

Carter, S., Shaw, E., Lam, W. and Wilson, F. (2007), 'Gender, entrepreneurship, and bank lending: the criteria and processes used by bank loan officers in assessing applications', *Entrepreneurship Theory and Practice*, 31 (3), 427–444.

Chodorow, N. (1971), *The Reproduction of Mothering: Psychoanalysis and the Sociology of Gender*. Berkeley, CA: University of California Press.

Cliff, J. E. (1998), 'Does one size fit all? Exploring the relationship between attitudes towards growth, gender, and business size', *Journal of Business Venturing*, 13, 523–542.

Cole, R. A. and Mehran, H. (2009), 'Gender and the availability of credit to privately held firms: evidence from the surveys of small business finances', *Federal Reserve Bank of New York Staff Reports*, No. 383.

Coleman, S. (2000), 'Access to capital and terms of credit: a comparison of men- and women-owned small businesses', *Journal of Small Business Management*, 38 (3), 37–52.

Coleman, S. (2007), 'The role of human and financial capital in the profitability and growth of women-owned small firms', *Journal of Small Business Management*, 45 (3), 303–319.

Constantinidis, C., Cornet, A. and Asabdei, S. (2006), 'Financing of women-owned ventures: the impact of gender and other owner – and firm – related variables', *Venture Capital*, 8(2), 133–157.

Croson, R. and Gneezy, U. (2009), 'Gender differences in preferences', *Journal of Economic Literature*, 47 (2), 1–27.

Deaux, K. and Lafrance, M. (1998), 'Gender', in Gilbert, D. T., Fiske, S. T. and Lindzey, G. (eds), 4th edition, *The Handbook of Social Psychology*, Vol. 1. (pp. 788–827), Boston, MA: McGraw-Hill.

Dwyer, R. F., Schurr, P. H. and Oh, F. (1987), 'Developing buyer-seller relations', *Journal of Marketing*, 51, 11–28.

Eagly, A. H., Wood, W. and Diekman, A. B. (2000), 'Social role theory of sex differences and similarities: a current appraisal', in Eckes, T. and Trautner, H. M. (eds), *The Developmental Social Psychology of Gender* (pp. 123–174), Mahwah, NJ: Erlbaum.

Fay, M. and Williams, L. (1993), 'Gender bias and the availability of business loans', *Journal of Business Venturing*, 8 (July), 363–376.

Fischer, E. M., Reuber, A. R. and Dyke, L. S. (1993), 'A theoretical overview and extension of research on sex, gender, and entrepreneurship', *Journal of Business Venturing*, 8 (2), 51–168.

Hurley, A. E. (1991), 'Incorporating feminist theories into sociological theories of entrepreneurship', paper presented at the Annual Meetings of the Academy of Management, Miami FL, August.

INSEE (2005), Tableau de l'Economie française au 01/01/2005, www.insee.fr

208 *Profiting from Diversity in the Banking Sector*

INSEE, DADS (2008), data published in July 2010, www.insee.fr

Kasen, S., Chen, H., Sneed, J., Crawford, T. and Cohen, P. (2006), 'Social role and birth cohort influences on gender linked personality traits in women: a 20-year longitudinal analysis', *Journal of Personality and Social Psychology*, 91, 944–958.

Kirchmeyer, C. (2002), 'Change and stability in managers' gender roles', *Journal of Applied Psychology*, 87, 929–939.

Légare, M. H. and Saint-Cyr, L. (1999), *Portrait statistique des femmes entrepreneures: les indicateurs de l'entrepreneuriat féminin et la disponibilité des données sur les femmes et leur entreprise*, Rapport d'expertise déposé et publié par le Ministère de l'Industrie et du Commerce, Montréal, décembre.

Macneil, I. R. (1980), *The New Social Contract*, New Haven, CT: Yale University Press.

Markus, H. and Wurf, E. (1987), 'The dynamic self-concept: a social psychological perspective', in Rosenzweig, M. R. and Porter, L. W. (eds), *Annual Review of Psychology*, Vol. 38 (pp. 299–337), Palo Alto, CA: Annual Reviews.

Marlow, S. and Patton, D. N. (2005), 'All credit to men? Entrepreneurship, finance and gender', *Entrepreneurship Theory and Practice*, 29 (6), 717–735.

Mcmanus, P. (2001), 'Women's participation in self-employment in western industrialized nations', *International Journal of Sociology*, 31 (2), 70–97.

Mills, A. J. (1989),' Gender, sexuality, and organization theory', in Hearn, J., Sheppard, D. L. and Tancred-Sheriff, P. (eds), *The Sexuality of Organization*, London: Sage.

Minnitti, M., Allen, I. E. and Langowitz, N. (2005), 'Global entrepreneurship monitor: 2005', Report on Women Entrepreneurship, Babson College, Center for Women's Leadership at Babson College, London Business School.

Mirchandani, K. (1999), 'Feminist insight on gendered work: new directions in research on women and entrepreneurship', *Gender, Work and Organization*, 6 (4), 224–235.

Muravyev, A., Talavera, O. and Schaefer, D. (2009), 'Entrepreneurs' gender and financial contraints: evidence from international data', *Journal of Comparative Economics*, 37 (2), 270–286.

Ogbor, J. O. (2000), 'Mythicizing and reification in entrepreneurial discourse: ideology-critique of entrepreneurial studies', *Journal of Management Studies*, 37 (5), 605–635.

Reed, R. (1996), 'Entrepreneurialism and paternalism in Australian management: a gender critique of the "self-made" man', in Collinson, D. L. and Hearn, J. (eds), *Men as Managers, Managers as Men* (pp. 99–122), London: Sage.

Robb, A. and Wolken, J. (2002), 'Firm, owner, and financing characteristics: differences between female- and male-owned small businesses', *Finance and Economic Discussion Series, Division of Research & Statistics and Monetary Affairs*, Federal Reserve Board, Washington, DC, No. 2002–18.

Ruble, D. N. and Martin, C. L. (1998), 'Gender development', in Damon, W. (ed.), *Handbook of Child Psychology*, 5th edition, Social, Emotional, and Personality Development, Vol. 3 (pp. 933–1016), New York: Wiley.

Saint-Cyr, L., Hountondji, S. and Beaudoin, N. (2003), *Mémoire présenté au Groupe de travail du Premier Ministre sur les femmes entrepreneures*, Chaire de développement et de relève de la PME – HEC Montréal et Réseau des femmes d'affaire du Québec, http://www.liberal.parl.gc.ca/entrepreneur/documents/030623_feedback_103.doc

Stevenson, L. (1990), 'Some methodological problems associated with researching women entrepreneurs', *Journal of Business Ethics*, 9 (4/5), 439–446.

Tajfel, H. and Turner, J. C. (1986), 'The social identity theory of intergroup behavior', in Worchel, S. and Austin, W. G. (eds), *Psychology of Intergroup Relations*, 2nd edition (pp. 7–24), Chicago, IL: Nelson-Hall.

Trebilcot, J. (1973), 'Sex roles, the argument from nature', Paper presented at the meeting of the American Philosophical Association, Western Division, April.

Treichel, M. Z. and Scott, J. A. (2006), 'Women-owned businesses and access to bank credit: evidence from three surveys since 1987', *Venture Capital*, Vol. 8, No. 1, 51–67, January.

Verheul, I. (2005), 'Is there a (fe)male approach? Understanding gender differences in entrepreneurship', ERIM PhD Series, Erasmus University, Rotterdam.

Walker, E. and Brown, A. (2004), 'What success factors are important to small business owners?', *International Small Business Journal*, 22, 577–594.

Watson, J. and Robinson, S. (2003), 'Adjusting for risk in comparing the performance of male and female controlled SMEs', *Journal of Business Venturing*, 18 (6), 773–778.

Disability

10
Deaf People in the Workplace

Marion Hersh

1 What does it mean to be deaf?

Most people probably consider deafness in purely audiological terms; that is, as a hearing impairment. However, there are alternative definitions based on culture, language use and community membership (Ladd, 2003; Lane, 2005; Obasi, 2008). The chapter will commence with a brief discussion of the different meanings of 'deafness' and some statistics. (As is frequent practice, 'deaf' with a small d will be used to indicate some degree of audiological deafness and Deaf with a capital D cultural and linguistic identification as Deaf and use of sign language.) However, the author is not deaf and therefore her perspective is that of an informed and sympathetic outsider.

There are a number of different estimates of the number of deaf people, depending on the definition used and how the data is collected. For instance, the Royal National Institute for Deaf People (RNID) in the UK considers that about one in seven (14.3 per cent) of the population has some degree of hearing impairment (RNID, undated a), whereas the National Association of the Deaf in the US uses a figure of 6.6 per cent, the World Christian Encyclopaedia 10 per cent (DEAF, undated) and the 1990 and 1991 US Health Interview Surveys 8.6 per cent (Holt et al., 1994). There is general agreement that the extent of hearing impairment increases with age.

As an illustrative example, the following statistics collected by the RNIB (undated a, b) for the UK will be presented. An estimated total of 8.9 million people have some degree of hearing impairment; 4 million of them could probably benefit from a hearing aid, but only 2 million people have aids and only 1.4 million use them regularly. Some 3.5 million people of working age (16–65) have some degree of hearing impairment, with 16,000 of them severely or profoundly deaf. In addition, half a million adults are severely affected by tinnitus, with most of them also having some degree of hearing impairment.

Only a very small proportion of deaf people are members of the Deaf community. The RNID estimates that there are 50,000 people in the UK who use British sign language as their first or preferred language (RNID, undated a). In the US, data on American sign language users is still based on the 1972 National Census of Deaf People, which found that there were about 277,000 deaf good signers (Mitchell et al., 2006). Many deaf people require some form of communication support, including speech-to-text conversion, subtitles, lipspeakers (who repeat what has been said with very clear lip patterns), notetakers and sign language interpreters. In the UK the ratios of British sign language interpreters (including trainees) and fully qualified interpreters for sign language users are 1 to 156 and 1 to 275 respectively (RNIB, undated b). This indicates the need for more sign language interpreters to be trained, as well as organisations to encourage some of their employees or members to learn sign language, to allow them to interact with Deaf members, employees and service-users, on at least a basic level.

Membership of the Deaf community is dependent on a combination of factors such as audiological deafness, political support for the goals of the Deaf community, fluency in sign language, contacts in the community and a positive attitude to Deaf people, their language and culture (Napier, 2002). The difference between audiological and cultural deafness is underlined by the fact that not all audiologically deaf people are part of the Deaf community, whereas some hearing people, particularly hearing children of Deaf adults (CODAs) and sign language interpreters, may be (Preston, 1995; Napier, 2002). Audiologically deaf individuals can become culturally Deaf at any time in their lives. However, the difficulties in acquiring a new language in later life, as well as the very significant differences between oral and visual communication, make it unlikely that people who become deaf later in life will acquire sign language and join the Deaf community.

Many Deaf people see themselves as part of a cultural and linguistic and sometimes also an ethnic minority rather than disabled (Ladd, 2005; Lane, 2005; Obasi, 2008), though they may make alliances with organisations of disabled people. Only about 10 per cent of deaf people are born in Deaf families (Sparrow, 2005), and therefore most Deaf people acquire Deaf culture from residential schools for deaf children (Ladd, 2003). However, the trend is towards mainstream schools and the closure of separate residential deaf/Deaf schools, leading to a concern among many Deaf people about a loss of their culture (Moores and Meadow-Orlans, 1991).

Deaf people who use spoken language generally welcome devices that will improve their hearing. However, they may be reluctant to wear hearing aids. The reasons include not admitting to themselves that they are becoming deaf and/or getting older; not recognising the potential benefits of an aid; cosmetic factors; negative perceptions of hearing aids and/or not wanting to seem to be different or stigmatised; and, where aids are not supplied free, cost (Atcherson, 2002; Kochkin, undated). This shows the importance of the appearance of assistive devices, which should be attractive, inconspicuous or resemble commonly used appliances.

Deaf people share the diversity of the rest of the population with regards to gender, ethnic origin, (other) impairments, age and interests, although those who identify as Deaf are more likely to engage in activities with other Deaf people. Being Deaf is the primary identity for many Deaf people, whereas for others another identity, such as being black, is more important (Foster and Kinuthia, 2003). There are a number of different sign languages, just as there are different spoken languages. However, Deaf people using different sign languages generally find it much easier to communicate with each other than do hearing people using different spoken languages.

Many deaf people have poor reading and writing skills (Kronreif et al., 2000; Debevc, 2002; Lang and Steely, 2003). This lack of functional literacy forms a barrier to their further careers, as well as their participation in leisure activities. Although their educational potential and cognitive skills are similar to those of their hearing peers (Paul and Quigley, 1984; Rodda and Grove, 1987; Bradley-Johnson and Evans, 1991), deaf people are much less likely to complete higher education (Lang, 2002) and have low expectations of promotion (RNID, 1987; Bradshaw, 2002).

One of the causes of poor literacy is poor language skills. There is, therefore, a need for appropriate strategies for language and literacy development for deaf children, and language and literacy improvement for deaf adults. These strategies should recognise both that sign language is the natural communication mode for deaf people (Sacks, 1990) and the benefits of spoken language for facilitating access to education and employment.

2 A brief survey of the current employment situation of deaf people

A small number of surveys have been carried out of deaf people's experiences in the workplace. A survey by Foster and MacLeod (2003) of communication in the workplace among deaf supervisors identified the following three factors that facilitate or impede communication: the characteristics of the organisation, and those of its hearing employees; and the strategies used by deaf employees to overcome barriers. The availability and quality of accommodations were considered important, as were organisational size, policy, culture and physical environment. However, surveys have found that the required accommodations were not always available and that the quality of available accommodations was often uneven or poor (Foster and MacLeod, 2003; Punch et al., 2007). The most commonly provided accommodations were found to be assistive devices such as amplified telephones and text telephones, with support frequently available on an informal rather than a formal basis. For instance, a co-worker might make a phone call for a hearing-impaired colleague (Scherich and Mowry, 1997). Even where high-quality assistive technology or support professionals were available, some respondents considered, for instance, using a text-phone or relay service to be insufficiently professional and the delays involved a barrier to communication. In addition, even the presence of interpreters did not always fully bridge the communication gap and interpreters were considered to be not particularly useful in informal social situations.

The attitudes of hearing colleagues and supervisors and their knowledge of deafness was very important, with supportive colleagues with positive attitudes and an understanding of the communication needs of deaf people making a real difference. Deaf people considered flexibility and the ability to change strategies important, as well as taking control of the situation to enhance communication. One respondent stressed the importance of reading and writing for deaf people, particularly to enable them to engage in learning on their own (Foster and MacLeod, 2003). This indicates the importance of measures to improve the education of deaf people, including, but not restricted to, the areas of literacy and numeracy. A small-scale survey of mentoring for deaf people in employment (Sheill, undated) showed that it was very beneficial, and recommended the development of a strategy for mentoring Deaf people and the setting up of a network of mentors with accredited training.

Noisy workplaces and group situations cause difficulties for deaf people (Scherich, 1996). A survey of deaf people and employers of deaf people (ibid.) showed that difficulties were experienced by more than half the respondents in work-related social functions, meetings, in-service training, socialising with co-workers and receiving instructions and supervisions, and led to the following recommendations:

- Problem-solving training to assist workers in identifying appropriate workplace accommodations.
- Training for workers in using 'marketing' approaches to obtain accommodations, with marketing approaches based on long-term associations and stressing the benefits to both parties.
- An accessible source of information for workers and employers on effective accommodations.

3 Benefits of employing deaf people

While this section will discuss what is often called the 'business case' for employing deaf people, it should be recognised that the reasons for doing so go beyond this business case, with the wider reasons relating to human rights, social justice and fairness. It should also be noted that both maximising the benefits to organisations and increasing social justice require that deaf people are employed throughout them and in senior and not just entry-level positions.

There are a number of studies which show that policies that successfully promote equality and diversity have positive impacts on organisations (EEOT, 2008), but much of the discussion has related to gender and race rather than disability. For instance, studies show that high achievers prefer to work in organisations with diversity policies, practices and values (Ng and Burke, 2005) and that such policies, practices and values generally result in improvements in productivity, sales, morale, staff retention, human capital, market access, reputation and employment relations (Kirton and Greene, 2005; Monks 2007). More than half of the 200 companies surveyed by the European Commission identified the benefits as improved long-term competitiveness, as well as sometimes improved short-term performance. However, other studies (quoted in EEOT, 2008) showed neutral or negative outcomes. Studies noted the importance of providing information on dealing with differences constructively in order to achieve the benefits, and the need to develop conditions which minimise performance barriers and maximise performance enhancement from a diverse workforce (Cox, 2001). Factors which lead to poor business outcomes from diversity (Sinclair, 2006) include entrenched discriminatory attitudes and beliefs, lack of awareness of systemic discrimination and the need for structural change, and a focus on other people's differences rather than changing organisational policies and practices. Thus, this brief discussion indicates that increasing the diversity of the workforce will generally have significant benefits for an organisation, unless it is badly managed and/or the organisation is marked by systemic discrimination.

There is some evidence that employers are concerned about employing people who are profoundly deaf and are not always aware when they are employing people who are hard of hearing (Scherich, 1996). However, employing deaf people generally has a number of benefits, which can be categorised as follows:

- Extending the talent pool
- Retaining skilled employees who become deaf
- The skills, aptitudes and approaches which deaf people may bring to the organisation
- Positive impacts on the organisation of a more diverse workforce
- Improved public relations and wider markets

Since deaf people have the same extent of variation of skills as hearing people, employing them increases the pool of potential employees (HREOC, 2005a), thereby increasing an employer's choices and chances of finding a suitable employee with the desired skills and qualities. While of value in general, this is particularly important when there are either general or specific skills shortages. It also increases the talent pool and consequently the likelihood of finding unusually talented and creative employees or employees with specialised skills who are likely to make a very significant contribution to the organisation.

Since the incidence of deafness increases with age (RNID, undated a), it is important that organisations are 'deaf friendly' so that they are able both to retain skilled employees who have become hard of hearing or deaf with age and make the best use of the skills and experiences of these employees. Employers who do not provide appropriate adjustments, practices and policies or where the attitudes of managers and co-workers are hostile, may lose the skills and accumulated experience of valuable employees due to age-related hearing impairment. Alternatively, these employees may stay with the organisation, but take great pains to hide their hearing impairments. This will prevent them accessing appropriate accommodations and may subject them to stress, lead to misunderstandings and possibly even conflict with co-workers and a deterioration in performance as communication becomes more difficult.

In addition to their job-related skills, training and experience, many deaf employees may additionally have particular skills, aptitudes and approaches as a result of their experiences of deafness. Like other disabled people, many deaf workers will have had to learn a range of strategies and techniques for doing things in order to cope in environments and use facilities that are designed for non-disabled people, and poorly adapted to them. In the case of deaf people, these strategies and techniques relate to communication. Deaf (and other disabled) people are likely to bring this adaptability and creativity into the workplace with them and may therefore be better at finding innovative and useful solutions to a range of workplace problems.

Several small-scale studies show that deaf and hearing people have different 'preferred' hemispheres for processing complex stimuli, such as pictures and letters, as well as detecting target shapes in the peripheral visual field (Phippard, 1977; Reynolds, 1993). In addition, there are indications that deaf people have less cerebral asymmetry than hearing people (Reynolds, 1993). While further research is required to investigate what these differences mean for the problem-solving and creative processes of deaf and hearing people, there are likely to be advantages to organisations which employ both deaf and hearing people so that both preferences are fully represented. Many deaf people use largely visual communication strategies. They are therefore likely to use visual thinking processes and approaches to problem solving. Thus, deaf people with relevant aptitudes and qualifications may be particularly suited to professions such as architecture, design, fine arts, surgery and astronomy, where visual perceptions, visual judgements and/or hand–eye coordination are important.

Studies (Loke and Song, 1991; Reynolds, 1993; Rettenbach et al., 1999; Bavelier et al., 2001; Proksch and Bavelier, 2002) show that deaf adults (but generally not also deaf children) have faster responses or otherwise perform better than hearing people in attention-dependent visual tasks, particularly those involving their peripheral visual field. Evidence (Proksch and Bavelier, 2002; Bavelier et al., 2006) that deaf signers shift attentional resources to peripheral vision, compared to hearing people, gives support to suggestions that deaf people have enhanced peripheral vision. Although signing may augment the transfer of visual attention to the peripheral field, it is deafness rather than signing experience that is significant, as native hearing signers who sign daily do not have enhanced peripheral visual attention (Proksch and Bavelier, 2002; Bavelier et al., 2006).

Employing a disabled person can act as a catalyst for beneficial change (Graffam et al., 2002). In the case of deaf people, the need to rethink the various communication strategies and approaches used, while initially difficult, can lead to new ways of thinking and problem solving and an increase in creativity and innovation. Employing disabled workers frequently leads to an improvement in organisational performance. The factors responsible probably include a combination of greater expectations and standards for all employees; the presence of disabled workers acting as a catalyst for change; improved morale, worker and customer relations; and the discovery of inefficient workplace processes. The safety and insurance costs of disabled workers have been found to be marginally less than those of non-disabled workers. The flexibility required to employ disabled workers also has benefits for all workers and the organisation in general (HREOC, 2005a).

Adapting the practice of carefully matching the job to the skills of a deaf person is likely to increase the overall efficiency of the organisation (HREOC, 2005a). When extended to hearing employees this has the benefits of ensuring that all employees are well suited to their jobs. The one caveat is the need to ensure that the matching process allows for growth and development within the job. More careful staff training and supervision for deaf employees can increase productivity and improve workplace and customer relations (HREOC, 2005a). However, it is important to ensure that more careful staff training and supervision does not become intrusive or controlling. Further organisational advantages of employing disabled workers (HREOC, 2005a), which are presumably relevant to the specific case of deaf workers, include increased workplace safety, performance and retention, as well as reduced absences and turnover.

A more diverse workplace can lead to more diverse markets (HREOC, 2005a). In particular, employment of deaf people is likely to increase marketability to deaf and hearing-impaired people. Due to the cohesiveness of the Deaf community and the importance of signed communication, businesses that employ Deaf people are likely to be particularly attractive to other Deaf people. However, all deaf people are likely to prefer and find it easier to patronise businesses which are deaf friendly. In addition to employing deaf people, organisations will require appropriate accommodations, practices and policies to ensure that they are truly welcoming to deaf people and enable them to have full access to information and to communicate on equal terms.

Like hearing people, deaf people are individuals with a wide range of different characteristics, interests and aptitudes. Despite the very real benefits of employing deaf people discussed above, it can happen that the employment of a particular deaf person is unsuccessful. This does not imply that all or even many deaf people are poor workers, any more than lack of satisfaction with a hearing worker would imply that all or even many hearing people are poor workers. In addition, the problem may be due to the lack of appropriate job accommodations or organisational practices rather than with the particular worker.

4 Inclusion: contextual factors

Full inclusion in the workplace should be considered a right for deaf people as much as for any other group of workers. In addition, lack of full inclusion may lead to frustration, isolation and underperformance, and could have significant disadvantages for both the particular worker and their employer, as well as their co-workers. Full inclusion of deaf workers will generally require one or more of the following:

- A good local acoustic environment.
- The provision of assistive technology (Hersh and Johnson, 2003).
- The provision of support professionals, such as sign language interpreters, lipreaders and notetakers.
- Changes in organisational polices and/or practices.

It should be noted that the provision of assistive technology and support professionals may be alternative means of achieving the same outcome, and that some deaf people will prefer support professionals and others assistive technology. In addition, there is a need for a local and national context which encourages and supports employers to carry out appropriate adjustments and to make their workplaces accessible and welcoming to deaf people.

4.1 Local context: acoustic environment and lighting

A well-lit quiet working environment is beneficial to all workers, but particularly important for deaf workers to enable them to communicate effectively. Communication by deaf people generally has a visual component, whether signing or lipreading. They therefore require bright but not dazzling and appropriately sited lighting in order to see details of the hands and faces of the people they are talking to and communicate with them. Social aspects of the workplace are often as important as more formal job-related aspects. Therefore, the need for good lighting extends to all the areas where communication takes place, such as corridors, social spaces, cafeterias, the stairs, entrances, sports facilities and toilets/washrooms. Care should be taken to choose quiet, well-lit restaurants or other venues for social or networking events and to provide deaf employees with the same type of communication support as they would have in a formal meeting. However, full inclusion of deaf employees will generally require all the real decisions to be made in formal meetings, where communication is likely to be easier, rather than in these social venues.

Most people find it more difficult to understand spoken communications in noisy environments but this is particularly problematical for deaf people who use spoken language (Walden and Walden, 2004; Sunitha and Udayashankara, 2005). (Deaf signers are generally unaffected by noise.) Proactive approaches to reducing noise levels (Hersh, 2010) will improve working conditions for all workers. Where discussion in small groups occurs, it is important that each discussion group takes place in a separate room, to avoid interference from the discussion in other groups. Deaf people who do not have their own office space will probably require access to a quiet room to make phone calls (if they are able to use the phone) and have discussions with colleagues and clients.

4.2   National and legislative context

This discussion is based on a number of surveys. An inquiry by the Australian Human Rights and Equal Opportunities Commission into the measures required to improve the participation, recruitment and retention of disabled people in the open workplace produced a list of 30 recommendations (HREOC, 2005b), which largely covered actions at the public policy level. Two of the most significant recommendations, which subsumed many of the others, were a national strategy for the employment of disabled people, and the setting up of a one-stop information shop. This national strategy should involve a whole-of-government approach and ensure the following:

- Adequate income support and transport, equipment and health-care subsidies and concessions.
- Adequate workplace supports and modifications, and personal assistance in the home and workplace.
- Improved transition to work schemes for disabled people in education and training.
- Increased recruitment and retention of disabled people in the public sector and improved relationships between private sector employers and government-funded information, recruitment and employment support services.
- Development of a benchmarking, monitoring and reporting system for accountability and continuous improvement of the incentives, supports and services for disabled people and employers.

The one-stop information shop should be fully accessible, including by having publications in different formats and media. It should be adequately served by appropriately trained personnel and have a freephone number, minicom number and email service that respond promptly to enquiries. There should be ongoing consultation with disabled people, employers and employment services on developing the information site and advisory service and the strategy for maintaining, updating and developing the service, and it should be widely publicised. Other recommendations include researching good practice in other countries, mapping existing services, and developing guidelines and strategies for promoting flexible workplaces which meet the needs of different groups of employees.

Evidence of the lack of availability of necessary accommodations in the workplace (Foster and MacLeod, 2003; Punch et al., 2007) indicates a need for measures to ensure that adjustments are available to all employees regardless of their job or status. These measures should include appropriate funding in the case of more expensive accommodations, such as interpreters or lipspeakers, as well as information about the benefits of employing deaf people and appropriately resourcing their employment (Punch et al., 2007).

A study of the work transitions of deaf adolescents with significant hearing impairments who communicate orally (Punch et al., 2004) noted the importance of part-time jobs or work experience in developing understanding of career-related issues and career search skills and the need for options which are accessible to deaf people. Many after school and holiday jobs require understanding of rapid oral instructions and requests, making them unsuitable for deaf people. There is also a need for parents (and career advisers) to encourage deaf young people to explore the world and to investigate potentially challenging career options. Currently many of their parents are over-protective, have low career expectations of them and either give little guidance on career choice or discourage deaf young people from careers which require a high degree of interaction with other people (Danermark et al., 2001; Punch et al., 2004). There is also a need for considerably greater support, expectations and counselling about higher education (Danermark et al., 2001).

A number of studies show both higher rates of unemployment for deaf than hearing people and severe underemployment, with deaf people in employment not working full time or at a level below their ability (Winn, 2007). Although a comparison of four studies of the employment situation of deaf people between 1960 and 2005 showed some increase in the percentage of deaf people in professional occupations from zero, deaf people continue to be under-represented in professional occupations, underemployed, and earn less than their hearing peers despite significant anti-discrimination legislation (Schroedel and Geyer, 2001; Winn, 2007). Thus, though important, anti-discrimination legislation is insufficient, not appropriately targeted or not enforced. However, there is evidence that completing secondary and post-secondary education leads to better-paid employment and lower rates of unemployment (Dauman et al., 2000, Winn, 2007). Among deaf people with post-secondary education, advanced degrees have been found to lead to better jobs and increased job satisfaction (Geyer and Schroedel, 1998).

Consequently there is an urgent need for research in the following areas and measures to implement its findings:

- The lack of effectiveness of disability discrimination legislation in removing discrimination and approximately equalising employment outcomes for deaf (and other disabled) and non-disabled people. (The author suspects that the lack of significant enforcement measures with stringent penalties for non-compliance is an important factor.)
- Why the education system is failing many deaf (and other disabled people), leading to lower rates of literacy and numeracy and fewer qualifications than their hearing peers, and the measures required to change this. Language and communication issues are clearly a factor, but probably not the only factor.

5   Assistive technology and personal assistance in the workplace

The activities component of the Comprehensive Assistive Technology (CAT) model (Hersh and Johnson, 2008) will be used to structure the discussion of the use of support professionals and assistive technology in the workplace. The hierarchically structured model has the four high-level components of Person, Context, Activities and Assistive Technology. The discussion will be based on the Activities component, which is illustrated in Figure 10.1, and, in particular, the communications and access to information component of the model, as this is one of the areas which is particularly important to deaf people.

However, it should be noted that safe working conditions require that deaf people are aware of fire (and other) alarms. They can be alerted

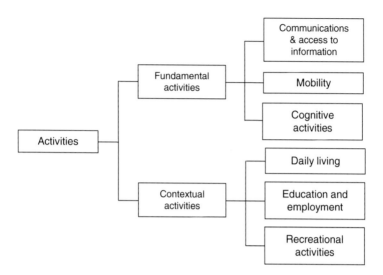

Figure 10.1   Activities component of CAT model

to these alarms through the use of either visual signals in the form of flashing lights or tactile signals in the form of a vibrating pager. The tactile version has the advantage of also being accessible to deaf-blind people and provides additional options such as door bell and telephone alerts. It also avoids the potential safety issues which could result if the organisations employ workers with autism spectrum conditions who are sensitive to both noise and light.

5.1   Communications and access to information

The activities under communications and access to information are further categorised as follows:

- Interpersonal communication
- Access to print media
- Telecommunications
- Computers and Internet accessibility
- Communications using other technology

Many deaf people require an appropriate combination of assistive technology and support professionals to carry out many of these activities in a society in which hearing people predominate. The support required for interpersonal communication depends on the deaf person's communication strategies and skills. Most deaf people have a visual element to their communication strategies. However, the specific strategies used and the balance between visual and oral strategies depend on the person, their personal and educational history and contextual factors, such as whether they have been encouraged to (try to) learn to sign, speak or both. While the accessibility of speech generally decreases with increasing hearing impairment, education and family background have a strong influence on the choice of signing or speech as the primary communication method.

5.2   Interpersonal communication

Supporting interpersonal communication for deaf people generally involves one or both of the following:

- Providing the information in a format that can be perceived visually. This includes sign language, text and lip speech.
- Improving the quality or intelligibility of the speech or other audio signal, for instance by removing noise, amplification or processing the speech signal.

For deaf signers the preferred option is generally a sign language interpreter. There have been a number of projects, such as ATLAS, ViSiCAST and Esign, to develop computer-based systems for automatic conversion between text (or speech) and sign language. However, progress to date has been limited and generally restricted to small vocabulary sets on particular topics. Most of the systems developed to date have the further disadvantage of being based on avatars (realistic or fictional two-dimensional representations of a person, animal or other animate object). They have rather stiff robot-like movements, unlike the fluidity of fluent signing, and lack facial expression, which is a crucial part of sign language. This makes avatars unpopular with deaf people and more difficult to understand than native signers. Therefore, considerable further research is required for automatic interpretation which could be used at workplace meetings or social events. However, existing systems could be used in limited communication situations with, for instance, a restricted set of instructions.

However, there is a commercially available system, Signtel Interpret (2008), which is able to produce sign language (or text) output from spoken English or English text, but which does not take account of the differences in word/sign order and grammatical structure. Although the lack of attention to sign order and grammar could make the meaning ambiguous, there is some evidence that Deaf people prefer it to text. It uses a database of signed words and phrases recorded on video. Therefore the individual signs will appear more natural than those produced by avatars and also have appropriate facial expressions, but the transition between signs may not always be fluid. There is also a Signtel Sign Language Public Address and Emergency Alert System based on Signtel Interpret. While there seems to be limited research into end-user attitudes to Signtel Interpret, the further development of interpretation systems which take account of sign language grammar and word order and use video clips of real signers rather than avatars may be the way forward.

Deaf people who use spoken language generally use a combination of visual and auditory approaches. The visual approach is based on 'lipreading' or the interpretation of a speaker's lip and facial movements. Support for lipreading can be provided by lipspeakers who have particularly clear and distinct mouth movements, facilitating lipreading.

Systems in common use to improve the intelligibility and quality of audio signals include hearing aids and infrared, induction loop and frequency modulated (FM) assistive listening systems. Hearing aids can be worn on one or both ears. In addition to amplifying sound, they apply a variety of (digital) signal processing algorithms to try to maximise information to the listener while avoiding the signal becoming uncomfortably loud at any frequency. Although the use of hearing aids can enable many hearing impaired people to understand speech (when used together with lipreading) and increase their enjoyment of music, they rarely give hard of hearing people the same quality of hearing as hearing people.

Both hearing aids and assistive listening systems have transmission and receiving components. However, in the case of assistive listening devices, the two components are separated, with the transmission microphone close to the speaker and the receiver worn by the user. In the case of hearing aids, direct transmission of the sound signal occurs, though it is digitised in the case of the increasingly commonly used digital hearing aids, whereas infrared, induction loop and FM assistive listening systems transmit the sound signal as an infrared, magnetic or radio wave respectively. The difference in transmission medium and the consequent differences in the transmission and receiver components differentiate the different assistive listening systems from each other.

The combination of the distance between the receiver and transmitter/microphone and the use of non-acoustic signal transmission technology allows the system to amplify and improve sound quality with reduced background noise and reverberation over a distance. This improves audibility and reduces listening fatigue. Induction loop systems are normally used with the telecoil setting of the user's hearing aid and therefore do not require an additional receiver, although receivers are available. The need to provide and maintain receivers for infrared and FM systems and the increased conspicuousness of the receivers compared to hearing aids are considered to be disadvantages of these systems compared to induction loop ones (Ross, 2002). However, some hearing aids now have incorporated FM receivers (Warick et al., 1997), though they are not necessarily compatible with all FM systems. The lack of intercompatibility between FM systems at different dedicated frequencies and between wide and broad band systems are further disadvantages of this approach, while infrared transmitters and receivers, and hearing aid telecoils and induction loops are always compatible.

However, FM systems are generally easy to set up, whereas infrared transmitters need to be carefully positioned and induction loops to be installed correctly and checked regularly. There is some anecdotal evidence that induction loop systems in public buildings often do not work properly or at all. FM systems are popular for one-to-one interactions, whereas infrared and induction loop systems are more commonly used in public settings, such as lectures and performances. There are therefore advantages in (larger) workplaces providing both.

For assistive listening systems to work properly, all members of staff in the workplace need to be sensitised to the importance of speaking into a microphone and to be made aware that speaking very loudly will not activate the system if a microphone is not used. There also needs to be someone in the organisation with responsibility for regularly checking the system and ensuring it is working. In large organisations this person could be trained to carry out repairs themselves, but this may not be feasible in smaller organisations.

Training for all staff in communicating with deaf people is also important. However, the requirements for effective communication with deaf people who use speech could be considered good practice for oral communication. In particular, only one person should speak at a time to avoid interference from competing speech signals, and the speaker should look at the deaf person and avoid covering their mouth or the lower part of their face or moving objects in front of them to allow for lipreading. Speakers who need to write on a board, should turn back to the audience in order to speak and not speak while writing with their heads turned away from the audience. Speakers should speak clearly and at a reasonable volume, but avoid shouting, which distorts lip patterns and makes lipreading difficult. They should also speak at a moderate pace, and avoid speaking either very slowly or too quickly (Warick et al., 1997). It is important to introduce a new topic gradually rather than changing topic abruptly, as understanding is generally facilitated by knowing what is being talked about. Speakers should also be patient if they have to repeat things, sometimes more than once, and may find that the need for repetition reduces as the deaf person becomes more familiar with the sound of their voice.

In the case of Deaf signers, while interpreters will be required for anything but the most basic communication, a basic knowledge of signed greetings, simple questions to which the answers are yes/no and good/bad (or ok/not ok), or some knowledge of the fingerspelling alphabet used by deaf people can make a deaf person feel welcome in an organisation. One of the recommendations produced by research on the support provided by the police to deaf people in the context of travel and road safety (Ohene-Djan et al., 2010) was the production of a booklet of words and expressions commonly encountered in road traffic and transport policing with their sign language equivalents. This could be generalised to the workplace context, where it should cover expressions relevant to social as well as commonly occurring work-related interactions in the particular workplace. However, this should be additional to rather than replace the use of interpreters.

Speech to text systems can be used to support both deaf people who sign and deaf people who speak in poor acoustic environments. The four main technologies for speech to text conversion are speech recognition, summary transcription, stenography, and standard word processing software (Downs et al., 2002). All four systems involve the conversion of spoken words to text using software. In the case of speech recognition the original signal is received by a microphone or telephone without modification and then processed using a speech to text conversion algorithm to produce text output. Summary transcription involves an operator or captionist repeating an edited version of the speech into a microphone and processing of this edited version using a speech to text conversion algorithm. The captionist edits the text to condense it without losing important information or distorting the meaning and adds punctuation and formatting, including an indication of who is speaking. An abbreviation-based typing system can be used to add words not in the system dictionary or correct misrecognised words.

In stenography, a steno operator or stenographer listens to the speech and inputs it phonetically to a steno machine using a specially designed ergonomic keyboard which allows entire words to be input by chording or hitting several keys together. The machine outputs a phonetic version of the words, which are then translated into standard text output using a laptop computer. In real time recording the output appears on a computer screen seconds after being spoken and can be transmitted to remote locations via the Web or telephone. Trained and experienced stenographers input data faster than the speed of speech in slide presentations and conversations (Anon 2011a; WPM, 2011). Since typing is generally considerably slower than speaking, information is likely to be lost, as well as errors made, when a typist and standard word processing software are used. This is therefore the last-resort option for use when better options are not available.

There are a number of commercially available speech recognition programs, including Dragon Dictate, Kurzweil and IBM. The accuracy of word recognition is still improving, but speech recognition rates are generally lower in public settings than in an office environment (Bennett et al., 2002; Leitch and MacMillan, 2003). The accuracy of stenography systems depends largely on the stenographer's accuracy. Accuracy of summary transcription systems, such as C-Print and Typewell (Downs et al., 2002; Francis and Stinson, 2003), should be defined in terms of low loss of information and distortion of meaning, as it does not give a word for word representation of the text. The use of summary transcription speech recognition software can significantly reduce speech recognition errors in a lecture or meeting, as the captionist is able to speak in a uniform way and can use the typing abbreviation system to make corrections and further reduce the errors.

Speech recognition, summary transcription and stenography are able to produce output on a text display a few seconds after the words are spoken. At least in principle, this gives deaf participants access to the spoken content of a meeting, class or training session at the same time as other participants. This, again at least in theory, makes it possible for them to interact with other participants, ask questions and participate in discussions if interpreters are available for deaf signers. How well this works in practice will depend on a number of factors, including the deaf person's ability to read and understand text (which may have some errors) at speed, any interpreters' facility with any specialist terminology, and the openness of other participants to interaction with the deaf person, including when they use an interpreter or their comments are slightly delayed.

5.3 Telecommunications

Standard telephones are not designed for deaf people since they do not support lipreading, and the reduced bandwidth of telephone speech signals may lead to a reduction in clarity and intelligibility. Therefore, many hard of hearing people find telephone use stressful and avoid it as much as possible, other than with people they know well and who speak clearly. The use of a standard telephone is clearly impossible for people who sign rather than speak. However, texting is popular among deaf people (Anon, 2010a).

The following approaches can be used to support telephony for deaf people:

- Video phones
- Text phones, often called minicoms
- Support professionals, for instance to relay telephone conversations in sign language or clear speech which can be lipread
- Relay services
- Telephone features, such as amplification
- Computer-based video and text telephone systems

Since they are able to transmit both audio and video signals, video phones can be used to support deaf people who use both sign language and speech with lipreading. For many deaf people, particularly signers, video is the preferred option, as it allows them to use their natural communication approach. Textphones, which are related to modems, have a keyboard and a small screen, allowing the transmission of text conversations. While there are several commercially available telephones that can be used for the transmission of either text or speech, a telephony system which gives automatic conversion between text and speech has not (yet) been developed.

Since few hearing people have textphones, relay services, such as Typetalk in the UK, are required to support communication by deaf people using textphones, with hearing people using standard telephones. The operator speaks the typed communication from the deaf person for the hearing person, and types the spoken message from the hearing person for the deaf person. There are also video relay services, which support telecommunications between a Deaf person who signs and a hearing person, but they are less widespread than text relay services. Sweden was the first country to provide a video relay service, with a pilot project in 1996. There is now a nationwide service fully funded by the government, with an average of 135,000 calls a year. A video software application is available for downloading from the service providers, and the government also supplies video phones to the deaf community free of charge (Anon, 2011b). The services in other countries are generally less well developed.

Telephone features which are likely to be particularly useful to deaf people (Hersh and Johnson, 2003) include amplification of both the conversation and the ringer, a low- rather than high-frequency ringer, since many deaf people hear low frequencies better than high ones, and an additional receiver. A second receiver will allow a deaf person to speak directly to the caller and a hearing assistant to relay the caller's responses to them in speech or text either in general or on request from the deaf person. Whether a dedicated professional is required, or a friend, colleague or family member could do this on an informal basis, will depend on a number of factors, including the frequency and duration of calls.

Text-over IP provides a real-time text service that operates over the Internet and networks that use it (Anon, 2010b). It complements voice and voice-over IP. It can be used instead of textphones and has a number or advantages relative to them. In particular it is designed to be used as a mainstream service which can be used on standard computers or mobile terminals. However, proper alerting systems and hardware and software interfaces are required to meet the needs of deaf people. Text-over IP can also be used to provide real-time captioning for spoken conversations.

5.4   Access to print media, computers and Internet accessibility

Although print media are purely visual they raise issues for deaf people due to the low literacy of many of them, resulting from inadequacies of the education system (Kronreif et al., 2000; Debevc, 2002; Lang and Steely, 2003). In addition, sign language does not have a written equivalent. Consequently, native signers have to read print material in a foreign language with all the associated difficulties. Computer and Internet access raise similar issues. In addition, the audio content of multi-media computer and Internet materials will need to be made available in a visual format, for instance through text or sign language.

The use of clear language is of benefit to everyone. Some deaf people may require versions of texts in simplified language, though care will be required to avoid (subtle) shifts in meaning or patronising them. Deaf signers would benefit from sign language sections of websites. Other options include text to SignWriting and text-to-fingerspelling conversion. SignWriting is a system of writing sign languages, developed by Valerie Sutton, which uses symbols to describe the movements of signing. Although both Open Source SignWriter Tiger (undated) and commercially available SignPuddle (undated) software have been developed to support SignWriting, and it could be considered a more natural form of output than printed or handwritten text for many Deaf signers, it is not widely used.

Fingerspelling or the spelling of words using the fingers is used by Deaf people to spell proper names and technical terms for which no sign is available. While it could be used for whole conversations, this would be much slower than signing. However, it has the advantage of being much easier to learn than signing and could therefore be used to support simple communication between Deaf and hearing people and thereby help to counter the isolation of Deaf people and support their integration into organisations. Consequently, there would be significant advantages with regards to the social integration of Deaf people in fingerspelling being taught to all schoolchildren. The development of text-to-fingerspelling conversion algorithms is a relatively simple proposition and there are existing systems, such as the SMS messaging Finger-chat system (Ohene-Djan and Mould, 2004), which could be adopted.

6 Conclusions

This chapter has discussed the inclusion of deaf people in the workplace and shown that there are considerable benefits to organisations in employing deaf people with regards to extending the talent pool, retaining skilled employees, the skills, aptitudes and approaches deaf people may bring to an organisation, positive impacts from a more diverse workforce, and improved public relations and wider markets. Since the prevalence of hearing impairment increases with age, measures are required to avoid losing the skills and expertise of long-time employees with age-related hearing impairments. In addition, deaf and hearing people have different preferred hemispheres for processing complex information, which may give them different and complementary problem-solving strategies, and deaf adults perform better than hearing adults on attention-dependent visual tasks, particularly those involving the peripheral visual field.

The chapter was introduced by a brief discussion of what it means to be deaf from the perspective of a sympathetic outsider. The fact that deafness may be based on culture and language rather than hearing impairment was noted. The importance of visual communication methods and the need to consider the different interpersonal communication strategies used by different groups of deaf people – namely audiovisual access to speech through lipreading and hearing aids, and signing – were stated. The significant proportion of the population, particularly in the older age groups, with some degree of hearing impairment was also noted.

The communication section of the activities component of the Comprehensive Assistive Technology (CAT) model (Hersh and Johnson, 2008) was used to structure the discussion of the assistive technology and support personnel required for inclusion in the workplace, giving the categories of interpersonal communications, telecommunications, print media, and computer and Internet access. Under access to interpersonal communications, three different types of assistive listening systems were discussed, the four main technologies for speech text conversion were considered, the current state of the art in automatic sign language conversion was evaluated, and a commercially available sign language translation system which does not take account of word/sign order and grammar was introduced. A number of different approaches to making telecommunications accessible to deaf people were considered, including video phones, text telephones, relay services, computer-based video and text telephone systems, and features such as amplification. The use of SignWriting, text-to-fingerspelling conversion, the use of clear, simple language and sign language sections of websites were considered under print media, computer and Internet accessibility.

The importance of a national, legislative and local context which supports deaf people was also stated. Under the local context appropriate lighting and acoustic environments were considered, as well as the need for visual or tactile fire and other alarms. The need for a national strategy, improved transition to work from education and training, improved education for deaf people and improved financial support for workplace accommodations for deaf people were discussed under the national and legislative context.

Acknowledgements: I would like to thank Professor Mike Johnson for his very helpful comments and suggestions.

References

Anon (2010a), 'For Deaf, texting offers new portal to world', http://www.cbsnews.com/stories/2010/09/20/tech/main6883857.shtml, accessed 11.01.2010.

Anon (2010b), 'Text over IP', http://en.wikipedia.org/wiki/Text_over_IP, accessed 11.01.2010.

Anon (2011a), 'Court reporter', http://en.wikipedia.org/wiki/Court_reporter, accessed 22.07.2011.

Anon (2011b), 'Video relay service', http://en.wikipedia.org/wiki/Video_Relay_ Service, accessed 11.01.2010.

Atcherson, S. R. (2002), 'Stigma and misconceptions of hearing loss: implications for healthcare professionals with hearing loss', *Journal of the Association of Medical Professionals with Hearing Losses*, Vol. 1 (1), http://www.amphl.org/articles/ atcherson2002.pdf, accessed 12.01.2009.

Bavelier, D., Brozinsky, C., Tomann, A., Mitchell, T., Neville, H. and Liu, G. (2001), 'Impact of early deafness and early exposure to sign language on the cerebral organization for motion processing', *Journal of Neuroscience*, Vol. 21, pp. 8931–8942.

Bavelier, D., Dye, M. W. G. and Hauser, P. C. (2006), 'Do deaf individuals see better?', *Trends in Cognitive Science*, Vol. 10 (11), pp. 512–518.

Bennett, S., Hewitt, J., Kraithman, D. and Britton, C. (2002), 'Making chalk and talk accessible', *ACMMM SIGGAPH Computers and the Physically Handicapped*, pp. 73–74, 119–125.

Bradley-Johnson, S. and Evans, I. D. (1991), *Psychoeducational Assessment of Hearing Impaired Students: Infancy through High School*, Pro-Ed.

Bradshaw, W. (2002), *The Experience of Employers: Research into Deafness and Employment*, RNID, London.

Cox, T. (2001), *Creating the Multicultural Organisation. A Strategy for Capturing the Power of Diversity*, University of Michigan Business School Management Series.

Danermark, B., Antonson, S. and Lundström, I. (2001), 'Social inclusion and career development – transition from upper secondary school to work or post-secondary education among hard of hearing students', *Scandinavian Audiology*, Vol. 30 (suppl. 53), pp. 120–128.

Daumann, R., Daubech Q., Gavilan, I., Colmet, L., Delaroche, M., Michas, N., Baldet, F., Saget, F., Diallo, A., Duriez, F., Olegaray, F., Soriano, V. and Debruge, E. (2000), 'Long-term outcome of childhood hearing deficiency', *Acta Otolaryngol*, Vol. 120, pp. 206–208.

DEAF (undated), 'Deaf Evangelism and Fellowship. Inc.', http://www.deafinf. com/internationaldeafstatistics.html, accessed 26.11.2008.

Debevc, M. (2002), 'Video supported online communities', *Proc. Int. Ed. Conf. on Computers*, MiRK 02, Piran, Slovenia.

Downs, S., Davis, C. D., Thomas, C. and Colwell, J. (2002), 'Evaluating speech-to-text communication access providers: a quality assurance issue', http://www. sunsite.utk.edu/cod/pec/products/2002/downs.pdf, accessed 05.11.2008.

EEOT (2008), 'Diversity and equality, a review of the literature', Equal Employment Opportunities Trust.

Foster, S. and Kinuthia, W. (2003), 'Deaf persons of Asian American, Hispanic American and African American backgrounds: a study of intra-individual diversity and identity', *Journal of Deaf Studies and Deaf Education*, Vol. 8 (3), pp. 273–290.

Foster, S. and MacLeod, J. (2003), 'Deaf people at work: assessment of communication among deaf and hearing persons in work settings', *International Journal of Audiology*, Vol. 42, pp. S128–S139.

Francis, P. and Stinson, M. (2003), 'The C-Print speech-to-text system for communication access and learning', CSUN 2003, http://www.csun.edu/cod/conf/ 2003/proceedings/157.htm, accessed 05.11.2008.

Geyer, P. D. and Schroedel, J. G. (1998), 'Early career job satisfaction for full-time workers who are deaf or hard of hearing', *Journal of Rehabilitation*, Vol. 64 (1), pp. 33–37.

Graffam, J., Smith, K., Shinkfield, A. and Polzin, U. (2002), 'Employer benefits and costs of employing a person with a disability', *Journal of Vocational Rehabilitation*, Vol. 17, pp. 251–263.

Hersh, M. A. (2010), 'Disabled people and employment: barriers and potential solutions', in Moss, G. (ed.), *Profiting from Diversity*, Palgrave Macmillan.

Hersh, M. A. and Johnson, M. A. (2003), *Assistive Technology for the Hearing Impaired, Deaf and Deafblind*, Springer Verlag.

Hersh, M. A. and Johnson, M. A. (2008), 'On modelling assistive technology systems part I: modelling framework', *Technology and Disability*, Vol. 20 (3), pp. 193–215.

Holt, J., Hotto, S. and Cole, K. (1994), 'Demographic aspects of hearing impairment: questions and answers', http://gri.gallaudet.edu/Demographics/fachsheet.html, accessed 26.11.2008.

HREOC (2005a), 'Workability part I: barriers', Human Rights and Equal Opportunity Commission', http://www.

HREOC (2005b), 'Workability II: solutions, people with disability in the open workplace', Final Report of the National Inquiry into Employment and Disability, Human Rights and Equal Opportunity Commission.

Kirton, G. and Greene, A. (2005), *The Dynamics of Managing Diversity. A Critical Approach*, 2nd edition, Elsevier.

Kochkin (undated), 'Hearing solutions – why people delay a solution', http://www.betterhearing.org/hearing_solutions/delaySolution.cfm, accessed 12.01.2008.

Kronreif, G., Dotter, F., Bergmeister, E., Krammer, E., Hilzensauer, M., Okorn, I., Skant, A., Orter, R., Rezzonico, S. and Barreto, B. (2000), 'SMILE: Demonstration of a cognitively oriented solution to the improvement of written language competence of deaf people', *Proceedings of ICCHP*, Karlsruhe, Germany.

Ladd, P. (2003), *Understanding Deaf Culture, In Search of Deafhood*, Multilingual Matters Ltd.

Ladd, P. (2005), 'Deafhood: a concept stressing possibilities, not deficits', *Scandinavian Journal of Public Health*, Vol. 33 (suppl. 66), pp. 12–17.

Lane, H. (2005), 'Ethnicity, ethics and the deaf-world', *Journal of Deaf Studies and Deaf Education*, Vol. 10 (3), pp. 291–310.

Lang, H. G. (2002), 'Higher education for deaf students: researching priorities in the new millennium', *Journal of Deaf Studies and Deaf Education*, Vol. 7 (4), pp. 267–280.

Lang, H. G. and Steely, D. (2003), 'Web-based science instruction for deaf students: what research says to the teacher', *Instructional Science*, Vol. 31, pp. 277–298.

Leitch, D. and MacMillan, T. (2003), 'Liberated learning initiative innovative technology and inclusion: current issues and future directions for librated learning research', Year IV report, St Mary's University, Nova Scotia, http://www.liberatedlearning.com/research/Year%20IV%20research%20report%202003.pdf, accessed 05.11.2008.

Loke, W. H. and Song, S. (1991), 'Central and peripheral visual processing in hearing and non-hearing indivuals', *Bulletin of the Psychonomic Society*, Vol. 29, pp. 437–440.

Mitchell, R. E., Young, T. E., Bachleda, B. and Karchmer, M. A. (2006), 'How many people use ASL in the United States?', *Sign Language Studies*, Vol. 6 (3), pp. 306–335.

Monks, K. (2007), *The Business Impact of Equality and Diversity. The International Evidence*, Dublin: Equality Authority.

Moores, D. F. and Meadow-Orlans, K. P. (1991), *Educational and Developmental Aspects of Deafness*, Gallaudet University Press.

Napier, J. (2002), 'The D/deaf-H/hearing debate', *Sign Language Studies*, Vol. 2 (2), pp. 141–149.

Ng, E. S. W. and Burke, R. J. (2005), 'Person-organisation fit and the war for talent: does diversity management make a difference?', *International Journal of Human Resource Management*, Vol. 16 (7), pp. 1195–1210.

Obasi, C. (2008), 'Seeing the deaf in "deafness"', *Journal of Deaf Studies and Deaf Education*, Vol. 13 (4), pp. 455–465.

Ohene-Djan, J., Hersh, M. A. and Navqi, S. (2010), 'Road safety and deaf people: the role of the police', *Journal of Prevention and Intervention in the Community*, Vol. 38 (4), pp. 316–331.

Ohene-Djan, J. and Mould, A. (2004), *Finger-chat: A Multi-mode Finger Spelling Chat System*, CVHI 04, Granada, Spain.

Paul, P. V. and Quigley, S. P. (1984), *Language and Deafness*, 2nd edition, San Diego: Singular Publishing Group.

Phippard, D. (1977), 'Hemifield differences in visual perception in deaf and hearing subjects', *Neuropsychologia*, Vol. 15, pp. 555–561.

Preston, P. (1995), 'Mother father deaf: the heritage of difference', *Social Science and Medicine*, Vol. 40 (11), pp.

Proksch, J. and Bavelier, D. (2002), 'Changes in the spatial distribution of visual attention after early deafness', *Journal of Cognitive Neuroscience*, Vol. 14 (5), pp. 687–701.

Punch, R., Hyde, M. and Creed, P. A. (2004), 'Issues in the school-to-work transition of hard of hearing adolescents', *American Annals of the Deaf*, Vol. 149 (1), pp. 28–38.

Punch, R., Hyde, M. and Power, D. (2007), 'Career and workplace experiences of Australian university graduates who are deaf or hard of hearing', *Journal of Deaf Studies and Deaf Education*, Vol. 12 (4), pp. 504–517.

Rettenbach, R., Diller, G. and Sireteanu, R. (1999), 'Do deaf people see better? Texture segmentation and visual search compensate in adult but not in juvenile subjects', *Journal of Cognitive Neuroscience*, Vol. 11 (5), pp. 560–583.

Reynolds, H. N. (1993), 'Effects of foveal stimulation on peripheral visual processing and laterality in deaf and hearing subject', *American Journal of Psychology*, Vol. 106 (4), pp. 523–540.

RNID (1987), *Communication Works: An RNID Enquiry into the Employment of Deaf People*, RNID, London.

RNID (undated a), 'Facts and figures on deafness and tinnitus' (factsheet), http://www.rnid.org.uk/information_resources/factsheets/deaf_awareness/ factsheets_leaflets/facts_and_figures_on_deafness_and_tinnitus.htm, accessed 26.11.2008.

RNID (undated b), Statistics, http://www.rnid.org.uk/information_resources/ aboutdeafness/statistics/, accessed 10.12.2008.

Rodda, M. and Grove, C. (1987), *Language, Cognition and Deafness*, Hillsdale, NJ: Lawrence Erlsbaum.

Ross, M. (2002), 'Telecoils: the powerful assistive listening device', *Hearing Review*, September.

Sacks, O. W. (1990), *Seeing Voices: A Journey into the World of the Deaf*, revised edition, Pan Books Ltd.

Scherich, D. L. (1996), 'Job accommodations in the workplace for persons who are deaf or hard of hearing: current practices and recommendations', *Journal of Rehabilitation*, April/May/June, pp. 27–35.

Scherich, D. L. and Mowry, R. (1997), 'Accommodations in the workplace for people who are hard of hearing: perception of employees, *Journal of American Deafness and Rehabilitation Association*, Vol. 31 (1), pp. 31–43.

Schroedel, J. and Geyer, P. (2001), 'Long term career attainments of deaf and hard of hearing college graduates: results for a fifteen year follow-up survey', *American Annals of the Deaf*, Vol. 145 (4), pp. 303–314.

Sheill, T. (undated), 'The effects of mentoring on the career development of deaf people', http://www.deafskills.co.uk/papers.html, accessed 11.01.2011.

SignPuddle (undated), http://www.suttonshop.com/ecommerce/pages/products_ sw_detail.jsp?id= 60.0, accessed 05.11.2008.

Signtel (2008), http://www.signtelinc.com/main1/id28.html, accessed 05.11.2008.

SignWriter Tiger (undated), http://www.signwriter.org/, accessed 05.11.2008.

Sinclair, A. (2006), 'Critical diversity management practice in Australia romanced or co-opted?', in Korad, Prasad and Pringle (eds.), *Handbook of Workplace Diversity*, Sage.

Sparrow, R. (2005), 'Defending deaf culture: the case of cochlear implants', *Journal of Political Philosophy*, Vol. 13 (2), pp. 135–152.

Sunitha, S. L. and Udayashankara, V. (2005), 'Fast factored DCT-LMS speech enhancement for performance of digital hearing aid', *Proceedings of World Academic of Science, Engineering and Technology*, Vol. 10. pp. 253–257.

Walden, T. C. and Walden, B. E. (2004), 'Predicting success with hearing aids in everyday living', *Journal of American Academy of Audiology*, Vol. 14, pp. 342–352.

Warick, R., Clark, C., Dancer, J. and Sinclair, S. (1997), 'Assistive listening devices', *Journal of Visual Impairment and Blindness*, Vol. 90 (5).

Winn, S. (2007), 'Employment outcomes for people in Australia who are congenitally deaf: has anything changed?', *American Annals of the Deaf*, Vol. 152 (4), pp. 382–390.

WPM (2011), 'Words per minute', http://en.wikipedia.org/wiki/Words_per_ minute, accessed 22.07.2011.

Section C

11

Diversity's Contribution to the Bottom Line: Assigning a Monetary Value to Diversity Initiatives

Ian Dodds, Alan David, Gloria Moss, Valeriya Kanuk and Peter Unwin

1 Introduction

It is important at all times, but particularly during economic downturns, for businesses to prioritise strategic objectives by calculating the different return on investment (ROI) of each. Equality, diversity and inclusion (EDI) activities have often been considered outside of these 'bottom-line' calculations although, in fact, EDI interventions have the potential to make big contributions, for instance through:

- raising productivity by inclusively engaging diverse workforces;
- attracting and retaining talent, thereby reducing recruitment, induction and training costs;
- generating more creative and longer-lasting solutions to business problems;
- gaining competitive advantage from meeting the needs of diverse customers.

These are just some of the ways that firms can capture the economic impact of EDI initiatives. This chapter describes the development and piloting of a Diversity Scorecard and Value Analysis Tool that enables businesses to calculate and prioritise the diversity ROI (DROI) of different initiatives.

The DROI process begins by capturing a firm's key success requirements for the business, in terms of industry success and survival factors

(ISSFs). It then maps existing and potential EDI initiatives, which can offer performance gains and competitive advantage against these ISSFs. The process can also expose blind spots where EDI initiatives have not yet been applied but may nevertheless have significant DROI potential. The development of a Diversity Scorecard, Stage 1, by pinpointing the data that is needed to estimate the diversity ROI, Stage 2, and permits the movement to Stage 3, the completion of the Value Analysis Tool.

The DROI tools were piloted among the seven companies that participated in the research project: Adecco; Alpine Interim; Ariadne Designs; Cisco Systems; MITIE; Pitney Bowes; Simons Muirhead and Burton Solicitors (SMAB). These cover a range of operating environments from micro-businesses such as Ariadne Designs, to global corporations such as Cisco Systems.

2 Review of the research underpinning this approach

The potential for top- and bottom-line benefits from diversity was first demonstrated in a Harvard Business Review case study of IBM, which spanned the 1990s and early 2000s (Thomas and Kanji, 2004). This showed how IBM had leveraged diverse groups of employees to drive incremental revenue returns from diversity blind spots that had failed to link diversity to business opportunities. Part of their success was attributed to the creation of task forces for diverse groups, for example groups for African-Americans, Hispanics, Native Americans, those with disabilities, lesbian and gay people, those who were 50+, and women. Each group had been tasked to build business from minority-owned businesses for their particular affinity group over a five-year period and it was found that each group had generated $150 million in incremental revenue.

3 Strategic implications of diversity ROI to business performance

The results of the IBM experience suggest that organisations can broaden their understanding of diversity beyond legal compliance, accessing instead a strategic dimension to diversity which can deliver competitive advantage. In order to calculate the DROI it is important to establish how much of any improvement (say, to productivity) is caused by a specific diversity, as against another, initiative. One helpful approach to isolating the effects of diversity on 'bottom-line' improvement is to depart for a moment from a diversity perspective and enquire as to the type of 'capabilities that a typical company in the sector would be expected to exhibit in order to survive and succeed'. In the strategic management literature, these are known as industry success and survival factors (ISSFs), and in our sample companies the ISSFs were specified for all of the sectors in which these companies operated. The analysis yielded a set of desired capabilities, which could be used in interviews with the target companies in order to throw into relief areas that were likely to yield bottom-line improvements to the organisation. A further benefit of ISSF analysis is facilitating the identification of strategic diversity 'blind spots', an example being a mass retail fashion business that adopted inclusive policies (with wide and inclusive recruitment policies in its retail stores) but nevertheless used a supplier in its value chain that was adopting questionable employment practices which could inflict serious damage to its reputation.

The research discussed here has led to the development of a methodology for assessing the DROI from EDI initiatives and identifying potential blind spots. In the course of this, it has developed enabling tools: a Diversity Scorecard and a DROI Value Analysis Tool.

3.1 The Diversity Scorecard

The Diversity Scorecard is a tool that assists in the creation, management, valuing and leveraging of factors that allow EDI to contribute to competitive advantage (Wheeler, 1998). It forms the first part of a two-stage process and takes a strategic rather than a compliance perspective. Progress can be measured through an EDI audit which, first, captures key success requirements for a business in a given sector, and then, from these ISSF factors, maps these against existing EDI initiatives with an impact upon the ISSFs. It also exposes blind spots where EDI initiatives have not yet been applied. This audit draws on the original balanced scorecard concept developed by Kaplan and Norton (1996), and adapted by Hubbard (2004) to specifically include EDI. Alan David (2010) has further developed a model that unites Wheeler's concepts of the 'phases' over which diversity is introduced (creating, managing, valuing and leveraging diversity) (1998) with Hubbard's typology concerning the 'types' of diversity introduced (workplace diversity, behavioural diversity, structural diversity and business diversity).

In terms of its benefits, the scorecard allows organisations to measure and assess the impact of strategic diversity initiatives with the same rigour as other operational, 'bottom-line' issues. It also enables the alignment of EDI initiatives with other critical business efforts. The benefits of initiatives are audited in relation to six categories of activities:

EDI vision and strategy This first level of audit explores the current EDI vision and strategy or EDI action plan within the company. It seeks out information relating to organisational targets at the corporate level, as well as to HR function and marketing and sales, and details the initiatives in place to deliver the EDI strategies or action plans for each of these areas.

Workplace diversity This level of audit looks at the organisation's workforce profile and its 'diversity density', that is, the extent to which the variables of the six diversity strands are represented at all levels of the organisation. It measures initiatives to increase diversity density, whether through single-threaded initiatives (for example, diversity awareness courses), or through deeper initiatives (for example, performance measurement and reward systems) that will embed diversity within the organisation. It looks, too, at how the company retains and motivates its diverse workforce by sustaining a productive, engaging and inclusive workplace climate.

Marketplace diversity: customers and clients This aspect of the audit examines how workforce diversity relates to customer or client diversity, with a view to meeting segmented, marketplace needs. It examines how the company is delivering products and services to its diverse marketplace and what further actions it might take to better meet segmented needs. In doing this, it considers the extent to which existing initiatives (for example, ascertaining the needs of minority ethnic customers or client groups) are satisfying the diverse requirements of stakeholders. It also assesses what potential initiatives might drive incremental revenue from marketplace, diversity blind spots.

Leadership commitment to business development This level of audit looks at both how the company will sustain leadership accountability for EDI and also where the responsibility for associated initiatives lies within the organisation. In doing this, it examines EDI leadership change drivers (for example, leadership behaviour and example); leadership message and communications styles; how employees are being empowered, engaged and supported in the company's EDI efforts; and the breadth and depth of the 'diversity mindset' within the senior management group (for example, the extent and ability of the organisation's senior management to demonstrate openness to, and awareness of, diversity across cultures and markets).

Financial impact This part of the audit is concerned with how the company endeavours to appear to its shareholders from an EDI perspective and how it aspires to use EDI to succeed financially in terms of investment and external support. It also examines the mechanisms employed to gain shareholder understanding of its EDI strategies and the benefits obtained or anticipated.

EDI learning and growth This final level of audit looks at how the company will sustain and improve its ability to change. It includes a focus on the extent to which the learning culture supports cognitive and demographic diversity, the efforts taken to learn from EDI initiatives and to disseminate the learning more widely, and the methods used to benchmark best practices elsewhere.

The Diversity Scorecard has proved highly adaptable to each of the specific, participating company situations and the findings are presented in a later section.

4 The Value Analysis Tool

The second stage of calculating the DROI involves assessing the costs and benefits of each EDI initiative. In order to do this, the DROI Value Analysis Tool was developed and piloted using hard data (for example, on turnover, recruitment and induction costs). Moreover, Hubbard suggests that the DROI is a product of soft as well as hard data, so those intangible benefits often associated with EDI initiatives, such as increased job satisfaction, reduced conflict, greater creativity and better problem solving, as well as improved closeness to diverse customers, need to be converted into monetary values. Conversion to monetary values can be achieved by collecting estimates from the main stakeholders as to the likely improvement values from initiatives, and percentages of confidence (see Section 9) as well as EDI isolation factor percentages need to be added to these estimates in order to achieve an adjusted value. Examples of how these concepts are applied to assess diversity ROIs are shown below:

- The introduction of 'flexible working' practices. Several of the participating companies introduced flexible working to attract and retain women in the workforce and it is possible to compare the 'before flexible working' and 'after flexible working' attrition rates (taking into account recruitment and induction costs) in order to derive a financial figure. However, other attributes associated with the employee resource, such as knowledge base retained through reduced attrition are, more difficult to quantify in purely financial terms, and estimates have to be obtained from the company's marketing and sales experts.

- The creation of a more diverse product design and development team. A diverse team would be likely to improve the sensitivity of a global company's marketing and sales efforts to local cultural differences and also differences between the preferences of other market segments (for example, men and women). This is likely to produce improved responsiveness (that is, corporate marketing agility), producing gains in competitive advantage. However, an attempt to measure the financial benefits of such actions presents difficulties, including the lack of a control group and the fact that the output (and future discounted cash flows) from some product developments may take several years to play out. This benefit requires targets to be assigned to revenue from new products and market penetration of products over a reasonably lengthy period, say three years. Experienced sales and marketing professionals in the company then need to offer confidence factor estimates on these targets being achieved.

- Building a productive and engaging workplace climate through the company's leadership, focusing on developing an inclusive workplace climate. A DROI initiative of this kind is likely to result in significant performance gains, some of which are amenable to measurement (for example, reductions in turnover and absenteeism) but some of which are less so (for example, the productivity and improved problem-solving gains delivered to the bottom line). In the project considered in this chapter, two questionnaires designed to measure organisational engagement were piloted: the Glowinkowski International (GIL) engagement style indicator (ESI) and the GIL organisational climate questionnaire. It should be noted that GIL has data based on work with a number of diverse organisations and this indicates that a 10 per cent increase in the ESI score for a company will tend to deliver a 20 per cent increase in workplace climate, and up to a 40 per cent incremental contribution to the bottom line. The use of these two GIL instruments enables the targeting of an ESI score improvement over, say, 12 months and an estimate of the resulting, expected performance gain.

Once the data has been collected into the Value Analysis Tool, the usual approach to evaluating investments is applied, with the DROI calculated as earnings divided by investment costs. Once the DROIs for the different initiatives have been calculated, it is possible to prioritise the initiatives so that available effort can be targeted on those with the best forecasted returns.

5 The project findings

In this section, the focus is on the results obtained from an in-depth review of EDI initiatives at the seven companies selected for the project described. These are the participating companies:

> **Ariadne Designs** a London-based web design company, which also specialises in the creation of e-newsletters for communicating to customers and for email marketing (four employees including the owner).
>
> **Alpine**: an agency providing resourcing through Alpine Interim, an interims agency; Alpine Advantage, offering consultancy and advisory services; and Alpine Executive, an executive search agency (ten employees).
>
> **Simons, Muirhead and Burton** a multidisciplinary law firm providing a wide range of services to its clients (about 50 employees).
>
> **Adecco** an international recruitment agency serving a wide variety of job sectors, with an objective to set the standard for best practice in the recruitment industry (large company).
>
> **MITIE** a strategic outsourcing company that delivers a range of integrated services to support the buildings and infrastructure of its clients (large company).
>
> **Pitney Bowes** a global provider of office equipment, software and outsourced mail and document services (about 1600 employees at its headquarters).
>
> **Cisco Systems** a global provider of network systems; collaboration, voice and video products; data centre products (65,545 employees worldwide with 10,000 in Europe and approximately 2500 in the UK).

5.1   Diversity Scorecard and DROI implementation

It has already been mentioned in Sections 3 and 4 that an EDI audit involves two main stages:

- Building the Diversity Scorecard based on the ISSFs and existing EDI initiatives within the company, then
- Calculating the DROI using the Value Analysis Tool.

Building the Diversity Scorecard is a starting point of the DROI analysis since it helps to 'map' diversity initiatives within the company according to business areas such as vision and strategy, workplace, marketplace, leadership, finance, and learning and growth. Doing this helps to identify areas where the company is currently benefiting from EDI initiatives as well as areas for potential improvement. In fact, the scorecard can be used on its own as a powerful analytical tool, but the Value Analysis Tool is needed to permit the calculation of the DROI, taking into account both the benefits and costs of each EDI initiative.

Although the scorecard and the Value Analysis Tool list the same EDI initiatives, the Value Analysis Tool focuses on those initiatives that are likely to have an impact on business performance, identifying three to five diversity initiatives that have an impact on the business and, among them, one or two that significantly drive EDI within the company. It is therefore important to analyse these in detail, ideally, via using hard data such as turnover and recruitment, but, where it is not possible to have hard data, it is important to obtain relevant soft data. In addition, estimates need to be made concerning the reliability and significance of EDI factors and, for each of the selected initiatives, in order to produce a final ROI value, costs of design and delivery need to be estimated and deducted from identified benefits.

The following are some of our findings from implementing these tools and carrying out analyses.

1. Adjusting the analysis to company size and industries

During the analysis it was important to take into consideration the industry in which the company operated since this revealed the ISSFs that were likely to apply to the specific company. In the case of Pitney Bowes, for example, one likely ISSF was 'the ability to develop and maintain a high rate of innovative products and services'.

2. Difficulties in having precise data

As pointed out earlier, hard and soft data can be used for a DROI analysis and, while it is easier to work with hard data, many of the benefits associated with EDI initiatives are intangible benefits such as increased job satisfaction, higher productivity and better access to diverse customers. In relation to complex initiatives, such as setting up a diversity council or changing the supplier selection system, most of the time estimates have to be built around intangible benefits and this makes the process of conducting a DROI more lengthy and complex than it would be for more straightforward initiatives such as saving office space because of introducing flexible working. At the same time, the data showed that complex initiatives often lead to higher returns in the long term and, therefore, may well be significant in terms of returns to the organisation.

3. Value of Hubbard's scorecards

The Diversity Scorecard approach developed by Hubbard proved to be a powerful means of auditing current EDI initiatives and we modified it to include a measure for supplier diversity. This is important since many organisations put effort into supplier diversity, not only by way of motivating and engaging diverse stakeholders (for example, employees who in turn effectively serve diverse customers and clients) but also to obtain services from suppliers with diverse ownership. A related benefit is that minority-owned suppliers can often offer useful market and recruitment intelligence as well as offering more flexible and responsive services.

4. Compliance to ethical standards

In addition to obtaining services from suppliers with diverse ownership, the importance of including scorecard components to measure both supplier diversity and also appropriate compliance to required ethical standard practices was critical to many companies. An example mentioned earlier relates to the organisation that failed to do this in the mass retail fashion sector by paying greater attention to in-house inclusive policies than to supplier diversity screening. This resulted in serious damage to its reputation when it was discovered that a supplier in its value chain was paying its staff/workers below minimum wage salaries and adopting questionable contractual arrangements. The simple introduction of supplier diversity screening and ethical practices, monitoring and evaluation systems, would have prevented this unfortunate incident.

5. Holistic scanning of EDI efforts

A major benefit of completing the Diversity Scorecard is that it encourages an organisation to look holistically at its EDI efforts and, in the process, reveal EDI blind spots. For example, one of the areas to be audited in the scorecard is financial impact, an element which considers how the company should appear to its shareholders to succeed financially. MITIE was investing considerable effort into this through its CEO, speaking regularly at business conferences and to the media, and this enabled its EDI efforts and their contribution to business success to be communicated to its existing shareholders as well as to potential new ones. This enhanced its reputation to a wide audience.

6. Learning and growth

Another area, which is not always considered rigorously, is learning and growth, an area which assesses not only how the company will sustain its ability to change and achieve its EDI vision but also whether the learning culture supports both cognitive and demographic diversity. The scorecard analyses we conducted indicated that it is likely that organisations can enhance their DROI by considering how they will access and use the learning from past EDI efforts to enhance and renew their future efforts. Moreover, the requirement to consider cognitive diversity encourages organisations to examine how they are addressing different mental models and thinking styles to improve the innovativeness and effectiveness of their business problem-solving processes and leadership styles.

5.2 Overall lessons learned

1. Importance of competitive advantage indicators

The participating companies had a wide range of EDI initiatives from which they were seeking to obtain competitive advantage through performance or efficiency gains. These covered:

- Building best-practice capabilities. Examples included the following initiatives: being a diversity champion (Cisco Systems); leveraging EDI for competitive advantage in making bids (MITIE); developing value-added relationships with suppliers (Pitney Bowes); using EDI legal capability to gain new business (SMAB).
- Enhancing business processes to better encompass EDI. Examples included the following: candidate search processes (Adecco); engagement and reward processes (Ariadne Designs); customer and client management processes (Cisco Systems).
- Enhancing recruitment and management. Examples included building a recruitment system that was sensitive to diverse

candidates' capabilities, including those of disabled candidates (Adecco); having inclusive leadership behaviour exemplars (Alpine).

- Cognitive diversity. Attention to cognitive diversity can help diminish groupthink while at the same time enhancing creativity. Examples included: addressing unconscious bias in the workplace at the customer and client interfaces (Cisco Systems); positive action activities to increase minority representation in management (MITIE); promoting the use of cross-functional teams to address business issues (Pitney Bowes).
- Building EDI legitimacy in the eyes of customers. Examples included: marketing achievements to customers and clients (Adecco, Cisco Systems, MITIE, SMAB); targeted affinity group recruitment to meet specific diverse customer, or client needs (Ariadne Designs, MITIE, Pitney Bowes, SMAB).
- Engaging and motivating employees. Examples included: flexible working initiatives (Alpine, Cisco Systems, Pitney Bowes, SMAB); offering opportunities for personal growth (Alpine, Ariadne Designs); undertaking engagement surveys to prioritise effort (MITIE, Pitney Bowes, SMAB); employee award schemes (Pitney Bowes); family-friendly employment practices (SMAB); a diversity week (MITIE).
- Learning and growth. Examples included: EDI surveys (Cisco Systems, MITIE, Pitney Bowes, SMAB); promoting and sharing learning through organisational intranets (Cisco Systems, Pitney Bowes); external benchmarking (Ariadne Designs, Cisco Systems).

Interestingly, the participating companies appeared to have started these EDI efforts from a need to address a wide range of issues. These included diverse recruitment and retention needs, increasing minority group representation in management, engaging and motivating employees better, enhancing business problem solving and creativity, meeting diverse market segment needs, and being an EDI leadership company to enhance reputation.

2. Criticality of identifying ISSFs

An insight that emerged in the course of the project was the importance of starting from a perspective which takes into account the overall business goals and the external environmental context of the industry, since doing this is more likely to drive the EDI practice *beyond* legal compliance to having a major role in strategy and competitive advantage. As indicated above, many companies are already leveraging EDI for performance and efficiency gains, but so long as the driver is driven by *internally* perceived requirements without taking into account ISSFs, the outcomes from EDI initiates may result in only marginal benefits. Another useful benefit from the ISSFs' analysis is that it assists in identifying strategic EDI blind spots. Those companies still 'stuck' in the 'valuing diversity' phase, rather than the 'leveraging diversity' phase (Wheeler, 1998; David, 2010) are more likely to exhibit blind spots.

3. Identifying blind spots

A 'diversity blind spot' is a missed business opportunity linked to EDI. We found that the Diversity Scorecard forces a comprehensive review of existing and potential EDI initiatives and, therefore, offers the potential to uncover diversity blind spots. For example, 'workplace climate/culture' requires the scorecard audit to consider how best to motivate the workforce in order to help sustain a productive, inclusive work climate. It also asks about the culture of the organisation and whether it appears to support cognitive and demographic diversity. Alpine's leadership acted as exemplars of inclusive behaviour but this had not consciously been part of its leadership strategy. Glowinkowski's engagement styles indicator measured the engagement index of its minority staff and evidenced a highly engaging and inclusive workplace climate. This ability to influence the workplace climate positively through leadership behaviour is something the firm can now consciously leverage to drive performance gains from inclusion.

Another element on the scorecard relates to 'customers/clients' and the extent to which this is a diverse constituency. Addressing this issue requires a consideration of the diversity of the current client/customer base in terms of demographics such as age, gender and geographical location. A further consideration relates to how the company should deliver products and services to a diverse community. It could be that a primary marketing consideration in the past has been revenue bands rather than affinity group market segments and this could be a potential blind spot for the organisation, as was the case with IBM (see the Introduction above).

Where financial impact is concerned, a prime consideration relates to how the company should appear to its shareholders in order to ensure financial success. Of the seven project companies, only MITIE appeared to have seriously addressed this business opportunity area and it is endeavouring to raise the company via various PR activities such as talks, interviews and events. The area of 'learning and growth' focuses on the extent to which the learning culture supports cognitive and demographic diversity. Many organisations place the emphasis on demographic diversity and neglect to consider how they will drive cognitive diversity through an inclusive culture that embraces differences in 'mindsets' and thinking styles, and through that support-ive management practices and cross-functional collaboration. One of the seven project companies, Pitney Bowes, had various initiatives to enhance operational agility through the use of cross-functional teams, and another, Cisco Systems, developed this though employee resource groups (ERGS) which were encouraged to take an enterprising approach to addressing business problems that their members had encountered.

4. Effectiveness of a scorecard approach

While it is possible to measure the discounted cash flow using a measure such as net present value, other interventions that confer wider strate-gic benefit to the organisation may be difficult to express in financial 'bottom-line' terms. One of the core advantages offered by the score-card approach is that it deliberately adopts a multi-criteria focus, which enables balanced judgements to be made concerning the impact on organisational performance of key policy 'levers'.

Building on an earlier example, we pointed out that the financial return from introducing 'flexible working' practices could be moni-tored through several scorecard metrics (for example, proportion of staff choosing flexible working, days working from home) as well as met-rics indicating likely benefits from this particular diversity initiative (for example, attrition rates, staff recruitment and induction costs for vari-ous staff grades). However, even in this relatively simple case, various attributes associated with the staff resource, such as years of experience and knowledge base lost per time period through staff attrition, would also be critical, particularly in the case of a professional services firm.

Thus in order to arrive at a truly balanced judgement on the effi-cacy of a flexible working initiative, further metrics would be required to capture the nature of core staff attributes lost through attrition. For example, a flexible working initiative that encouraged more-experienced staff to leave would dilute the average level of staff experience within the professional staff resource pool if these staff were replaced by staff with less experience. It is also worth pointing out that these qualitative attributes are much more difficult to quantify in purely financial terms, although a good scorecard design would come up with a set of vari-ables that would give a good indication of the *quality* of skills/knowledge being lost.

The key lesson here is that the nature of the scorecard metrics chosen should focus on the priorities in any *particular* organisation to support its mission-critical objectives when designing the scorecard measures that are appropriate. After all, the idea behind the balanced scorecard is to enable organisations to align EDI initiatives with other critical business effort and mission-critical objectives. As a result, organisations are able to measure and assess diversity management with the same rigour as other operations critical to the 'bottom line'. We learnt that the actual process of developing appropriate metrics is useful in focusing thinking on objectives and the driving factors that lie behind their achievement. This makes a multi-criteria approach transparent to decision-makers, thereby providing a sensible guide to policy design and action.

5. Holistic approach to diversity

A great strength of the Diversity Scorecard is that it necessitates a holistic approach to auditing existing and prospective EDI initiatives. Indeed, the use of it with the seven participating companies highlighted that they were all pursuing workplace as well as marketplace initiatives. Moreover, several had, or were planning, initiatives in the community. By way of example, Alpine was incorporating EDI into its corporate social responsibility (CSR) strategy; Adecco was working with disabled communities to attract candidates to work with LOCOG for Olympics 2012; MITIE expected each employee to undertake two hours' volunteering a year around its CSR agenda; SMAB had a long tradition of working on human rights issues, including individuals sentenced to death by regimes which do not respect human rights.

6. Exploiting the full value chain

One of the lessons learned, widely supported by the strategic management and diversity literatures, is that internal (and external) policy interventions to encourage and foster EDI in organisations require a diversity-friendly organisational infrastructure. In fact, to achieve sustainable diversity-friendly systems, it appears that systemic and structural organisational components in the entire value chain need to change in tandem with the introduction of 'diversity policies'. A related conclusion is that single-threaded diversity solutions, for example, reliance simply on recruitment, or single-approach management techniques such as requiring every employee to take diversity training, do not create lasting change or sustainable advantage. To further explore the importance of diversity-friendly infrastructure, see David (2010).

Developing this last theme, the evidence from the participating companies, as well as from the literature, suggests that interventions focusing in only a general sense on 'valuing diversity', no matter how well intended, are not sufficient to deliver sustainable improvements in organisational performance. Similarly, even if some, or many, individuals develop diversity-friendly relationships in a large system, there is no certainty that this will bring about systemic change in behaviours and attitudes. The obstacles to change may include cultures, structural arrangements and embedded organisational routines that can blunt EDI-oriented transformations and inhibit their diffusion. By way of an example, the act of teaching an individual team-working skills will not, of itself, lead to a different style of working unless the organisation collectively determines that organisational performance is achieved through teamwork, and unless organisational design elements within the value chain are moved in line with the training. There are even examples in the literature of the way that organisations with non-diversity-friendly infrastructures can find themselves applying punitive measures to individuals whose learning is successful and ahead of that of the dominant peer group culture/organisational paradigm.

7. The contexts in which the tools work well

The work with the seven participating companies showed that the Diversity Scorecard worked effectively for all of them. As indicated earlier, the Hubbard scorecard does not explicitly encompass supplier diversity and so this was added and audited in the 'customer/community partnership' field. As a footnote, it is important also to understand the importance of obtaining an informed view when completing the scorecard about the degree of confidence in any improvement values (see Section 9 below). Also, there is a need to estimate the extent to which the targeted improvement will be attributable to EDI factors as against other strategic initiatives. For example, Cisco Systems provides training on unconscious bias to its sales managers, and while improvement in revenues and margins may be attributable to this training, the improvement could also be linked to a host of other factors, for example an improved sales and marketing strategy; other forms of training for sales staff; a Cisco Systems product having significant advantages over competitor products.

In the case of the Value Analysis Tool, Section 4 discussed how some aspects of an initiative lend themselves readily to financial quantification (for example, employee turnover reduction cost savings), while others are more challenging and need informed estimates (for example, non-dilution of the knowledge base through reduced attrition is difficult to quantify in purely financial terms and estimates have to be obtained from the company's marketing and sales experts). However, despite some of the difficulties, the authors found that overall it was possible to obtain estimates which could be relied upon with reasonably high levels of confidence.

8. Limitations

There are situations that can confound the simplistic thinking that good scorecard metrics equates to successful organisational performance.

For instance, it is often difficult to measure state-of-mind intangibles. In a law firm, for example, client *dissatisfaction* is not the same as *low satisfaction* and this difference needs to be noted when interpreting scorecard metrics. Moreover, some scorecard metrics appear to improve over time and this may be due to the fact that some problems can 'fix themselves'. On the other hand, there could be a more negative explanation, with a staff/workload ratio coming into balance on account of a loss of customers, an outcome that is certainly *not* a desired outcome for long-term reputation building.

All of the above points demonstrate the importance of applying common sense and systems thinking when interpreting scorecard metrics. It is vital that those interpreting performance figures have a deep understanding of the 'physics' of the business.

9. Isolating good practice

While the scorecard enables organisations to align EDI initiatives with other critical business initiatives, there are several difficulties in designing a measurement tool that assesses diversity management with the same measure of rigour as other operations critical to the 'bottom line'. As pointed out, the available metrics, whether or not expressed in financial cash-flow terms, will help to identify the contribution of EDI initiatives as well as infrastructure/and culture to organisational effectiveness. Moreover, a scorecard measurement tool approach that assigns both a *confidence level* to estimates as well as an *isolation factor* (for EDI's contribution) will also be of value. The confidence interval provides upper and lower limits to estimates of the present value of future cash flows and is a useful indication of the general level of uncertainty surrounding cash-flow estimates. The 'isolation factor' is of importance to the diversity manager (or 'champion') who is interested in the proportion of cash flows attributable to a single EDI initiative rather than the entire portfolio of related initiatives. The isolation of these EDI-related cash flows could be described as the *incremental* cash flows resulting from particular EDI initiatives and the availability of this data helps take an interest in diversity beyond the human resources management function.

10. Cross-sector lessons

The initiatives pursued by the participating companies did not tend to be sector-specific. Thus, Cisco Systems was the only organisation that endeavoured to enhance cognitive diversity by addressing unconscious bias in both the workplace and marketplace. Similarly, Pitney Bowes was the only organisation to introduce an employee award scheme to recognise exceptional achievement in the area of employee engagement; and Adecco, Cisco Systems, MITIE and Pitney Bowes were the only organisations to actively use their intranets to leverage EDI learning. This is notwithstanding the fact that this medium could probably be used more by SMEs for this purpose.

11. Organisational structure (ownership, roles, collaboration, and delivery)

The participating companies had all considered carefully the organisational structure needed to drive their EDI initiatives and a key factor appeared to be sponsorship of the initiative at board level or by the firm's managing partners. MITIE was setting up a diversity board, reporting to its executive, and in Cisco Systems the Inclusion & Diversity (I&D) director reported directly to the executive and was responsible for developing and monitoring I&D strategy on their behalf. The Cisco Systems' I&D director was assisted on certain initiatives by 'change ambassadors', employees who took on a part-time role in becoming experts in the policies for, and implantation of, a particular EDI initiative, for example flexible working. None of the SMEs had equivalents to diversity champions or the Cisco Systems ambassadors.

Another good practice adopted by many organisations was the formation of affinity network groups, for example a network for women, or for SMEs, or for lesbian, gay, bisexual and transgender employees, or for employees with carer responsibilities. These networks can ensure that the issues of their group are made known to management who can then consider initiatives to address them. They can also provide positive action development support for their members. Although the corporate participating companies did have various employee networks, there was no evidence of their having significant initiatives to enhance their contribution.

As stated previously, a critical aspect of cognitive diversity is developing an inclusive culture for different thinking styles and mental models to avoid group or silo thinking which is typical of a department or function. Developing this inclusive style of thinking enhances creative business problem solving and the practical mechanisms for doing this are demonstrated at Pitney Bowes through their emphasis on cross-functional teams and at Cisco Systems through the encouragement that is given to the formation of cross-functional employee resource groups to address business problems and opportunities. These are both initiatives that would prevent group or silo thinking.

12. Importance of cognitive diversity
Cognitive diversity encompasses work styles, leadership styles, learning styles and communication styles, including styles of design (Moss, 2009), aspirations, beliefs/value system, as well as employees' attitudes and expectations. It also includes the degree of diversity in thinking at both the individual and group level, and the subsequent richness of 'mental models' and ability to read signals from diverse environments that are developed through diverse thinking over time. Organisations often have paradigmatic models that are rooted in the cognitive behaviours of the dominant members of the senior group, but not those of other members of the organisation, or the customer base. For example, men may have a preference for transactional over transformational leadership, and the projection of this preference at recruitment may lead to the continued appointment of men, rather than women, to leadership positions, since women have a tendency to be more transformational in their leadership style and men a tendency to be more transactional (Moss et al., 2010). It may also lead to the perpetuation of the transactional style, which is less productive, in terms of long-term results, than transformational leadership.

In order to build a richer picture of the way that EDI can contribute to competitive advantage and innovation in organisations, it is useful to explore the link between the concepts of 'diversity' and the 'learning organisation'. A learning organisation is an organisation that acquires and transfers knowledge, its behaviour in the light of new knowledge and insights (Garvin, 1993). The literature on 'diversity' and the 'learning organisation' can be viewed as complementary since not only do both strive to release the potential of employees in the greater pursuit of organisational benefits but both rely on a supportive culture and infrastructure. The learning organisation, in fact, facilitates the full utilisation of the potential present in the organisation, but if the organisation is not diversity oriented there is a risk that the available pool of potential will be narrow. The learning organisation, therefore, needs to ensure that the organisation is successfully managing diversity, and Hall and Parker (1993) argue the need for taking a view in which managing diversity and the learning organisation are viewed as complementary.

13. Organisation Development (OD)/transformational change methodology

Building an inclusive culture to obtain the bottom-line benefits from EDI takes long-term strategic effort. The starting point will tend to be the formulation of an EDI vision aligned with the organisation's business aspirations. In fact, all the participating organisations in this project had an EDI vision, although in the SMEs it could be less formalised than in the large corporations. The next step is to communicate the vision and engage employees in its delivery, and in fact Adecco, Cisco Systems and Pitney Bowes had put structured effort into communication and engagement, for example through task forces, employee resource groups and change ambassadors. In Cisco Systems, there was considerable engagement activity, with sales managers trained to lead and manage their team members in delivering the vision, and the initiative ambassadors were another form of engagement. The company intranet was used extensively to involve employees in sharing EDI success stories and good practices, and in MITIE, the EDI vision was being introduced via a diversity week. During this period, executives would communicate with employees who would have the opportunity of, and be invited to, become involved in its delivery.

14. EDI leadership

Leadership is critical to the delivery of an EDI vision and strategy, and important elements include the clarity of the message and leading by example. In terms of the participating organisations, all had high levels of executive or managing partner sponsorship and the leaders in these organisations were described as being clear about their EDI messages. Moreover, Alpine, Adecco and Cisco Systems had initiatives in place to develop the capability of their leaders to set an example in the behaviours needed to drive their strategies. Since it has been demonstrated that 80 to 90 per cent of the behaviour in an organisation is influenced by that of its leaders (Schein, 1992), the correct, inclusive leadership behaviour could be considered a critical element in the successful implementation of an EDI strategy. In point of fact, the participating companies had engagement activities in place, although MITIE was only in the process of planning activities of this kind.

15. Diversity mindset

The concept of diversity mindset refers to the extent to which an organisation's senior executives view EDI as a *business strategy* rather than a *human resources* department issue. The EDI mindset leads to a better understanding of the needs of markets with a diverse customer base, and also produces a better understanding of the factors required to influence the buying decisions of customers comprising this market. This leads Hopkins and colleagues (Hopkins et al., 2008) to conclude that the higher the level of diversity density in an organisation, the easier it is for it to *assimilate* diversity knowledge. They further argue that transnational organisations using locally informed employees benefit from the country knowledge or 'diversity orientation' perspective they offer. These organisations access diversity density and use it to interpret the applicability of diversity knowledge in specific situations. It is important to point out that, in addition to an external market focus, a diversity mindset also includes the *motivation* to create a diversity climate within the firm, to support the strategy.

6   Conclusions

- The Diversity Scorecard and Value Analysis Tools provide practical means for businesses to prioritise and focus their EDI efforts in terms of the potential ROIs that they offer.
- The participating companies had a wide range of EDI initiatives from which they were seeking to obtain competitive advantage through performance or efficiency gains.
- The project sample included companies of different sizes, from large corporates (MITIE and Cisco) to micro-businesses (Ariadne Designs and Alpine). The pilot showed that both the scorecard and the Value Analysis Tool worked well regardless of company size, the only difference being the scale of the analysis and the level of detail.
- In the case of the Value Analysis Tool, some aspects of an initiative readily lent themselves to financial quantification, for example cost savings from a reduction in employee turnover. Others, however, were more challenging and needed informed estimates; for example, non-dilution of the knowledge base through reduced staff attrition. Overall, the research demonstrated that it is possible to obtain estimates from relevant internal experts with reasonably high levels of confidence.
- A major benefit of completing the Diversity Scorecard is that it encourages a discipline of looking holistically at the organisation's EDI efforts.
- The Diversity Scorecard forces a comprehensive review of existing and potential EDI initiatives and, therefore, offers the potential to uncover diversity blind spots, i.e., a missed business opportunity linked to diversity.
- To achieve sustainable diversity-friendly systems, the research demonstrated that structural components in the entire organisation

need to change in tandem with the introduction of 'diversity policies'. Hence, a single-threaded initiative such as giving all employees diversity training is unlikely to lead to sustained change unless organisational design elements within the value chain are moved in line with the training.

- Building an inclusive culture to obtain the bottom-line benefits from EDI takes long-term strategic effort. The starting point tends to be the formulation of an EDI vision, aligned with the organisation's business aspirations. All of the participating companies in this project had an EDI vision, although in the SMEs it could be less formalised than in the large corporations.
- In terms of the participating organisations, all had high levels of executive or managing partner sponsorship and the leaders in these organisations were described as being clear about their EDI messages.
- Some of the participating companies were developing the capability of their leaders to drive their strategies forward and, as evidence suggests that 80 to 90 per cent of the behaviour in an organisation is due to leaders (Schein, 1992), this is a critical way of cascading the implementation of the EDI strategy down through the organisation.

Organisations should be encouraged to take inspiration from the cases provided here to see how business benefits can accrue from the strategic use of EDI initiatives. The EDI approach to diversity can therefore pave the way to a more strategic use of EDI that will deliver significant competitive advantage to organisations. To achieve this, organisations need to:

- Invest more effort into cognitive diversity to obtain the business dividend available from more creative and effective business problem solving.
- Invest effort into marketplace as well as workplace diversity. This research demonstrated that high ROIs can be available from marketplace diversity.
- Avail themselves of the measurement tools available, and outlined in this chapter, for measuring the qualitative and quantitative benefits of strategic diversity initiatives.

References

David, A. H. (2010), 'Diversity, innovation and corporate strategy', in *Profiting from Diversity*, G. Moss (ed.), Palgrave McMillan, Chapter 2.

Garvin, D. A. (1993), 'Building a learning organisation', *Harvard Business Review*, July–August, 78–91.

Haberberg, A. and Rieple, Alison (2008). *Strategic Management: Theory and Application*. Oxford: Oxford University Press.

Hall, D. T. and Parker, V. A. (1993), 'The role of workplace flexibility in managing diversity', *Organisational Dynamics*, 22 (1), 4–18.

Hopkins, W. E., Gross, M. and Hopkins, S. A., (2008), 'A conceptual assessment of absorptive capacity through the lens of diversity', unpublished paper, Proceedings of the Decision Sciences Institute Annual Meeting, Baltimore, MD. For lead author contact: College of Business, California State University, Chico, CA 95929 001, 530.898.6272, wehopkinscsuchico.edu.

Hubbard, E. (2004), *The Diversity Scorecard*, Elsevier-Butterworth-Heinemann.

Kaplan, R. S. and Norton, D. P. (1996), *The Balanced Scorecard*, HBS Press.

Moss, G. (2009), *Gender, Design and Marketing*, Gower, Farnham.

Moss, G., Farnham, D. and Cook, C. (2010), 'Women managers in Latvia: A universal footprint for the future', in *Profiting from Diversity*, G. Moss (ed.), Palgrave Macmillan.

Schein, E. H. (ed.) (1992), *Organizational Culture and Leadership*, Jossey-Bass Publishers, San Francisco.

Thomas, D. A. and Kanji, A. (2004), 'IBM's diversity strategy: Bridging the workplace and the marketplace', *Harvard Business Review*, November.

Wheeler, M. L. (1998), 'Measuring diversity: A strategy for organisational effectiveness', *Employment Relations Today*, Spring, John Wiley and Sons Inc.

Name Index

Subject Index